Commerce, finance and statecraft

MANCHESTER
1824
Manchester University Press

Commerce, finance and statecraft

Histories of England, 1600–1780

BEN DEW

Manchester University Press

Published by Manchester University Press
Altrincham Street, Manchester M1 7JA
www.manchesteruniversitypress.co.uk

British Library Cataloguing-in-Publication Data
A catalogue record for this book is available from the British Library

ISBN 978 1 7849 9296 5 hardback

First published 2018

Typeset by
Servis Filmsetting Ltd, Stockport, Cheshire
Printed by Lightning Source

For Claire

J.U.S.N

Contents

Acknowledgements

I have received a good deal of help and support while completing this study. Jessica Dyson and Bronwen Price kindly and selflessly covered my teaching duties in the spring of 2016, thereby giving me a much-needed unofficial sabbatical. Richard Coulton and Matthew Mauger read through the bulk of the manuscript and provided detailed, perceptive and exceptionally helpful feedback. The two readers engaged by Manchester University Press offered both enthusiasm and excellent advice. The bulk of the research was completed at Senate House Library, the Bodleian Library and the British Library; I would like to thank the staff at all of these institutions.

I am also very grateful for the intellectual guidance and encouragement I have received over the years. At the University of East Anglia, I was inspired by Marina Mackay and Judy Hayden. At Queen Mary, University of London, I benefited greatly from working with Richard Bourke, Markman Ellis, Andrew Lincoln and Christopher Reid. I am also appreciative of the support I have received from Gregory Claeys, Emma Clery, Noelle Gallagher, Mark Salber Phillips and Nicholas Phillipson.

For their good cheer and enormous generosity I would like to thank Siân and Paul Brock, Vera and Francis Connolly, and Ann Brock. I am also very appreciative of the assistance I received from Patricia and Ivor Dew, and Marie Brodie. My parents Kathy and Chris have provided invaluable help, warm hospitality and excellent company.

My greatest debt is to Claire Brock who has been a willing and able discussant on all aspects of the project, a super editor, and an even better companion. Her love and friendship have made everything worthwhile.

Introduction

1. Economic statecraft

This book explores the accounts of commerce and finance developed by seventeenth- and eighteenth-century historians of England. Writers of the period, I argue, were engaged in a series of long-running and politically charged debates concerning a range of economic issues: the impact of popular and arbitrary forms of government on trade; the political and economic consequences of taxation; the development and value of England's trading companies and commercial empire; the relationship between war and commerce; and, more generally, the meaning of national prosperity and its significance for England's security, greatness and happiness. In discussing such questions, historians sought to present kings and queens as managers of the nation's monetary and trading interests, and economic issues themselves as aspects of statecraft. As a consequence, commerce and finance came to be considered alongside political and military affairs as matters in which monarchs could demonstrate their skill, virtue and even heroism. This historiographical approach, which I label 'the economic statecraft tradition', shaped the ways in which seventeenth- and eighteenth-century society conceived of politics, wealth and the meaning and function of the past, and helped to generate an important, but largely unexplored, variety of economic history.

Three characteristics of this mode of writing should be emphasised. First, its conceptions of commerce and finance were, in a sense, political. Writers did not view the economy as an autonomous or semi-autonomous system shaped by the forces of supply and demand. Instead, commercial and financial material was presented as a series of actions performed by government – primarily the instigation of laws, commercial regulations and taxes – which either helped or hindered England's interests. Economic statecraft's key concern, therefore, was with what can best be described as the history of economic policy. Second, and largely as a consequence of this, none of the writers who discussed economic statecraft conceived of it as an independent field of study. Rather, the achievements of particular statesmen in commerce and finance were shown to be connected to their political, religious and military roles. This meant that economic statecraft formed part of a wider study of statesmanship, and understanding it involves tracing its shifting relationship with other aspects of this subject. Third, the accounts developed by historians were premised on the idea that the past provided a series of good and bad examples of economic management. England's greatest monarchs, it was argued, through their skills in this area, had brought wealth, power and happiness to the nation. Its less successful rulers had allowed nationally beneficial forms of trade to decline and introduced morally and financially corrosive types of luxury. Consequently, their actions had weakened England in relation to its international rivals and had inaugurated periods of poverty and misery. Studying these examples was valuable as they could provide practical lessons for modern statesmen. Economic statecraft was, as a consequence, a self-consciously didactic form of writing.

The narrative that follows examines the emergence of economic statecraft in Jacobean historical writing (Chapters 1–3), charts its development through the seventeenth and eighteenth centuries (Chapters 4–7) and explores the circumstances that led to its ultimate demise (Chapters 8–9). In doing so, it considers the work of a broad range of the period's narrative historians, among them Francis Bacon, William Camden, Thomas Carte, William Guthrie, Edmund Howes, David Hume, Paul de Rapin de Thoyras and Thomas Salmon.[1] Such an account will provide, I believe, a useful addition to our knowledge of English historical writing. Recent scholarship has done much to emphasise the complex ways in which the term 'history' was understood in the seventeenth and eighteenth centuries, and in the process has uncovered a series of previously ignored, but important, historical genres.[2] The result of this is that we now know much more than we did twenty years ago about the historical content of modes of writing such as secret history,[3] satire and panegyric,[4] memoir,[5] biography,[6] and the history of women.[7] However, with the notable exception of the work of David Hume, the multi-volume narrative histories of England that constituted the period's most popular and prestigious historical form have been neglected.[8] And even those critical works that do deal with the narrative tradition have generally used it as a point of comparison to illuminate wider literary and historiographical trends. Thus, a number of accounts have contrasted the conventional approach to the past employed in historical writing with the radical innovations that were taking place in the early novel.[9] Others, meanwhile, despite providing useful discussions of the national histories of Rapin, Salmon and Guthrie, have seen the primary significance of such works as lying in their partial anticipation of the more substantial achievements of Hume, Edward Gibbon and the Scottish stadial historians.[10]

In contrast to such approaches, this analysis treats historical writing about England as a subject worthy of attention in its own right and aims to show that the writers of the period developed a sophisticated form of politico-economic history. Two clarifications need to be added to such a claim. First, I am not arguing that the works under consideration were 'doing' economic history in the modern sense of the term. There is, of course, a huge methodological gap between the approaches taken by William Camden and David Hume, and those of, say, J. H. Clapham, Phyllis Deane and W. A. Cole.[11] Equally, however, there are some connections. A particularly useful definition of the discipline is that developed by the late Donald Coleman. For Coleman, economic history, in its current form, is that which 'asks economic questions – be they about the demand and supply of goods and services, about costs of production, levels of income, the distribution of wealth, the volume and direction of investment, or the structure of overseas trade'.[12] As a result, 'it inevitably deals with large numbers, with aggregates' and 'has to contend with the task of identifying and measuring forces normally outside the conscious control of single, individual actors'.[13] I want to show that a number of these 'economic' questions, while not perennial, have substantial histories of their own, and have been answered using the conceptual vocabulary of neoclassical narrative history, as well as the 'modern' terminology of aggregates and forces.

Second, while the organisation of this account is broadly chronological, it does not treat the texts it discusses as a series of incremental steps through which historians gradually acquired the techniques of modern economic history. To do so would be to assume that the significance of a piece of historical writing lies in its contribution to a narrative of progress of which the historian who wrote it could have no knowledge. Rather, my approach is to locate the works in the specific contexts from which they emerged and to which they directly responded.[14] Narrative histories require a particular sort of treatment from the contextualising intellectual historian. This mode of writing was constructed through analysing, paraphrasing and transcribing archival sources and, more frequently, other works of narrative history. As a consequence, it corresponds closely to Roland Barthes' definition of a literary text as a 'multidimensional space in which a variety of writings, none of them original, blend and clash'.[15] Understanding such texts involves establishing the specific writings that historians chose to blend, and, in a sense, reconstructing in literary terms the real-life desks and libraries of specific authors. In addition to this, however, the choice of sources that historians made, and the way in which they organised their material, played a part in an ongoing series of discussions concerning the nature and function of history. There was a general consensus that history constituted 'a narrative of worthy deeds, polite and dignified, written to instruct the political elite with moral and political lessons'.[16] Nevertheless, both the nature of 'worthy deeds' and the moral and political lessons which history should provide remained vexed and politically charged issues. And in discussing such matters, writers frequently found themselves responding not just to other historians, but to a variety of works of political polemic and political economy.[17] As a result, to identify the contribution being made by a specific work of narrative history, we need to understand its relationship with its sources, and its interactions with contemporary historiography, broadly defined.[18]

2. Public and private realms

This book also contributes to wider discussions concerning historical and economic culture in the seventeenth and eighteenth centuries by developing a critique of what might be labelled neo-Aristotelian analyses of commercial modernity. Such ideas received their classic exposition in Hannah Arendt's work of 1958, *Vita Activa*.[19] For Arendt, ancient political thought rested on a 'self-evident and axiomatic' distinction between the private realm of the *oikos* or household and the public realm of the *polis*.[20] Drawing principally on Aristotle's *Politics*, Arendt went on to define the *oikos* as the association in which a householder ruled over his wife, children and slaves, noting that its distinctive trait 'was that in it men lived together because they were driven by their wants and needs'.[21] The *polis*, by contrast, was the community of householders who, through the rotation of offices, ruled and were ruled by one another as equals. It was created for the sake of the good life, a mode of living equated with political action and freedom from necessity. Such a division, Arendt argued, meant that according to ancient thought, 'the very term "political economy" would have been a contradiction in terms: whatever was "economic", related to the life of the individual and the survival of the species, was a non-political, household affair by definition'.[22] The key condition for political economy's emergence was the development in the eighteenth century of 'society'. This concept served to blur the 'public' and 'private' spheres and enabled peoples and political communities to be conceived 'in the image of a family whose everyday affairs have to be taken care of by a gigantic, nation-wide administration of house-keeping'.[23]

Arendt's thesis has been highly influential. In *The Machiavellian Moment* (1975), for example, J. G. A. Pocock drew on the language and conceptual framework of *Vita Activa* to examine how the Aristotelian ideal of the *polis* and its conception of civic participation shaped political ideas first in Renaissance Italy and later in the Anglophone world of the seventeenth and eighteenth centuries.[24] Through doing so, he endorsed the general chronology of Arendt's account and assumed, as Arendt had done, that Aristotelian virtue constituted a barrier to the emergence of modes of thought capable of justifying commercial and financial activities. Thus, for Pocock,

> Augustan political economics mark the moment when the trader – and, still more pressingly the financier – was challenged to prove that he could display civic virtue in the sense that the landed man could. It was easy to visualise the latter, anxious only to improve his estate for inheritance, engaging in civic actions which related his private to the public good; much harder to ascribe this role to one constantly engaged in increasing his wealth by exchanging quantities of fictitious tokens.[25]

Such ideas have gone on to play a major role in the history of political thought, and much of the best work by Pocock and others associated with the Cambridge School has been concerned with the difficulties that eighteenth-century writers faced in reconciling modern ideas of wealth with classical notions of virtue.[26]

Neo-Aristotelian ideas about the nature and value of the public realm have also shaped discussions of historical writing, most notably in the important work of Phillip Hicks and Mark Salber Phillips. Hicks's *Neoclassical History and English Culture* (1996) focused on the problems faced by narrative historians of England in the seventeenth and eighteenth centuries. Readers and writers of the period, he shows, continued to conceive of the genre in classical terms as 'a continuous, truthful story about important, public events'.[27] Its primary subject was 'war and politics' and its function 'was to instruct political society'.[28] However, despite numerous attempts, England's historians struggled to use these conventions to provide an adequate account of the nation's past. Part of the problem was modernity. Writers faced the challenge of using a 2,000-year-old classical idiom to describe a series of phenomena that had no classical precedents, among them 'the mariner's compass, modern commerce, Christianity, gunpowder, the printing press, political parties, a middle rank of citizens [and] modern antiquarian scholarship'.[29] Moreover, aspects of the modern world were fundamentally antithetical to ancient historiographical practice; for classical historians, issues relating to trade, manners and art were 'unworthy subjects in their own right cut off from politics'.[30] Most historians had come to grief in the face of such difficulties. And, Hicks argues, it was not until Hume was able to synthesise a public, political narrative with new forms of literary, artistic and economic analysis in his *History of England* that the nation was provided with a successful, large-scale narrative account of its past.[31]

A similar conception of early modern history's public orientation underpins Phillips's *Society and Sentiment* (2000). For Phillips, classical historiography, and its early modern revival, were 'predicated on a sharply drawn separation between public and private concerns'.[32] The focus of history was on public affairs and, as such, it restricted its attention to matters of 'statecraft and military manoeuvre'.[33] This ensured that commerce, which in the wake of Arendt's work we see 'as a principal agent in blurring the division between private and public', was ignored; it 'had no place in historical narrative because it had no legitimate place in the pursuit of the *vita activa*'.[34]

Phillips's main interest, however, is not (as Hicks's had been) in the durability of these models, but rather in the forms of writing that came to challenge them. From the mid-eighteenth century onwards, he demonstrates, pressure began to be placed on classical forms of historical discourse as Britain came to conceive of itself as a trading nation, whose status, identity and survival were dependent on financial factors. This situation contributed to both the development of a variety of philosophical history that emphasised the role that social and economic factors played in producing historical change, and the emergence of a series of more specialised types of historical writing.[35] While they incorporated elements of classical historiography, these innovative forms expanded the field of historical endeavour to include detailed analysis of trade, finance and commerce, and their interactions with politics and a range of other 'new' subjects such as navigation, customs and manners, and the arts and sciences. Trade, therefore, while it did not stand alone, functioned as 'the most visible sign of history's new direction'.[36]

This study builds on Hicks's and Phillips's accounts and provides a broad endorsement of both the former's emphasis on the continued importance of classical models and their shared characterisation of neoclassical history as, in Phillips's words, 'the story of the public actions of public men'.[37] In doing so, however, the book aims to show that rather than being a barrier to an engagement with economic affairs, the genre's public, political focus was highly conducive to a particular form of economic commentary. From the late sixteenth century onwards a growing awareness emerged of the link between a state's economic strengths and its capacity to wage war effectively.[38] Such ideas helped to ensure that commentary on the standard themes of classical history – war and politics – increasingly involved analysis of a nation's commercial and financial interests and that the management of these issues was viewed as a public, political issue. To an extent, an examination of these matters reveals a narrative that is the inverse of Arendt's. It is Bacon and Camden who come closest to representing the state as a nation-wide administration of housekeeping. By the eighteenth century, commerce was beginning to be conceived of as separate from the public political sphere, and as an activity with its own laws, its own literature and its own history. This separation, however, was never total. Much seventeenth- and eighteenth-century historical writing takes the form of a series of competing analyses concerning the relationship that existed, and should have existed, between government and commerce at various moments in England's history.

3. Mercantilism and economic policy

The economic statecraft tradition is also of significance for a series of debates in the field of economic theory. Key to Adam Smith's analysis in the *Wealth of Nations* was a coruscating critique of the mercantilist policies that had shaped, and continued to shape, England's approach to commerce.[39] In part the errors made were the product of an intellectual mistake. There was a tendency, Smith argued, to see the amassing of money and the establishment of a positive balance of trade as the best ways of producing national affluence. This, in turn, led writers and politicians to assume that the object of political economy was 'to diminish as much as possible the importation of foreign goods for home-consumption, and to increase as much as possible the exportation of the produce of domestick industry'.[40] Such a policy was, for Smith, fundamentally misguided. The majority of a nation's wealth lay not in overseas trade but in its 'lands, houses, and consumable goods of all different kinds'.[41] Controlling the nation's money supply was not just unnecessary – the forces of supply and demand would naturally secure the required amount – but also a potentially retrograde measure. Indeed, the various monopolies, drawbacks, tariffs and bounties instigated by states had, Smith sought to demonstrate, raised prices and slowed economic growth. Their perpetuation, meanwhile, was a deliberate attempt on the part of the mercantile interest to enrich itself at the expense of consumers.

Smith's critique did much to damage the credibility of mercantilist political economy, and it has never quite shaken off its post-*Wealth of Nations* reputation as an intellectual fallacy, rooted in self-interest. His ideas have also helped to shape attitudes towards the history of statecraft. As had been the case with Smith's own work, the classical, neoclassical and Marxist writers who built on the foundations he established tended to present their analyses as critiques of existing economic practice. From such a perspective, the history of economic policy, particularly in its seventeenth- and eighteenth-century forms, was a sorry tale of ineptitude. The influence of statesmen had generally been pernicious to the nations they ruled over and, where their actions had brought benefits, these had been unintended and unforeseen. As a consequence, there was little reason to turn to the past for inspiration when intellectual models of ever-increasing philosophical and mathematical sophistication could identify the failures of previous generations and prescribe better solutions for the future.

These ideas, while retaining their influence, have not gone entirely unchallenged. Central to a series of critiques of 'orthodox' or 'mainstream' economics has been an attack on the discipline's relationship with reality. Joseph Schumpeter, for example, claimed that economics suffered from the 'Ricardian Vice' of basing practical policy prescriptions on *a priori* assumptions that lacked any empirical basis.[42] Similarly, John Maynard Keynes noted that economists had become increasingly 'unmoved by the lack of correspondence between the results of their theory and the facts of observation; a discrepancy which the ordinary man has not failed to observe'.[43] For Robert Skidelsky, meanwhile, economics has cut itself off from 'the common understanding of how things work, or should work'.[44] Such claims have often run alongside an interest in pre-Smithian economics of a mercantilist bent. Schumpeter argued that mercantilism's faults were in a sense the opposite of those of orthodox modern economics; it was so rooted in the everyday that its practitioners were incapable of theorising.[45] Keynes, while acknowledging the mercantilists' practical leanings, was a good deal more sympathetic. Indeed, the latter sections of his *General Theory* contain a wide-ranging account of mercantilism, which defends the 'older theory' endorsed by 'the majority of statesmen and practical men' against the criticisms made of it by modern, free trade 'theorists'.[46] A similar division is at the heart of recent work by the Norwegian economist Erik S. Reinert.[47] Reinert distinguishes between two broad approaches to economic theory. On the one hand, there is the 'standard' Smith-influenced canon of economics, which relies upon abstract mathematical models, and assumes as an ideal a 'self-regulating system seeking equilibrium and harmony'.[48] On the other hand, however, there exists a counter-tradition. This 'other canon' draws inspiration from the mercantilists, the German historical school, and the work of writers such as Keynes, Schumpeter and Thorstein Veblen. Its ideas are derived from a series of historically informed examples and it assumes that economic stability is a product of the specific measures followed by individual governments. While Reinert acknowledges that both canons have a role to play in modern debates, his key point is that the latter approach has come to be neglected in favour of the former. As a consequence, economics has lost touch with reality and rich countries have come to advocate a series of economic panaceas to the developing world that are at odds with the actual policies through which they achieved their own affluence. These issues have also, Reinert argues, exerted an influence on the organisation of academic disciplines. As he notes: 'unlike the history of economic thought (what theorists said ought to happen), the history of economic policy (what policies were actually followed) is a non-existent academic discipline'.[49]

Reinert has made the first steps towards rectifying this situation through establishing the 'Other Canon Foundation', a network of heterodox economists and economic historians concerned with issues of economic development.[50] Key to the work of this group is an attempt to trace the types of economic policies that rich countries employed as they 'went from poverty to wealth'.[51] Such information, it is assumed, can then play a key role in helping modern-day poor nations generate strategies to improve their current living conditions. The account that follows is sympathetic to Reinert's project and aims to contribute to it by providing a study of the ways in which historians of the mercantilist era dealt with economic policy. In doing so, my objective is to show that while the history of economic policy may be extinct as an academic discipline, it is a mode of writing with a substantial, if largely ignored, pedigree. A knowledge of this pedigree, I contend, is useful for three specific reasons. First, an attempt to instigate an investigation of economic policy without an understanding of the history of this approach risks the very historical impoverishment that proponents of the 'other canon' have levelled at mainstream economics. This account aims to counter such dangers by providing a discussion of an important tradition in the study of economic policy. Second, there is a tendency in scholarly work on the 'other canon' to present mercantilist-era writers as having a shared, experienced-based method, and as being in broad agreement with one another on the lessons that experience taught. Such assumptions are highly problematic. As the work of Carl Wennerlind and Steve Pincus has shown, particularly from the 1640s onwards, analyses of commerce and finance were tied up with and shaped by wider party political debates.[52] This ensured that mercantilism was not so much an agreed economic theory or methodology, but rather a series of often fraught disputes between Royalist and Parliamentarian and, later, Whig and Tory polemicists. This book expands upon the work of Wennerlind and Pincus by showing that, running alongside the debates in 'economic' writing that they identify, there existed a parallel (if generally distinctive) series of discussions among seventeenth- and eighteenth-century historians. My aim is to reconstruct these debates and, by doing so, to provide further evidence about the ways in which political and polemical concerns shaped approaches to economic policy. Third, as Chapter 8 and, more pointedly, the discussion of David Hume in Chapter 9 show, over the course of the eighteenth century Enlightenment ideas concerning progress came to undermine the humanist conceptions that had previously structured historical writing about commerce and finance. One casualty of this process was the notion that examples drawn from economic history could provide a useful model of emulation for contemporary statesmen. As a consequence, the rise and fall of economic statecraft is also a key element in the wider story of the triumph of modern, more ahistorical analyses over an older, historically informed approach to statecraft.

4. Terminology and chapter outline

The terms that feature most frequently in this study are 'commerce', 'trade' and 'finance'. I treat 'commerce' and 'trade' as synonyms, as my sources do, and alternate between them for stylistic purposes. The historians discussed had very little interest in the domestic market, and, consequently, the 'commerce' and 'trade' they discussed were generally international in character. 'Finance' is used, as it was from the latter part of the eighteenth century onwards, to refer to the various ways in which states raised money and regulated its supply.[53] Key aspects of the former subject include taxes, duties on goods and government borrowing. Analysis of the latter leads me to discussions of usury, interest rates and the quality and quantity of coinage. The adjective 'economic' is used as a shorthand for matters relating to both commerce and finance. As a result, 'economic statecraft' refers to both the commercial *and* the financial practices of a particular monarch. As will be made clear, the relationship between commerce and finance could be conceived of in a wide variety of different ways; the term 'economic statecraft' is not, therefore, meant to imply the existence of a particular causal connection between commercial and financial policies.[54]

My focus in the chapters that follow is primarily on 'modern history', specifically debates concerning the reigns of Henry VII, Elizabeth I and James I.[55] Discussion of periods before, between and after the lives of these monarchs is included when required to illustrate the broader historical import of a particular work. The decision to concentrate on these monarchs was determined by the material; put simply, accounts of their reigns contain the most detailed and interesting discussions of commercial and financial affairs. This concern with economic issues was, in part, a product of contemporary attitudes to the history of English trade. Particularly from the mid-seventeenth century onwards, historians came to see the reign of Henry VII as inaugurating a new commercial age, the major events of which had taken place during the lives of Elizabeth and James. An account of these monarchs, therefore, allows for some detailed engagement with debates surrounding England's emergence as a commercial power.

The book is divided into three chronologically ordered parts. Part I looks at the emergence of the economic statecraft tradition through considering three highly influential works: Francis Bacon's *History of the Reign of King Henry VII* (1622), William Camden's *Annales* (1615, 1625) and the account of James I developed by the chronicler Edmund Howes in his edition of John Stow's *Annales, or General Chronicle of England* (1615, 1631). Each of these narratives provided an analysis of the role that particular monarchs played in managing the nation's commercial and financial interests, and assumed that achievements in economic statecraft had been central to the successes of the reign. Despite this, they offered contrasting accounts of what constituted good government. Bacon employed a realist, Tacitean mode of analysis to explore the public benefits that could be generated by amoral, or even immoral, financial management. Camden, in contrast, treated successful economic statecraft as a product of a ruler's willingness to subordinate his or her own private interests to those of the nation. As a consequence, he was able to show how the sort of ideas about exemplary virtue and honour that had underpinned Livy's *History*, and much Renaissance historiography, could be applied to modern commercial affairs. Howes, meanwhile, used the chronicle form to investigate the contribution to commercial affairs not just of England's monarchs, but also of its people. Through doing so he was able to advance a highly original account which emphasised the transformative role of recent innovations in trade and manufacture, and traced the origin of these developments to England's successful imitation of European practices. As the rest of this book shows, it was through borrowing from, expanding on and critiquing the ideas of Bacon, Camden and Howes that many later historians developed their own accounts of economic policy.

Part II traces the impact of the Civil War on ideas of economic statecraft. In the wake of the conflict, I argue, discussion of economic history was increasingly shaped by polemical, political concerns. As part of this process, two rival accounts of the state's economic management emerged, each based on an interpretation of the reign of James I. For Parliamentarian writers and their Whiggish successors, James's political absolutism and personal extravagance made him a calamitous administrator of England's commercial and financial interests. The result was a period of misery and poverty, which was in sharp contrast to the contentment and wealth experienced under Elizabeth. Royalist and Tory writers responded by arguing that James had followed the precedents of Elizabeth with regard to taxation and, through the wise use of monarchical prerogative, had surpassed her achievements in relation to commerce. The opposition he experienced, meanwhile, arose from a pernicious Puritan faction intent on advancing their own selfish interests and undermining the constitution. Chapter 4 explores the development of these modes of analysis in the second part of the seventeenth century through a discussion of accounts concerning James I by Anthony Weldon, Arthur Wilson, William Sanderson and Roger Coke. Chapters 5, 6 and 7 examine how the political divisions of the seventeenth century came to shape eighteenth-century accounts of economic statecraft. My aim here has been to provide analysis of a broad cross-section of political views, and alongside detailed accounts of histories by a Whig (Rapin), a Tory (Salmon) and a Jacobite (Carte), the discussion contains briefer accounts of Patriot and Court Whig writing.

Part III focuses on William Guthrie's *General History of England* (1744–51) and David Hume's *History of England* (1754–61). Political ideas about history also provided the framework through which these works were both constructed and read. What distinguished them from their predecessors, however, was a belief that advancements in commerce formed part of a wider and distinctively modern set of socio-cultural changes. The key to recent European history, it was argued, lay in a series of shifts in property ownership which had caused wealth, and with it power, to pass from the feudal barons to the commercial classes. These advances had led to the birth of the commercial age and transformed the political, legal, social and cultural landscape of the continent. As a consequence, narrative histories of England came to conceive of individual incidents in England's commercial past not simply as examples of monarchical achievement or failure. Rather, their significance lay in the contribution they had made – or failed to make – to national economic development and the social transfigurations it had inspired. Part of a historian's job was still to outline the policies that statesmen pursued with regard to taxation, and overseas and domestic trade. Indeed, the defining role that commercial affairs played in understandings of modernity meant that such a task was more important than ever. However, there was an awareness that, as well as shaping the economic sphere, the actions of statesmen were themselves shaped by their economic and intellectual environments. Tracing a nation's history, therefore, involved looking at the complex relationship between particular actions on the part of statesmen and their wider social context. My account examines the origins of this approach and its impact on the political, economic and narratological strategies that underpinned ideas of economic statecraft.

Part I

1

Tacitean history: Francis Bacon's *History of the Reign of King Henry VII*

On 30 April 1621, a 'Confession and Humble Submission' was read before the House of Lords. In this document, Sir Francis Bacon acknowledged that, as Lord High Chancellor, he had received bribes and was, therefore, 'guilty of corruption'.[1] The Lords responded with a harsh sentence: Bacon was given a fine of £40,000, imprisoned at the King's pleasure, and barred from holding office or high employment in the state and from coming within twelve miles of Court. In the weeks leading up to this verdict, and aware that punishment was inevitable, Bacon had made concerted efforts to cushion his fall.[2] Thus, in a letter dated 21 April, he provided the King with what Michael Kiernan has aptly labelled a 'brashly phrased offer':

> but because he that hath taken bribes is apt to give bribes, I will go furder, and present your Majesty with a bribe. For if your Majesty give me peace and leisure, and God give me life, I will present your Majesty with a good history of England, and a better digest of your laws.[3]

To an extent, this attempt at bargaining achieved the results that Bacon desired; he was to spend only three days as a prisoner in the Tower and his fine was never collected. And while the promised history of England was never completed, he did, true to his word, devote himself to historical research in the months following his release. From this emerged *The History of the Reign of King Henry VII*, an account written in fourteen weeks at Gorhambury, near St Albans, between the end of June and the beginning of October 1621, and presented in manuscript form to the King on 8 October.

The conditions in which Bacon found himself had important consequences for the kind of history he was able to write. Anxious to work quickly, and unable to access the main archival material held in London, Bacon based his narrative on earlier printed accounts, such as Polydore Vergil's *Anglica Historia* (1534), Edward Hall's *The Union of the two Noble and Illustrate Famelies of Lancastre* [*and*] *Yorke* (1548) and John Speed's *History of Great Britaine* (1611).[4] However, while Bacon was reliant on these narratives, his engagement with them was shaped by his reading of a variety of other sources, principally legal records, classical history (particularly Tacitus) and the writings of Machiavelli and his various critics. This chapter investigates how Bacon fused methods and ideas derived from these works and explores the consequences of this move. Central among them, I argue, was the development of a new approach to the representation of finance and commerce.

The chapter is divided into three sections. Section one discusses the humanist approach to history employed in pre-Baconian histories of Henry VII, most significantly Vergil's *Anglica Historia*. Section two looks at the challenge to conventional, humanist assumptions about history and politics posed by the late Elizabethan and Jacobean vogue for Tacitus, and explores how the employment of Tacitean ideas led Bacon to place financial affairs at the heart of his account. The final part is concerned with Bacon's use of the parliamentary statutes passed during Henry's reign. Through drawing on this source material, it will be shown that Bacon developed a detailed account of the King's achievements as a manager of England's commercial interests and, more generally, an original neo-Machiavellian analysis of the relationship between government and trade.

1. Polydore Vergil, humanism and Livian exemplary history

The most influential historical account of the reign of Henry VII prior to Bacon's was that contained in Polydore Vergil's *Anglica Historia*. Vergil was born c. 1470 at Fermignano, near Urbino, and studied at the universities of Padua and Bologna. By 1502 he was an employee of the Pope, and serving in London as collector of Peter's Pence.[5] Much of the rest of his life was to be spent in England and he began compiling a complete history of the country in around 1506. A manuscript copy of this work – now preserved at the Vatican Library in Rome – was completed in around 1513 and, after a series of amendments, this text was published in Basel in 1534 as *Anglica*

Historia. New editions followed in 1546 and 1555, which both revised the content and extended the narrative from its original end point of 1513 up to 1538.

Vergil's account exemplified a number of trends in humanist historiography and, aided by Thomas More's *History of King Richard III* (written c. 1513–18), was responsible for introducing this approach to English historical writing.[6] The most distinctive features of the humanists, as Antonia Gransden has argued, was their conception of themselves as members of an international scholarly community which drew 'its principal inspiration from Italy'.[7] Such a self-identification generally entailed a rejection, at least in part, of native stylistic and thematic conventions. Describing the chronicle tradition in England, Vergil noted that these 'almost day-by-day accounts' formed 'annals in which both the arrangement and the style was so threadbare that they justly strike us, as they say, as food without seasoning'.[8] His own work, he continued, sought to take this 'raw' material, and 'learnedly polish and adorn [it]'.[9] At one level, the process of refinement involved raising the quality of historical prose, through the use of a clear and elegant form of Latin and the addition of some rhetorical flourishes, most notably elaborate, invented speeches. Equally significantly, however, humanists sought to improve the organisation of historical writing. Medieval chronicles had prized comprehensiveness and the result, as one modern commentator has noted, was a 'baggy and disordered recitation of names, dates, and notable political and natural events'.[10] Vergil employed a much tighter structure. Following the approaches of Suetonius' *The Twelve Caesars* (AD 121) and Platina's *Lives of the Popes* (1479), he divided his post-Conquest narrative into books, each of which dealt with the reign of a particular monarch and employed the same basic form.[11] Discussion opened with a description of the King's ascent to the throne before providing a broadly chronological narrative of the principal occurrences in domestic and foreign affairs during his reign. The narrative then concluded with an account of his appearance, family and, most importantly, 'character' – his main virtues and vices.[12] These divisions enabled writers to emphasise that individual reigns had different distinguishing features, and that these features were, to a large degree, determined by the different personal traits of particular monarchs.

The *Anglica Historia* was also rooted in characteristically humanist ideas about the function of history as a source of morally edifying lessons or *exempla*. Central to this approach was the idea that the actions described in historical narratives provided useful examples of both virtuous and the non-virtuous conduct. The former, as Vergil explained in the first section of the *Anglica Historia*, could stimulate readers 'to achieve immortal glory and virtue', while the latter helped in 'deterring others from vice by fear of infamy'.[13] As a consequence, history served to pass 'judgements about what things are of the greatest use for the conduct of our lives'.[14] This conception of history had a long and illustrious heritage. The key discussion in the ancient world had come from Livy, who in the preface to his *History* had observed:

> The special and salutary benefit of the study of history is to behold evidence of every sort of behaviour set forth as on a splendid memorial; from it you may select for yourself and for your country what to emulate, from it what to avoid, whether basely begun or basely concluded.[15]

Such sentiments were, it should be emphasised, broadly in line with much medieval historical writing. However, whereas medieval historians conceived of history as a means of providing 'pious edification', classical and humanist authors sought to inspire a more active and explicitly political form of virtue.[16] Alexander Barclay, for example, in the dedication that prefaces his 1525 edition of Sallust, noted that every good example written in histories 'is set for a warnyng & monycion unto princes and governours therby to rule & order themselfe: & a commen wele'.[17] Similar notions inform Thomas Blundeville's *The True Order and Methode of Wryting and Reading Hystories* (1574), the first English work specifically concerned with the study of history. For Blundeville, history enabled men to gather judgement and knowledge 'as well to direct [...] private actions, as to give Counsell lyke a most prudent Counseller in publyke causes, be it matters of warre, or peace'.[18]

These ideas about historical writing's capacity to provide 'Counsell' also ensured that classical and humanist historians frequently dealt with issues relating to government finance. Within the works of Livy and Tacitus, for example, there are accounts of matters such as the mechanisms through which the state raised money,[19] the actions it performed in times of dearth and crisis to ensure that the population were fed and watered,[20] and its management of the system of private borrowing.[21] Polybius, meanwhile, argued that in relation to each of the specific nations discussed, a 'general sense of the wealth and resources [was] vital knowledge for a historian to have'.[22] Such comments were echoed by Blundeville. Alongside discussions of the 'force' and the 'maner' of government in a particular 'Countrie or Citie', it was necessary, he argued, for a historian to provide accounts both of 'the trade of lyfe' and the 'publique revenues'.[23] Knowledge of the former meant that we can 'learne howe to have lyke in like times', while the latter made us aware 'what things have bene done therwith' and, as a consequence, 'we come to know what the Countrye or Citie is able to doe'.[24]

Vergil's account of Henry VII, like the rest of the *Anglica Historia*, is in line with these ideas regarding history's moral function and political focus. His commentary on the King's character, as such, is principally concerned with identifying Henry's virtues and vices, and outlining the various ways in which they shaped his approach to government. In the manuscript draft of the text from 1513, Vergil provided a balanced account of both the King's merits and his failings. With regard to the former, it was noted that Henry's 'spirit was distinguished, wise and prudent; his mind [...] brave and resolute' and 'his hospitality [...] splendidly generous'.[25] The King's chief merit, however, was his respect for justice, which 'he cherished [...] above all things'.[26] This ensured that he punished the violent and wicked, and that his death was greatly regretted by his subjects, who under his protection 'had been able to conduct their lives peaceably, far removed from the assaults and evil doing of scoundrels'.[27] Such virtues, however, were, in part, counterbalanced by the King's principal vice: his avarice. To an extent, the *Anglica Historia* presented this trait as an unintended consequence of the King's successes. It was only after 1502, once he had subdued the last of the rebellions that blighted his reign, that Henry was shown to have become preoccupied with wealth. Two further explanations for this development were also provided. The King argued that he treated his people with harshness and severity 'to ensure they remained more thoroughly and entirely in obedience to him'.[28] The people, however, 'had another explanation', attributing these exactions to 'the greed of their monarch'.[29] Vergil had more sympathy with the latter interpretation, commenting that 'it is not indeed clear whether at the start it was greed; but afterwards greed did become apparent, so irresolute, vacillating and corrupted are all human purposes'.[30] The vice was then further accentuated, the

Italian continued, by a group of informers, who noting the turn in the King's behaviour, 'dangled before [him] ways of making money'.[31] This helped to ensure that 'the good prince by degrees lost all sense of moderation and was led into avarice'.[32] The implication, therefore, of Vergil's analysis was that the shift in Henry's behaviour was a product of a psychological change. This change, however, had been triggered and then exacerbated by specific political factors.

Such developments, Vergil argued, had highly pernicious consequences for the management of Henry's revenues. Primary among these was the appointment of two lawyers, Richard Empson and Edward Dudley, as judges. These individuals, 'realising that they had been given the job by the King not so much to administer justice as to strip the population of its wealth, without respite and by every means fair or foul vied with each other in extorting money'.[33] To this end, they embarked on a series of prosecutions and land seizures, seeking both to amass personal fortunes and to satisfy the rapacious desires of the King. For Vergil, therefore, Henry's avarice was 'truly burthensome to his people' who, as a result of the ongoing impositions, came to 'greatly [fear] for themselves and their interests'.[34] Concluding his discussion, he observed:

> Avarice is surely a bad enough vice in a private individual, whom it forever torments; in a monarch indeed it may be considered the worst vice, since it is harmful to everyone, and distorts those qualities of trustfulness, justice and integrity by which the state must be governed.[35]

Perhaps unsurprisingly, Vergil appears to have had reservations about making these comments public. There was a twenty-year gap between the completion of the first draft of the *Anglica Historia* and its publication. And when Vergil did go to press, he substantially revised his verdict on Henry. By the time of the final edition, the 'character' of the King had been entirely rewritten to accentuate Henry's virtues and his various achievements, and the account of Empson and Dudley had been greatly reduced in length.[36] Moreover, Vergil provided an endorsement of the King's claim that his exactions were a product of fears about national security. Suggestions that the King was driven by a 'lust for money-making', it was noted, had arisen from 'those who were wounded' by this policy.[37] These accusations were also fundamentally unfair:

> Indeed, this modest sovereign did not despoil his subjects of their fortunes immoderately, for he left behind him a kingdom most wealthy in all respects. This is made plain, among other things, by the immense amount of gold and silver annually brought into the island by merchants plying to and fro, whom he very frequently helped with interest-free loans, so that the flow of commerce, both useful and necessary for all men, would be more abundant in his realm.[38]

England's commercial success, therefore, was evidence that Henry could not have been an avaricious ruler.

Later discussions of Henry VII drew extensively on Vergil's account and developed its analysis of both the King's virtues and his vices. In relation to the former, as had been the case in the *Anglica Historia*, particular attention was paid to the King's legal reforms. Edward Hall, for example, noted Henry's desire to promote 'good and profitable lawes and statutes' and praised him as an 'indifferent and sure justicier'.[39] John Speed, meanwhile, making use of summations from a range of other historians, presented Henry as '*the Salomon, who brought peace to this Kingdome, long before oppressed by warre and tyranny*'.[40] His key princely virtues were his 'singular wisdome, excellent temperance, and moderate frugality' and his 'policy, justice and gravity'.[41] The chroniclers were divided, however, on the issue of the King's avarice. Hall endorsed Vergil's published account, noting that high taxation was part of Henry's attempt to 'pollitiquely' eradicate the causes of 'unquyetnes and mischief'.[42] Speed, in contrast, was sceptical. While Vergil provided a plausible analysis of the King's conduct, 'we can hardly find any commendable root thereof, the wayes being so importune and harsh, by which hee raised money'.[43] Despite this, Speed sought to temper his criticisms. Discussion of avarice was restricted to a single paragraph in the main narrative and, in the 'character' which preceded the narrative, avarice was presented as 'the naturall maladie of age'.[44] Moreover, Speed claimed, the 'splendor' of the public buildings that Henry erected served to divert the people's envy away from him.[45]

The existence of these competing accounts of royal avarice, and Vergil's abrupt *volte face* on this issue, imply that this was a matter of considerable importance to Tudor historiography. However, underpinning all the analyses were the same broad contentions. Henry's successes had been a product of his virtues, and were principally legal in character. His failures, if there had been any, related to his management of revenue and were a consequence of his avarice. As a result, his life provided a series of clear lessons for future statesmen.

2. Bacon and Tacitean history

Humanist conceptions of history retained their influence well into the seventeenth century. Bacon's generation of historians, like their predecessors, identified their work with Graeco-Roman approaches to the past, criticised the native chronicle tradition and saw history as a source of politically instructive examples. At the same time, humanist generic conventions – most notably the use of the monarch's character as the key organisational principle within narratives and the employment of invented speeches – retained their influence. In the late Elizabethan and Jacobean periods, however, ideas about the sort of lesson the past might teach began to shift. It was this alteration in attitudes to history's didactic function, as we shall see, that opened the way to Bacon's highly innovative approach to economic statecraft.

The key force driving developments in historical writing during these years was the growing influence of Tacitus. Over the course of the sixteenth century his work achieved popularity across Europe, and in the first half of the seventeenth century he became the most frequently published of the ancient historians and the subject of numerous commentaries.[46] While an interest in Tacitus developed rather later in England than elsewhere, by the early 1580s he was being read and discussed by an influential group of scholars with connections to Oxford, among them Thomas Savile, Jean Hotman, Henry Cuffe and William Camden.[47] A more active form of engagement emerged in the 1590s from the circle of politicians surrounding the Earl of Essex, a coterie with close connections to the Oxford Taciteans.[48] One of Essex's supporters, Henry Savile, an elder brother of Thomas, completed the first English translation of Tacitus' work, a 1591 edition of the first four books of the *History* and the *Agricola*. This was supplemented by a pseudonymous preface, which in the view of some contemporary observers, Ben Jonson among them, was authored by Essex.[49] Moreover, a number of those individuals associated with Essex, including John Hayward and Bacon, went on to produce distinctively Tacitean histories.

What was Tacitus' appeal and what did it mean to write Tacitean history? One answer to this question came in the 1601 discussion of historical writing by the essayist Robert Johnson.[50] For Johnson, history is 'the mixture of profite and delight'.[51] It proceeds by noting 'causes and effects, counselles and successes, likenes betweene nature and nature, action and action, fortune and fortune'.[52] This enables history to teach its readers 'to deliberate with ripenes of judgement'.[53] Johnson went on to emphasise the diverse ways it might achieve this, distinguishing between two broad approaches. The first of these is a Livian variety of exemplary history. In it:

> as it were in *Cleanthes* table, vertue is set out in her best ornamentes, as in the describing of famous battelles, where specious wars, the ruine of nations, the scituation of Countries, the uncertaine traverses of fortune, the death of brave Commanders, have a certain kind of Majesty linked with delight, and the mind by conversing in them is not onelie delighted, but also lifted up with a spirite of better resolution, and raysed to thinke of imitating: These fil a man with better courage, but faile in inabling him for the manage of civill actions.[54]

The second type of history is:

> like labyrinths, relating cunning and deceitfull friendshippes, how rage is suppressed with silence, treason disguised in innocence, how the wealthy have beene proscribed for their riches, and the worthy undermined for their vertue. These provoke us to eschew their viletie and lacke of vertue, and to be rather viceles[s] than greatly vertuous: and although they bee distasted by those who measure Historie by delight, yet they are of most use in instructing the minde to the like accidentes. And sithens men prostituting their wittes to all hopefull endes of gaine, are ready to adventure themselves in the like actions, they are the most necessarie thinges, that can be warned us, to the intent that in the like practises, we may seeke meanes of prevention and frustrate all the attempts of such subtlely evill companions. In this ranke I preferre *Tacitus* as the best that any man can dwel upon.[55]

Johnson's comments, and the more detailed discussion of Tacitus' work that followed, identified a number of characteristics of Tacitean history, three of which are particularly significant for this study. First, it took as its subject some of people's less desirable forms of behaviour, principally deceit and injustice, and sought to analyse their operation and the impact they had on the state. As a result, it had a close resemblance to the approach that modern sociologists have labelled 'social pathology'.[56] Second, this form of writing was premised on the idea that there was a disjunction between the appearance of actions and their true meaning and significance. The function of history was to delve beneath the surface, and uncover the psychological drives and *arcana imperii* (state secrets) which really shaped events. Tacitean writing was concerned, therefore, with causation, specifically the interaction between character and action. It maintained, however, that this relationship would be complex and, until revealed by the historian, concealed from public view. Third, the value of this approach lay in its realism. Underlying this suggestion was a fundamentally pessimistic view of political life. Great virtue of the sort inspired by exemplary history was presented as unsuitable for the world of 'civill actions'. Instead, 'viceles' conduct was required which, while it avoided direct immorality, was adapted to life in a world where treachery and unfairness were the norm. Realist histories both 'provoke' their readers to engage in such behaviour and provide a guide to the nefarious actions that they can expect from others.[57]

Bacon's relationship to the Livian and Tacitean traditions was a complex one. In a letter to Sir Fulke Greville, written in the 1590s, he praised Tacitus as 'simplye the best' of the historians, noting also that Livy was 'verye good'.[58] This judgement was overturned in *The Advancement of Learning* (1605), where it was claimed that, among the historiographers, it was Livy who was 'best'.[59] References to both Livy's *History* and Tacitus' *Annals* and *History*, meanwhile, abound throughout Bacon's published work, and in *De Augmentis Scientiarum* (1623) he included both writers in his discussion of the capacity of the 'wiser sort of historians' to trace the connection between the actions of historical personages and their natures.[60] Despite his praise for Livy, however, Bacon remained highly critical of exemplary forms of history, and his own approach to historical writing was distinctively realist and, in this sense, distinctively Tacitean in character.

The thinking behind this preference was perhaps explained most clearly in the typologies of history developed in *The Advancement* and *De Augmentis*.[61] Figure 1 summarises Bacon's account as advanced in the latter text. The highest distinction was that between 'Natural History', which dealt with 'the deeds and works of nature', and 'Civil History', which concerned itself with 'those of men'.[62] This second mode was itself divided into 'Ecclesiastical', 'Literary' and 'Civil' varieties.[63] The last of these was 'pre-eminent among human

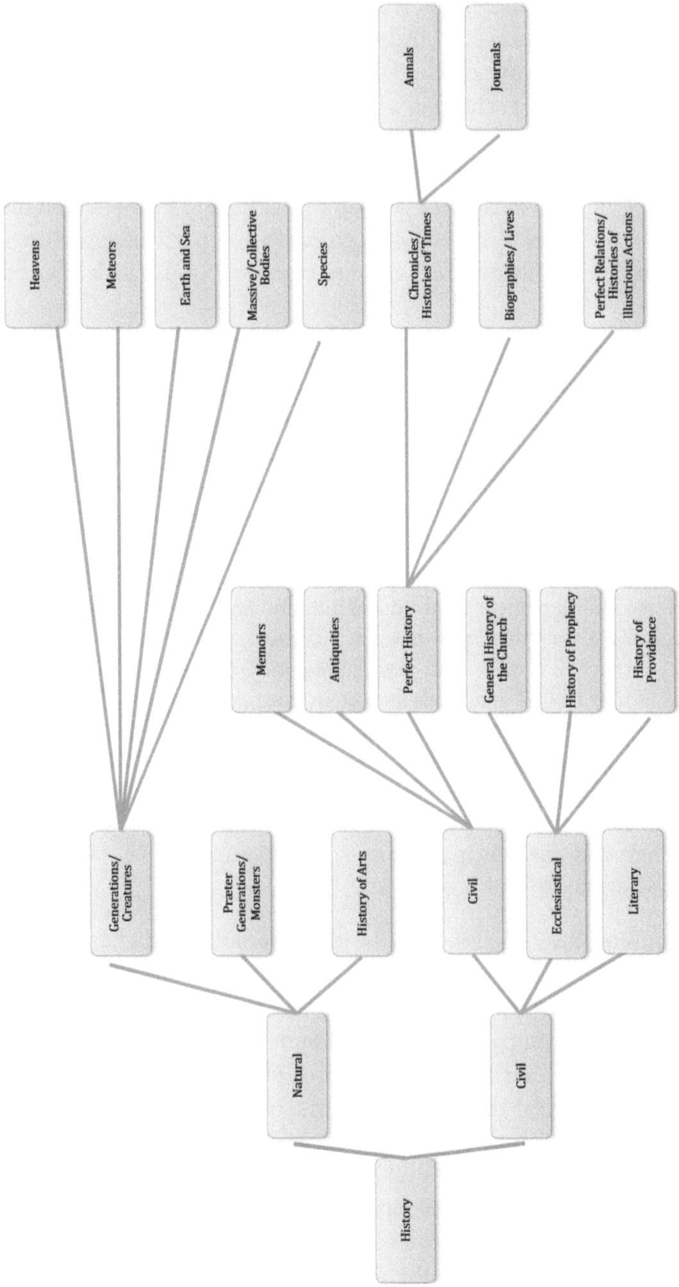

Figure 1 Bacon's typology of history
Derived from *De Augmentis Scientiarum* (1623)

writings', but to be successful, it needed to ensure that 'events [were] coupled with their causes'.[64] Indeed, such causal analysis constituted 'the ornament and life of Civil History'.[65] More generally, its role was to relate 'the revolutions of times, the characters of persons, the fluctuations of counsels, the courses and currents of actions, the bottoms of pretences, and the secrets of governments'.[66] Discussing the various subdivisions that made up this category, Bacon stated his preference for 'lives' – history concerned with a particular person – over 'chronicles' – history that was concerned with a particular period of time:

> For History of Times represents the magnitude of public actions, and the public faces and deportments of persons, but omits and covers up in silence the smaller passages and motions of men and matters. But such being the workmanship of God, that he hangs the greatest weights upon the smallest wires, it comes commonly to pass that such a history, pursuing greater things alone, rather sets forth the pomp and solemnity of business than the true inward springs and resorts thereof. Moreover, when it does add and insert the counsels and motives, yet from its love of grandeur it introduces into human actions more gravity and prudence than they really have; so that a truer picture of human life may be found in a satire than in some histories of this kind. Whereas Lives, if they be well and carefully written (for I do not speak of elegies and barren commemorations of that sort), propounding to themselves a single person as their subject, in whom actions both trifling and important, great and small, public and private, must needs be united and mingled, certainly contain a more lively and faithful representation of things, and one which you may more safely and happily take for example in another case.[67]

In describing 'lives' in this manner, Bacon emphasised that realism constituted their chief merit. While not necessarily pathological in approach, 'lives' avoided false attributions of 'gravity and prudence' and, in this sense, employed a model of human nature closer to satires than chronicles. Their aim was a form of psychological uncovering; they sought to reveal the hidden but 'true inward springs' of human behaviour, and to show how these 'springs' influenced actions and events. Such a focus allowed 'lives' to fulfil many of the functions that Bacon associated with civil history, most significantly the relation of 'characters of persons', 'the courses and currents of actions' and 'the secrets of governments'. At the same time, 'lives', as distinct from chronicles, presented a true picture of humankind and, as a consequence, provided worthy and realistic objects for imitation.

Bacon's historiographical practice in the *History* was closely connected to his theoretical discussions. The task he set himself, in effect, was to transform the 'exemplary', Livian-style analysis of his source material into a new, Tacitean narrative. Avarice was key to such an endeavour. Indeed, it was through placing discussion of this vice at the very centre of his analysis that Bacon was able to provide the sort of pathological, psychological and character-based analysis associated with Tacitus. A key effect of such a manoeuvre, meanwhile, was to ensure that the *History* became a study of the financial interactions between the King, Parliament and the populace, and the various benefits and losses that accrued to the nation as a result.

At the heart of Bacon's reworking of his source material was a new approach to the relationship between character and action. Discussing the 'springs' that had shaped the King's actions, he observed:

> No doubt, in him as in all men (and most of all in Kings) his fortune wrought upon his nature, and his nature upon his fortune. He attained to the crown not only from a private fortune, which might endow him with moderation, but also from the fortune of an exiled man, which had quickened in him all seeds of observation and industry. And his times being rather prosperous than calm, had raised his confidence by success but almost marred his nature by troubles. His wisdom, by often evading from perils, was turned rather into a dexterity to deliver himself from dangers when they pressed him than into a providence to prevent and remove them afar off. And even in nature, the sight of his mind was like some sights of eyes, rather strong at hand than to carry afar off. For his wit increased upon the occasion, and so much the more if the occasion were sharpened by danger. Again, whether it were the shortness of his foresight, or the strength of his will, or the dazzling of his suspicions, or what it was; certain it is that the perpetual troubles of his fortunes (there being no more matter out of which they grew) could not have been without some great defects and main errors in his nature, customs, and proceedings, which he had enough to do to save and help with a thousand little industries and watches.[68]

For Bacon, therefore, action was conceived as the product of a dialectic between 'fortune' – by which he meant 'circumstance' – and 'nature'. The two elements of this dialectic, however, had contrasting qualities. Fortune was shown to be in a constant state of flux. An individual's nature, while it responded to changes in fortune, retained a fixed inner core. This idea was important to Bacon's analysis of Henry's avarice. Vergil and other earlier historians, as we have seen, either denied that Henry was led by this trait or presented it as something that developed in the latter part of his life.[69] In contrast, Bacon saw avarice as an innate aspect of the King's personality and one that had informed his actions throughout his political career. As was noted with regard to the Parliament of 1485, 'points of profit to his coffers' were something of which 'from the very beginning [Henry] was not forgetful'.[70] Consequently, although Bacon accepted Vergil's claim that the King's post-1502 impositions were triggered by the political stability of the period, he did not see this shift in circumstances as changing the King's nature. Rather, it simply allowed Henry's character to reveal itself more clearly; whereas in the first part of his reign he was 'happily contained and refrained by some bands of fortune', later he became free to act as he pleased.[71]

The suggestion that avarice underpinned the King's character did much to shape the *History*'s narrative, and led Bacon to emphasise the fundamentally mercantile nature of the King's approach to statecraft. On occasions, this simply involved expanding upon the arguments of previous historians. Bacon's discussion of Empson and Dudley, for example, both endorsed and borrowed from Vergil's account, and supported its core contention that Henry's desire for self-enrichment had been the driving force behind their extortions. However, as well as making reference to a wider range of legal records than other historians, Bacon concluded with a unique detail. Switching to first-person explanation, he observed:

> I do remember to have seen long since a book of account of Empson's, that had the King's hand almost to every leaf by way of signing, and was in some places postilled in the margent with the King's hand likewise, where was this remembrance:
>
> > Item, Received, of such a one, five marks, for a pardon to be procured; and if the pardon do not pass, the money to be repaid; except the party to be some other ways satisfied.
>
> And over against this memorandum (of the King's own hand):
>
> > Otherwise satisfied.[72]

The image presented of the King, therefore, is that of a punctilious petty tradesman busying himself over his account book.

Elsewhere, Bacon departed more abruptly from his predecessors. Vergil, and the chroniclers who drew on his work, had offered overwhelmingly positive accounts of Henry's approach to military affairs, emphasising that, while he sought to avoid unnecessary loss of life, he had done everything in his power to protect English interests and behave justly. This was particularly true with regard to French attempts to seize Brittany in the late 1480s and early 1490s. Henry's initial willingness to go to war, Vergil argued, was a product of his desire to 'check, curb, and defeat the French, who were threatening the liberty, life, and blood of the [Bretons]'.[73] Ultimately, however, when the French sued for peace, Henry consented; he was aware that Brittany was already lost, and that an end to the conflict would mean that 'he could more readily confront [...] coming domestic troubles'.[74]

Bacon's account was entirely at odds with this. The King, he argued, had no intention of fighting, and only declared himself in favour of military intervention in order to secure a generous allocation of revenue from Parliament. As a result, he 'did but traffic with that war, to make his return in money'.[75] When it came to the peace negotiations, meanwhile, Henry's approach was driven by the prospect of further financial inducements rather than considerations regarding the nation's interests and, as such, he obtained 'rather a bargain than a treaty'.[76] This behaviour, Bacon concluded, meant that the King had aimed at acquiring two distinctive types of 'profit': 'upon his subjects for the war, and upon his enemies for the peace'.[77] In doing so, he had run England 'like a good merchant, that maketh his gain both upon the commodities exported and imported back again'.[78]

Such representations, of course, constituted direct criticisms of Henry's conduct; to be a merchant, it is implied, is to prioritise selfish financial desires over more honourable, kingly concerns. Running alongside such commentary, however, is a more Tacitean-style analysis concerning the benefits of an amoral, avarice-led form of statesmanship. It was Henry's desire to enrich himself, for example, that is shown to be at the root of his promotion of commerce: as 'a King that loved wealth and treasure he could not endure to have trade sick'.[79] The *History*'s discussion of the law moves in a similar direction. While Bacon maintained that the King's desire to augment the royal coffers led him, on occasions, to ignore or pervert standard judicial practices, he also saw this desire as having contributed to Henry's successes as a legislator.[80] The King, it was noted, conceived of law-making as a process of financial exchange whereby he would provide 'good laws' as 'retribution' for the treasure he exacted from the populace.[81] Moreover, a number of the King's successful laws, most notably the measures designed to counter depopulation, were shown to have their origins in a desire to maintain tax revenue.[82] Equally significantly, the vast fortune that Henry accrued – Bacon estimates it at 'near eighteen hundred thousand pounds' – is, in part, justified in the *History* by the close relationship between monarchical wealth and power.[83] The influence, for example, of Lady Margaret, Duchess of Burgundy – the chief promoter of the impostor kings Lambert Simnel and Perkin Warbeck – is said to arise from the fact she was 'abounding in treasure'.[84] By the same token, Maximilian, King of the Romans, was a largely ineffective monarch because he was 'feeble in means'.[85] Henry, Bacon implied in his conclusion, was aware of these examples: 'having every day occasion to take notice of the necessities and shifts for money of other great Princes abroad, it did the better by comparison set off to him the felicity of full coffers'.[86] Consequently, whereas Vergil saw the King's fortune as bringing him only misery, for Bacon it represented both Henry's moral failings and a pathway to political stability and, potentially, happiness.

As a result of this, avarice, or rather avarice-as-statecraft, is key to the *History*'s originality. Vergil and his predecessors had treated Henry's financial exactions, his military record and his legislative achievements as separate phenomena; Bacon, by contrast, conceived of them as products of a single desire. This approach not only altered the impression given of the King's character, it also constituted a rejection of the moral framework that had been central to early humanist history. Vice, for Bacon, did not necessarily create private and public misery, but instead was the source of a complex assortment of gains and losses. To an extent, the *History*'s innovations are a product of its fashionable, Tacitus-inspired approach. Avarice enabled Bacon to make the sort of causal connections between character and action that were often seen by Jacobean writers as the defining feature of the best Roman history. It also allowed him to engage in a series of Tacitean reflections on deceit and duplicity, and to emphasise the gap between the King's public acts and demeanour, and the drives that shaped his behaviour. The lessons that this unmasking demonstrates, meanwhile, are worldly and realistic, rather than straightforwardly moral; consequently, they are a good deal closer to Tacitean *arcana imperii* than Livian *exempla*. What distinguishes Bacon's work from classical accounts, however, is its focus on avarice. Such a move leads him to place money, and with it issues of finance, at the heart of his narrative in a manner that has no direct precedent in Graeco-Roman or English history. Moreover, and equally uniquely, the image that ultimately emerges of Henry is that of a merchant monarch, carefully managing his coffers and ensuring that his financial gains outweighed any losses.

3. The law and neo-Machiavellian trade

The second feature that distinguished Bacon's analysis from earlier accounts of Henry VII was its analysis of the law. Previous historians, as we have seen, had drawn attention in general terms to Henry's desire to promote 'good and profitable lawes and statutes'.[87] Bacon, however, provided a much more detailed form of analysis, temporarily halting the main chronological narrative in order to outline the causes, provisions and ultimate effects of the principal legislation passed in the King's Parliaments. Such an approach, as this section will demonstrate, allowed him to develop both an original account of the King's achievements as a legislator and a distinctively neo-Machiavellian analysis of economic statecraft.

Bacon's source with regard to Henry's legislation was the Rolls of Parliament. He could have viewed these parchment manuscripts in person at the Tower of London before the terms of his impeachment prevented him from coming within twelve miles of Court. Alternatively, and as seems more likely, he may have taken advantage of an offer from the antiquarian John Seldon to forward the notes that he had taken concerning 'divers proclamations, & commissions touching state of Henry 7. his time in the rolls'.[88] The inclusion of such material in a work of history was unconventional and controversial. John Hayward was later to provide a direct criticism of the use of statutes in histories, and in the *History* itself Bacon felt obliged to include a paragraph-long defence of his own practices.[89] Three principal reasons were given:

> [1] because it was the pre-eminent virtue and merit of this King, to whose memory I do honour, and [2] because it hath some

> correspondence to my person; but chiefly [3] because in my judgement it is some defect even in the best writers of history, that they do not often enough summarily deliver and set down the most memorable laws that passed in the times whereof they write, being indeed the principal acts of peace.[90]

The emphasis here on 'memorable' laws is particularly significant. A discussion of history, Bacon was aware, should not be a tedious list of legal regulations. Rather it was necessary to identify the most important statutes, while avoiding reference to laws that were 'of a more private and vulgar nature than ought to detain the reader of an history'.[91] Ideas about vulgarity were also of central importance to Bacon's discussion of Henry's achievements as a lawmaker. The King's regulations, it was noted, were

> deep and not vulgar; not made upon the spur of a particular occasion for the present, but out of providence of the future; to make the estate of his people still more and more happy, after the manner of the legislators in ancient and heroical times.[92]

This reference to 'ancient and heroical' legislators served to associate Henry's practices with the achievements of figures such as Solon and Lycurgus, and by extension, Bacon's own work with the historians who described them. Ultimately, however, his engagement with the statutes led his work in a different direction to that of other classical and neoclassical writers. Among the material contained in the Rolls was a substantial body of commercial and financial law. In relation to trade, this covered issues such as the import and export of goods by English and foreign merchants,[93] the taxation of overseas traders,[94] the prices of particular goods,[95] the use of weights and measures[96] and the management of trading companies.[97] With regard to finance, there were statutes concerning usury,[98] the exchange of foreign money,[99] coinage,[100] as well as various measures relating to taxation.[101] Bacon, in a manner no previous historian had done, engaged with these regulations, sometimes briefly discussing their principal provisions, elsewhere offering more lengthy analysis. Given the criteria he had established for the inclusion and exclusion of particular laws, such a move makes a clear statement. For Bacon, these were not 'vulgar' pieces of legislation, but rather the sort of 'deep' laws from which precepts could be drawn, and which, as a consequence, merited consideration in a serious work of history.

In dealing with these laws, one of Bacon's key aims was to judge the merits of particular statutes. His approach to this task was, in a sense, fundamentally un-empirical. He did not seek alternative forms of evidence to examine whether a certain law had promoted or hindered trade, enriched or impoverished the people. Rather, the laws were his only source material and – as was standard practice in classical and neoclassical history – judgements were made using a series of seemingly pre-conceived ideas regarding what constituted good government.[102] With regard to economic issues, Bacon's understanding of good government was derived from his engagement with an ongoing European debate concerning the relationship between wealth and *grandezza* (national greatness). Key to this discussion was the work of Machiavelli.[103] For the Florentine, to achieve *grandezza* it was necessary to create a 'numerous and well-armed people'.[104] In his discussions of how this might be achieved, Machiavelli dismissed what he referred to as 'the popular opinion' of wealth as the 'sinew of warfare'.[105] Rather, while money was clearly necessary for a prince or republic to enter into a war, it was 'good soldiers' who were key, as 'gold is an insufficient means of finding good soldiers, but good soldiers are a more than sufficient means of finding gold'.[106] These good soldiers, he maintained, were generally infantrymen not cavalrymen, and always free citizens driven by a desire for glory rather than mercenaries who fought for a 'bit of salary'.[107]

Underpinning such comments were a series of core assumptions. Machiavelli associated wealth and the desire for wealth with selfishness and corruption; indeed, excessive riches are presented as incompatible with 'well-organised republics'.[108] The poverty of Rome's citizens, meanwhile, was shown to have been central to its success, with Machiavelli placing particular emphasis on the selection of two small-landowner farmers, Cincinnatus and Regulus, as Roman generals.[109] Such appointments demonstrated both the virtue of the republic, which valued merit over wealth, and the virtue of these individuals, who sought honour from battle rather than material reward. Concluding his account of the generals, Machiavelli observed: 'it would be possible to demonstrate with a long discussion how much better are the fruits of poverty than of wealth and that poverty has honoured citizens, provinces, sects, while wealth has destroyed them, if this subject had not on many occasions been celebrated by other writers'.[110]

Machiavelli's arguments were to be subjected to considerable criticism in the years following their publication, as various writers sought to demonstrate that wealth was not just compatible with greatness, but fundamental to its existence.[111] In his *Politics* (1589, published in English in 1594), for example, the Flemish humanist Justus Lipsius rejected the notion that a state required a spirited citizen militia to advance its interests. Rather, he argued, the foundations of military success lay in acquiring a disciplined professional army and the money to pay and arm it. As a consequence, a provident prince should carefully consult his army about the financial costs of war before entering into it: for as the '*phisitions do denie that men cannot walke without sinewes*, so warre cannot set forward without coine'.[112] A similar argument was developed by the Italian writer Giovanni Botero in his *A Treatise, Concerning the Causes of the Magnificencie and Greatnes of Cities* (1588, published in English in 1606).[113] As Machiavelli had done, Botero maintained that a state's greatness was a product of the 'multitude' of its inhabitants.[114] However, for Botero it was not just liberty that drew individuals to a metropolis, but also plenty. In particular, a state that promoted manufacturing would not only generate money, but also attract people to make, trade and transport goods, and supply the needs of labourers. Consequently, a statesman had two important functions to fulfil. First, he needed to lure manufacturers who were masters of 'Art and cunning'.[115] This could be achieved

> *if he bring out of other countries excellent artificers, & give them enterteinment & convenient seate to dwell upon: if he reckon of good witts, and esteeme of singular and rare inventions and workmanship: if other while also he doe reward perfection and excellency in things of Art and cunning.*[116]

Second, he had to prevent '*rude & unwrought things*', such as 'Wooll', 'Silke', 'Timber' and 'Metall', from being exported.[117] If this was not done, artificers would abandon a city, thereby reducing its population, and the prince's revenue would be diminished, as manufactured goods sold for more than the unwrought natural products.[118] Concluding his discussion, Botero praised the laws against the 'carrying out of Woolles out of their dominions' made by the kings of England and France, arguing that such regulations contributed to the 'riches and the greatnes of the King' and advanced the interests of his people.[119]

Bacon was clearly interested in the issues raised by such analyses, and he accepted the notion that one of the key roles of a statesman was to administer the wealth and plenty of a polity in a manner that advanced its greatness. In relation to military affairs, however, he rejected the sort of arguments developed by Lipsius and Botero and, albeit with some qualifications, sided with Machiavelli.[120] His most detailed engagement with this subject before the *History* came in his unfinished work of c. 1608: 'Of the True Greatness of Britain'.[121] Bacon's analysis began by outlining the errors and excesses 'of certain immoderate opinions' regarding a nation's military power, and repudiating the suggestion that size of territory, fruitfulness of soil, fortification of towns and riches might, of themselves, promote greatness.[122] To demonstrate this he turned directly to 'the authority of Machiavel', and endorsed both his rejection of the claim that '*money was the sinews of war*' and his contention that 'there are no other true *sinews of war*, but the *sinews and muscles of men's arms*'.[123] Support was also provided for the Florentine's comments regarding the connection between poverty, physical hardship and military success. Thus concluding his discussion of a range of successful kingdoms – among them the Persians, Spartans, Turks, Goths and Vandals – Bacon noted that 'in case of foreign wars, you shall scarcely find any of the great monarchies of the world, but have had their foundations in poverty and contemptible beginnings'.[124] This was not to say, however, that treasure and money were inherently pernicious. Rather, Bacon went on to argue, they could assist in bringing 'true greatness and strength to a state' if three conditions were met:

> First, [. . .] *that they be joined with martial prowess and valour.*
> Secondly, *That treasure doth then advance greatness, when it is rather in mediocrity than in great abundance. And again better when some part of the state is poor, than when all parts of it are rich.*
> And lastly, *That treasure in a state is more or less serviceable, as the hands are in which the wealth chiefly resteth.*[125]

To an extent such comments remain firmly in the Machiavellian tradition. Poverty is presented as a condition of military virtue, and Bacon favours the even division of wealth that Machiavelli associates with a republic – his preferred form of government. Nevertheless, for Bacon, such conditions might be made to exist within a modern commercial society. Indeed, when searching for an example of a society where wealth had been distributed evenly, he turned not to the farms of ancient Rome, as Machiavelli had done, but rather to the warehouses and shops of the Dutch. For Bacon, it was the fact that wealth had been distributed between 'merchants, burghers, tradesmen, freeholders, farmers in the country, and the like' that had been key to Dutch survival and success.[126]

Such arguments were to be developed a good deal further in the various discussions of Henry's statutes which punctuate the *History*'s narrative. These sections of the discussion emphasised that the wealth derived from commerce had the potential to enervate a nation and was, as a consequence, a potential threat to national greatness. Bacon's contention, however, was neither that trade should be ignored, nor poverty embraced. Rather, he sought to show that through the careful management of commerce, Henry had been able to make wealth support and augment power.

This concern with economic management meant that there were parallels between Bacon's approach and that of Botero. For both writers, one of a monarch's key functions was to promote a form of nationally beneficial commercial activity. Bacon emphasised the importance of this role in an invented speech he gave to Henry, supposedly delivered to Parliament in the late 1480s:

> And because it is the King's desire that that this peace wherein he hopeth to govern and maintain you do not bear only unto you leaves, for you to sit under the shade of them in safety, but also should bear you fruit of riches, wealth, and plenty; therefore his Grace prays you to take into consideration matter of trade, as also the manufactures of the kingdom […][127]

Underpinning Bacon's account here was the assumption that a 'lawful and royal' form of trading could contribute to a nation's interests. And in his discussion of the ways in which Henry had succeeded in promoting trade, the *History* came to endorse a number of Botero's views on good practice. For example, Bacon praised Henry's statutes for 'the keeping of wools within the realm', assuming, as Botero had done, that exporting raw materials was a commercially ill-advised move.[128] Equally, the *History* endorsed measures restricting the import of silk. Key to the analysis here was a series of widely held assumptions about 'worked up' (already manufactured) goods. Making and selling these goods to other countries, it was agreed, achieved a profit. Buying them from abroad, however, enriched foreign manufacturers and, particularly as they were generally luxury and disposable items, wasted native resources. Such an argument could then be used to justify bans on foreign imports. As Bacon observed, Henry's regulations preventing certain types of silk from entering the country pointed to a 'true principle': 'that where foreign materials are but superfluities [by which he means 'luxuries'], foreign manufactures should be prohibited, for that will either banish the superfluity or gain the manufacture'.[129] For Botero, therefore, as for Bacon, 'gaining' the manufacture constituted a sensible goal for government policy.

Despite these similarities, however, the bulk of the commercial directives that Bacon described had a different goal than those endorsed by Botero. Botero's primary concern had been with how a city might attract artificers and merchants and protect the interests of its tradesmen. Bacon, in contrast, focused on and applauded the various laws that Henry used to regulate these sections of the population, paying particular attention to measures used to prevent individuals enriching themselves to the detriment of 'lawful and royal trading'.[130] Reference is made, for example, to the 'good and politic laws' made to prohibit usury and illegal money exchanges, which are referred to as the 'bastard use of money' and 'bastard usury' respectively.[131] Also summarised and endorsed are measures taken to limit the price of cloth,[132] to restrict the power and wealth of London's trading companies,[133] and to ensure that overseas tradesmen both paid taxes and were prevented from withdrawing money earned in England out of the nation.[134] Underlying these comments is the Machiavellian idea of a tension between excessive private wealth and the interests of a well-run state. Traders and manufacturers, as Bacon presents them, are not simply sources of greatness, but also threats to it. To increase their profits, usurers might charge outlandish rates of interest, clothiers set unfairly high prices, trading companies take advantage of monopolistic trading practices, and foreign merchants enrich themselves at the expense of the English. Where Bacon differed from Machiavelli, however, was in his interest in the ways that trade might be managed to alleviate these problems. For Bacon a vital and – as Henry's reign demonstrated – achievable task for government was to restrict those forms of commerce that harmed a nation's interests. Through doing so, it was emphasised, a monarch could promote beneficial forms of trade and advance a nation's interests.

A revised form of Machiavellian analysis aimed at circumventing the tension between wealth and virtue was also of central importance to Bacon's approach to the relationship between economic and military affairs. Although Machiavelli is not invoked directly, his influence is readily apparent in the *History*'s discussion of regulations regarding the importation of 'wines and woads' from Gascony and Languedoc.[135] The law under consideration was the 1489 statute 'An act against bringing wine into this realm in foreign vessels'.[136] This had decreed that only English, Welsh and Irish ships could import these goods, with the measure being justified on the grounds that 'there has recently been a great diminution and decay of the navy of this realm of England'.[137] While Bacon followed his source material in noting that the measure was 'for the better maintenance of the navy', he placed it in a broader historical context.[138] Whereas the 'ancient policy' of the kingdom had sought to secure cheapness by allowing international merchants to bring in all sorts of commodities, Henry looked 'to the point of state concerning the naval power'.[139] Through doing so, he wisely subordinated 'consideration of plenty to consideration of power'.[140] Such claims are based on the assumptions that there is a tension between power and plenty and that in choosing the latter over the former, Henry had made the correct, Machiavellian decision. This tension, however, is conceived of as partial rather than absolute. Bacon did not maintain that Henry should have banned the trade in wine and woads entirely; rather, it was necessary that it continued in order to create demand for English shipping. The task for statesmen, therefore, was not to ignore or reduce the nation's 'plenty', but rather to manage it in a manner that ensured that it contributed to power.

An even more explicitly Machiavellian analysis was to be developed in Bacon's discussion of the 1489–90 'Act against pulling down towns'.[141] This statute sought to combat depopulation by decreeing that 'houses of husbandry' with more than twenty acres of land 'should be maintained and kept up for ever' or face 'seizure of the land itself by the King and lords of the fee, as to half the profits'.[142] For Bacon, however, the law's real significance lay in its wider historical implications. Two points are of note here. First, in a way that the law did not, Bacon traced the origins of the changes in land usage that had reduced the population back to the increased use of enclosure. The merit of the King's legislation lay in the fact that it did not directly prohibit this practice, which had also augmented agricultural productivity, but rather sought to offset its pernicious consequences. For Bacon, therefore, Henry's achievement was to pioneer a regulated and improved form of enclosure that maintained improvements in the nation's 'patrimony', but avoided depopulation.[143] Second, Bacon greatly expanded the statute's brief reference to the enfeeblement of the nation's defences to provide a detailed, and distinctively Machiavellian, analysis of England's armed forces. His key contention was that, through establishing the conditions necessary for a citizen militia, the law had done much to 'advance the military power of the kingdom'.[144] The opinion of the 'men of best judgement', Bacon noted, alluding directly to Machiavelli, was that the principal strength of an army lay in its infantry.[145] And for Bacon, as for Machiavelli, an infantry was the product of a certain type of social stratification. A good cavalry might be had in nations such as France and Italy, where the people were divided between 'noblemen and gentlemen' and 'cottagers'.[146] An infantry, however, required men 'bred not in a servile or indigent fashion, but in some free and plentiful manner'.[147] By ensuring that farms were of sufficient size to maintain an able body 'out of penury', the depopulation act had put 'a great part of the lands of the kingdom unto the hold and occupation of the yeomanry or middle people'.[148] As a result, Henry's reform had 'secretly [sown] Hydra's teeth'.[149] England, despite its relatively small territories, had no need for mercenaries and was able to field a large and able body of armed men.[150] Bacon, therefore, clearly imagined that the law on depopulation had helped to produce just the sort of armed, small landowners that Machiavelli had praised. However, not only did he emphasise that such measures were compatible with increased agricultural productivity, an issue of little interest to Machiavelli, but he also avoided the praise for poverty that had been a key feature of Machiavelli's analysis. This move was to be of central importance for English historiography. It was Bacon's association of Henry's reign with the emergence of a prosperous 'middle people' that enabled this section of the *History*, as we shall see in later chapters, to play a key role in seventeenth- and eighteenth-century accounts of the rise of commerce and the commercial classes. Bacon, of course, knew nothing of such developments, and they are based, in a sense, on a misreading of his work; he is clearly discussing rural, agricultural developments, not changes to trade. However, such a misreading would itself have been impossible had Bacon not offered a partial rejection of Machiavellian ideas regarding wealth and poverty.

Conclusion

Underlying Bacon's analysis of Henry's management of English trade is a series of assumptions about commerce, politics and history; I would like to conclude this chapter by briefly delineating these. Bacon's account is based on the notion that there exist 'good' and 'bad' forms of commercial activity. The former are those which advance the interests of the kingdom; the latter those which work against them. This distinction was of key importance to the form of 'reason of state' theory that emerged in the latter part of the sixteenth century and, through discussing commercial affairs at length and drawing on such concepts, Bacon's work aligns itself with this tradition. However, his contentions that an effective army could not be obtained purely through financial means, and that a pernicious form of commerce would be one that prioritised plenty over power, ensured that he took such ideas in a distinctively Machiavellian direction. In sum, therefore, Bacon rejected both Botero's assumption that plenty and power were necessary concomitants and the extreme Machiavellian position that private plenty and public power were inherently incompatible. Rather, the key task for the lawmaker was to manage and restrain commerce in a way that reconciled power and plenty and wealth and virtue. The stakes in such an activity were high. Commerce could bring riches and wealth to a nation and, through augmenting the royal coffers, determine its international power and influence. Equally though, it was a potentially enervating force; 'bad' types of trade could drain a state of wealth, destroy its armed forces and enrich its competitors. Documenting attempts to regulate commerce, Bacon assumed, was one of the principal roles for a modern historian. Key to this idea was the claim advanced by Machiavelli and much humanist historiography that the study of history could provide a series of examples from which general principles of the utmost value to modern statesmen could be drawn. Bacon, however, in a way that Machiavelli did not, conceived of the administration of trade as a branch of politics worthy of detailed analysis and capable of being distilled into a practical and useful form of knowledge.

2

Exemplary history: William Camden's *Annales*

William Camden's *Annales of Queen Elizabeth* (1615, 1625) are prefaced by a short essay entitled 'The Authour to the Reader'. In this discussion, Camden sought to associate his own approach to historiography with those of Polybius and Tacitus. The chief merit of the former, it was noted, was his understanding of causation, specifically his awareness that only through developing an account of causal processes could history function as a didactic mode of writing. As Camden observed:

> Circumstances I have in no wise omitted, that not onely the Events of Affairs, but also the Reasons and Causes thereof, might be understood. That of *Polybius* I like well *Take away from History Why, How, and To what end, things have been done, and Whether the thing done hath succeeded according to Reason; and all that remains will be an idle Sport and Foolery, than a profitable Instruction: and though for the present it may delight, for the future it cannot profit.*[1]

His understanding of historical form and style, Camden continued, had been derived from Tacitus:

> My Work I have intitled by the Name of ANNALS, in regard I have disposed every thing in its proper Year: for I have learn'd of *Tacitus*, that Weighty and remarkable Occurences are to be digested by way of Annals; and that the principal Business of Annals is, to preserve Vertuous Actions from being buried in Oblivion, and to deter men from either speaking or doing what is amiss, for fear of after-Infamy with Posterity.[2]

Such ideas about history ensured that Camden's conception of the subject had some significant similarities with Bacon's. Both saw affairs of state as their principal subjects and, in discussing them, drew inspiration from classical historiography. Moreover, both were attracted to the works of Tacitus. And although Bacon had relatively little to say on Polybius, he, like Camden, entirely endorsed the Polybian claim that it was through analysis of cause and effect that history could teach men political wisdom.

The similarities between their work have led the two writers to be conceived of as part of the same Tacitean, 'politic' school of history.[3] However, while an admiration for the Roman historian undoubtedly shaped their historical outlooks, there are some important differences between them. Whereas Bacon's exile meant that he had access to limited archival sources, Camden received direct support from Court, specifically from Lord Burghley, and wrote surrounded by a wealth of archival material. They also approached Tacitus' work in different ways. Bacon's account, as we saw in the previous chapter, was rooted in a fashionable, 'realist' form of history based around psychological and pathological analysis. Camden, however, showed little interest in exploring the human psyche. As he noted in 'The Author to the Reader': 'Things secret and abstruse I have not pried into' as '*The hidden Meanings of Princes* [...] *and what they secretly design to search out, it is unlawfull, it is doubtfull and dangerous.*'[4] Their attitudes to Tacitus' moralism also contrasted sharply. Bacon conceived of the Roman as a useful guide to the murky labyrinths of an amoral form of politics. In contrast, Camden, as his comments show, viewed him as a straightforward moralist whose work sought to preserve virtuous actions and deter posterity from 'doing what is amiss'. As a result, Camden's approach to didacticism had more in common with the 'exemplary', Livian tradition of Vergil and Hall than it did with the more world-weary history of Bacon.

Finally, as the rest of this chapter will explore, the two historians developed very different analyses of economic statecraft. For Bacon, the successful administration of the nation's revenues was a skill, a product of a ruler's political cunning and understanding of the complex workings of finance. By contrast Camden, in similar fashion to Burghley, saw good financial management as a virtue, dependent not on specialist forms of knowledge, but rather on the monarch's commitment to the interests and welfare of the commonwealth. Indeed, Camden's key claim was that the Queen's careful administration of the nation's revenues, coin and commerce had brought her the sort of 'honour' and 'glory' conventionally associated with military victories and political successes. The first part of this discussion looks at how, through drawing on ideas from Burghley, Camden developed an account of Elizabeth's honourable economic statecraft. The second section explores his treatment of those areas of policy – mercantile avarice, monopolies and the growth of luxury – which sat less comfortably within this framework.

1. Commerce, finance and honour

Camden's conceptions of commerce and finance were shaped by his relationship with William Cecil, Lord Burghley. Born in 1551, Camden was educated at Christ's Hospital and St Paul's School, the latter an institution run by two of Cecil's associates, John Cooke and Alexander Nowell.[5] He went on to study at the University of Oxford, before eventually gaining employment at Westminster School, where he served first as an under-master (1575–93) and later as headmaster (1593–97). It was here that Camden moved directly into Burghley's orbit. Burghley had been Elizabeth's principal agent when she re-established the school in 1560, and continued to act as its patron, regularly presiding over scholarly gatherings, and retaining a residence nearby. Consequently, as Camden's biographer Wyman H. Herendeen has argued, the school was 'deeply imbued with the political, scholarly, and religious vision of [Burghley]', and he came to act as 'the presiding genius over the community in which Camden lived'.[6] Burghley's support and patronage also did much to shape Camden's career as an antiquarian and historian. Through helping to bring together a like-minded circle of scholars, among them Nowell, Gabriel Goodman and William Latimer, and providing access to his extensive collection of antiquarian material, Burghley provided a fertile intellectual environment within which Camden could work. It was only fitting, therefore, that Camden dedicated the first editions of the *Britannia* (1586) to Burghley.[7] Moreover, it was Burghley, as Camden explained in the preface to the *Annales*, who at some point in the 1590s had passed on to him 'first his [Burghley's] own, and then the Queen's Rolls, Memorials and Records, willing me to compile from thence an Historical Account of the Reign of Queen ELIZABETH'.[8] Camden 'obeyed' Burghley's request, he continued, 'lest I might seem either to neglect the Memory of that most Excellent Princess, or to fail his Expectation'.[9]

The long and complex development of the *Annales* has been well covered in the existing scholarly literature, and readers interested in the subject are advised to consult the excellent accounts by Hugh Trevor-Roper and Daniel Woolf.[10] All that needs to be added here is that, after progress on the project ground to a halt following Burghley's death in 1598, Camden returned to it in the early years of James's reign at the request of the King and the French historian Jacques-Auguste de Thou. The first three parts of the *Annales*, covering the period 1558–88, were published in 1615; a final part dealing with the period 1589–1603 emerged posthumously in 1625. Aspects of the *Annales*' content were clearly shaped by the Jacobean context in which Camden wrote. In particular, its account of Mary Stuart was, in effect, written to order for James as part of his attempt to rescue his mother's reputation from the scandalous accusations levelled at her by the Scottish historian George Buchanan.[11] The rest of the text, meanwhile, has been alternatively presented by modern historians both as part of the King's strategy to identify his approach to government with that of Elizabeth, and as an oblique criticism of James's statesmanship.[12]

The primary influence on Camden's accounts of commerce and finance, however, was not James, but Burghley. This influence took a number of forms. At a very general level, by handing over a series of government records, Burghley shaped the type of history that Camden was able to write. And while the original batch of archival sources was later supplemented by further papers from Sir Robert Cotton, Camden essentially received more of the same kind of material. This, therefore, was a history written through consultation with 'Charters and Grants of Kings and great Personages, Letters, Consultations in the Council-Chamber, Embassadours Instructions and Epistles, [and] Parliamentary Diaries, Acts and Statutes'.[13] These documents enabled Camden, as numerous commentators have noted, to create an impressively wide-ranging commentary on the age of Elizabeth, and one that paid particular attention to economic affairs.[14] What needs to be remembered, however, is that while Camden had access to an unprecedented selection of archival material, the bulk of this information was derived from government sources. As a result, he saw events from a distinctively political perspective, and his concern was not so much with commerce and finance *per se*, but rather the state's management and regulation of these activities.

In discussing such issues Camden provided a broad endorsement of the statesmanship of Lord Burghley. Burghley's interest in financial affairs was a long-standing one.[15] As a clerk of council under Edward VI he had concerned himself with monetary problems, compiling extensive lists of domestic and foreign debts and schedules for discharging them. He left this position following Mary's ascent to the throne, but returned to government with Elizabeth in 1558, as Secretary of State. Although William Paulet, the marquess of Winchester, served as Lord Treasurer during this period, Burghley, as Frederick C. Dietz argued, had 'the real initiative and control in matters of revenue policy'.[16] When Winchester died in 1572, Burghley succeeded him as Lord Treasurer, holding the post and, with it, direct responsibility for government revenue for the rest of his life.

A flavour of the philosophy that underpinned Burghley's work can be gained from a collection of thirty-four of his aphorisms and sayings assembled shortly after his death by his first biographer.[17] Key to these observations was a conventional Christian view of human beings as, by nature, selfish, greedy creatures, who could expect this-worldly punishments for their sinful actions.[18] Thus Burghley observed that 'he seldom sawe goods yll gotten, but weare quicklie ill spent'; 'Riches weare God's blessings to such as use them well, and his curse to such as did not.'[19] Moreover, 'Private gaine is the perverting of justice, and pestilence of a Commonwealth.'[20] Equally significant to his comments, however, was a form of Christian humanism that valued the *vita activa* and *vivere civile*, and understood good statesmanship as a product of a ruler's capacity to, in some sense, transcend his fallen status, and subordinate his private interests and desires to the common good. Thus the Lord Treasurer is said to have commented: 'He can never be a good Statesman, who respecteth not the publique more than his owne private.'[21] Moreover: 'Good Princes ought first to preferre the service of God and his Church, and next of the Commonwealth, before theire own pleasure or proffit.'[22] The assumption here was that, while monarchs needed to 'follow the best counsell' and secure the love of their people, they were also required to be 'better than other men, because they command and rule all others'.[23] This ensured that 'Noe wise Prince can be a tyraunt' and that 'a happie King' was one that 'can governe and moderate his affections'.[24] Elizabeth, Burghley argued, was the perfect embodiment of such a monarch, and the list of sayings concluded with a paean to her:

> She had so rare gifts, as when her Counsell had said all they cold, she wold find out a wise Counsell beyond all theires, and that she shew'd her wisdome and care of her Contrie; for there was never anie great consultation, but she wold be present herself, to her great profitt and praise.[25]

Burghley was to develop a more extended analysis of the Queen's approach to government in 'A Meditation on the State of England', a thirty-eight-page 1595 manuscript which provided both 'a resumé' of the Queen's policy and an 'apologia' for Burghley's career as secretary and Lord Treasurer.[26] The Queen's management of the nation's finances, he argued in this document, was a source of wonder. She had spent substantial sums of money on the nation's defences, funding both an expansion of the navy and a series of new garrisons. Despite this, 'Her Majesty is not indebted but is able with the power of her own people with out the help of strange force to defend her realm.'[27] This state of affairs, he continued, had attracted the attention of a variety of 'curious heads' who 'although they know this to be true yet are inquisitive by what means she doth possess soe much riches'.[28] To satisfy these individuals, Burghley developed a three-pronged explanation rooted in the same ideas regarding 'public' good and private 'vice' that had underpinned his sayings. The primary reason for Elizabeth's achievement, he argued, was her absolute commitment to the commonwealth; she 'had regard not to expend her Treasure but either for the honor of her estate, [...] or for publique defence of her realm, or to ayde her neighbors tyrannously oppressed'.[29] Such 'parsimony', Burghley continued, 'hath been a great cause of her Majesty's riches' and had enabled her 'to perform those actions whereof heads are inquisitive'.[30] Second, Burghley maintained that the Queen had been able to regulate the selfish desires of her populace by reforming 'great abuses in such as had charge of her revenues and namely of her customs'.[31] This had been achieved through preventing officers from engrossing money, and reducing the sums left uncollected, moves which brought in large yearly sums to the state.[32] Third, Elizabeth abandoned the system of tax assessment under which individuals were forced to undergo inquisitions by 'oath or others coercion'.[33]

While this 'voluntary' system may have reduced income, it helped to develop trust in the monarchy and ensured that the 'subsidies as they were collected did also increase [the Queen's] power'.[34] The success that Elizabeth enjoyed with regard to revenue was, therefore, a product of both her own commitment to the public's welfare, and her capacity to generate a similar public spiritedness from her subjects.

Camden's narrative was based on the same core assumptions regarding financial good practice as Burghley's account, and drew directly on the Lord Treasurer's 'Meditation'. This can be seen particularly clearly in the *Annales*' record for 1590. The discussion opens with a list of the large sums of money that Elizabeth had spent in support of Protestant interests in mainland Europe.[35] Such generosity attracted the attention of 'many' observers who, like the 'curious heads' referred to by Burghley,

> admired whence this Wealth came to serve all these Turns, seeing she was in no man's Debt (as all other Princes almost were,) and was able to defend herself and hers without any foreign Helps, which not one of her neighbour-Kings could doe.[36]

Camden then went on to use and develop the 'Meditation's' analysis of Elizabeth's successes, referring, in sequence, to the same three causes as Burghley. He began, therefore, by discussing the Queen's parsimony, arguing that she was 'providently frugal, and scarcely spent any thing, but for the Maintenance of her Royal State, the Defence of her Kingdom, or the Relieving of her Neighbours'.[37] The discussion next proceeded to deal with reforms to 'customs'. Camden agreed that reforms in this area had been important, but attributed them to Burghley rather than to Elizabeth, noting that the Lord Treasurer had 'looked narrowly unto those who had the Charge of Customs and Imposts, by whose Avarice many things were under-hand imbezeled'.[38] Finally, Camden endorsed and developed Burghley's comments on taxation. The Queen, he observed, 'detested Extortions, and all Rigidness in exacting extraordinary Contributions', and did not use unpopular forms of revenue such as benevolences or poll taxes.[39] This ensured that the 'People always granted Subsidies chearfully' and their subsidies were 'rather voluntary, without Demanding or any Constraint'.[40]

In addition to the material derived from Burghley, Camden added one further explanation for the Queen's financial successes.[41] Through following the advice of 'one Caermarden', he noted, 'an understanding and subtil Fellow, of the Mysteries of the Farmers of her Customs', Elizabeth was able to raise the income she derived from customs from £14,000 to £42,000.[42] The decision to turn to Carmarden was opposed by Burghley, Leicester and Walsingham, who maintained that it 'would tend to the Disgrace and Disparagement of her and her Council, if she should hearken to the Accusations of so inconsiderable an Informer'.[43] Elizabeth, however, defended her actions by noting that 'it was the Duty of a Prince to hold an equal Hand over the highest and the lowest' and that she would not 'endure that the Farmers of the Customs should like Horse-leeches suck themselves fat upon the Goods of the Commonwealth, whilst the poor Treasury waxed lean and was exhausted'.[44] Camden's sympathies in this passage are clearly with the Queen, and there is an irony in the fact that the one section of his discussion on revenue not derived from Burghley contained a direct criticism of him. Ultimately, however, even this passage provides a vindication of the conception of Elizabeth that Burghley and Camden shared. The successful management of the nation's finances, both agreed, was dependent on acting against self-interested practices, and ensuring that people and government worked in amicable partnership with one another to secure the safety and prosperity of the commonwealth.

Camden and Burghley's ideas about the public interest were closely connected to another aspect of their approach to statecraft, namely their understandings of 'honour' and the cognate term, 'glory'. In his highly influential discussion of 'honour', Mervyn James argued that the late sixteenth and early seventeenth centuries were the time of a key shift in the concept.[45] 'Honour' in the early Tudor period had been conceptualised in relation to an individual's bloodline. Although any individual might earn honour for themselves on the battlefield, an exalted lineage, it was assumed, 'predisposed' individuals to honourable forms of conduct. To behave with 'honour', meanwhile, was to engage in self-assertive, masculine and martial actions, which simultaneously secured one's own reputation and that of one's family. Such ideas had an ambivalent relationship with the king and the commonwealth. Honour societies revered kingship. However, family ties and the symbolic rite of '"giving one's word" – the word of honour' committed individuals to courses of action which could not, at least without dishonour, be violated.[46] As such, they helped to reinforce a system of social relations that were beyond the direct jurisdiction of the state, and had the potential to generate a series of motives and justifications for opposition to the will of the Crown. Towards the end of the Tudor period, James contended, this understanding of honour yielded to a new 'moralized' approach.[47] At one level, although lineage remained an important concept, honour became partially detached from its anchorage in pedigree and descent, as the privileges of honour were increasingly sought not just by men of war but 'lawyers, officials, merchants, even husbandmen and artisans'.[48] Equally significantly, the growing influence of humanism and religion, 'itself the result of a deeper penetration of lay society by literacy and education', helped to redefine ideas of honour, which came to be associated with learning, virtue, godliness and, perhaps most significantly, public service to the state.[49]

Such ideas are broadly in line with the accounts of scholars working on the influence of humanist ideas.[50] In particular Markku Peltonen has shown that a form of humanism emerged in England during the 1570s and 1580s which assumed that the 'main aim of human life was [...] the advancement of the common good' and that this could only be achieved 'by the relentless pursuit of a virtuous *vita activa*'.[51] While many humanist writers continued to define virtue in relation to military activity, and it was generally agreed that citizens had a duty of honour to defend the fatherland from attack, more irenic conceptions of public service also emerged. Thus for some writers, particularly the authors of moral treatises such as Haly Heron, Thomas Pritchard and William Blandy, 'to take part in the political life of the commonwealth and to act as its governor was the way in which men could acquire the greatest amount of worldly glory'.[52]

Camden's account is rooted in these ideas and, more specifically, the notion that an individual's contribution to the commonwealth might be based on the financial aspects of statecraft. This can be seen particularly clearly in the lengthy 'character' of Burghley included in the *Annales*. Discussing his former patron, Camden noted that

> (though [Burghley] detested to scrape Money together by base and corrupt ways) he increased both his private Estate and the publick Treasure by his Industry and Frugality. For he hardly suffered any thing to be expended but for the Queen's Majestie's Honour, the Defence of the Realm, or the relief of neighbouring Allies. He looked strictly, yet not over-rigidly, to the Farmers of the Customes. He never

> liked (as he was wont to say) that the Treasury should grow too great like the Spleen,whilst the rest of the Members languished and pined away: and he made it his great Endeavour, not without good Success, that both Prince and People might grow rich: saying oftentimes, that nothing is truly for a Prince's Profit which is not conjoyned with Honour. Wherefore he would have no Rents raised upon Lands, nor the old Farmers and Tenants put out. Which also he observed in his own private Estate, which he managed with that Integrity, that he never sued any man, nor any man ever sued him. But I will not goe too far in his Praises: yet may I say truly, that he was one of those few who have both lived and died with Glory.[53]

Key to Camden's comments here is an implied contrast between honourable and dishonourable approaches to wealth. On the one hand, a statesman could use 'base and corrupt' means or overly rigid revenue-collection to amass a fortune. In such circumstances, the interests of statesman and populace would be in opposition to one another, and honour and glory would be sacrificed to avarice. On the other hand, political figures could, as Burghley had done, forego opportunities to seize money and seek to honourably administer the nation's finances. While such an approach required 'Industry and Frugality', through it the people, their government and their monarch could simultaneously grow rich, and a variety of potentially conflicting financial interests could be reconciled. In Camden's account, therefore, we see the emergence of what might be called a 'negative' conception of 'honour' and 'glory'. Rather than requiring specific 'positive' actions on the part of an individual, honour and glory could be acquired, as they had been by Burghley, through the fair management of monetary and property relations and the avoidance of measures aimed at avaricious forms of self-advancement.

These ideas underpinned the *Annales*' general discussion of Elizabethan economic affairs. Indeed, Camden sought to show that through prioritising the welfare of the public in matters of finance, the Queen had earned herself 'honour' and 'glory'. With regard to commerce, these attributes had been acquired in a number of ways. On occasions, Elizabeth gained honour, as Burghley had done, through protecting property rights. Thus, following the confiscations they had suffered at the hands of the Duke of Alva, the Queen intervened to restore property to her tradesmen in the Netherlands; consequently, matters are said to have 'turned to her exceeding great

Honour'.[54] Alva, in contrast, presumably to his equally great dishonour, 'restored not a Farthing to the *Netherlanders*'.[55] Elsewhere, mercantile activity, particularly the development of new commercial institutions, was shown to have the capacity to bestow more 'positive' forms of prestige. Discussing the foundation of the East India Company in 1600, Camden observed that 'The Queen nevertheless, for the increase of Navigation, the Honour of the Kingdom, and the propagation of Trade, about this time set up a Company or Society of *East-India* Merchants with large Privileges.'[56] The establishment of a factory in Surat by the Company, meanwhile, is described as being 'to the Honour of the English Nation'.[57] Also of significance here is Camden's account of the Russian Tsar, John Basilides (Ivan IV). Summarising a letter from Ivan to Elizabeth, for example, Camden noted that Ivan 'twittingly upbraided' the English for, among other things, being 'too mindfull of the Merchants Business (which were matters unbeseeming a Prince)'.[58] Camden had no sympathy for such views, arguing that the Tsar had 'contemptuously and disgracefully charged [merchants] as a sordid kind of people, that rather gaped after Wealth than sought their Prince's Honour'.[59]

Honour was also shown to be a key issue in relation to a nation's coinage, and here, once again, Burghley's influence was of central importance. In the years between 1544 and 1551, the government had 'enhanced' England's coins by raising their face value without altering their bullion content, and 'debased' them through lowering the metal content, but maintaining the same face value.[60] This situation was remedied between 1560 and 1561 when Elizabeth reduced the face value of a range of enhanced coins and recalled the debased money, replacing it with new coin. Burghley played a key role in this process, both advising the Queen and helping to draft *A Summary of Certain Reasons* (1560), the government publication that explained to the populace the rationale behind the re-coinage.[61]

At the time Camden wrote, discussion of reforms to the money supply was already a standard feature of historiography on Elizabethan England. John Stow had introduced a brief comment on the issue in the 1570 edition of his *Chronicle*, describing the changes to the value of individual coins produced by Elizabeth's 1560 proclamation, and noting that 'her grace restored unto all her subjectes fyne and pure sterlinge moneye, both of gold and sylver for theyr corrupt and base coyne'.[62] These remarks were then repeated by 'Holinshed' and gradually expanded in later editions of Stow's *Chronicle* and *Annales*, first by Stow himself and then by his successor, Edmund Howes.[63] Camden's account, however, was not merely a good deal more detailed than that of his predecessors, it also interpreted events through the lens of humanist ideas concerning 'honour' and 'glory'. His key assumption was that a nation's coinage constituted a marker of its reputation and that of its monarch. Problems with England's currency had their origins, Camden argued, in the actions of Henry VIII who, 'to the great Dishonour of the Kingdom, and the Damage of his Successours and People', had mixed the coin with brass 'leaving thereby a notable example of Riot and Prodigality'.[64] Edward VI could not act to restore this situation and Mary 'durst' not.[65] Such a situation was not just embarrassing for England, it also worked to the detriment of its people. To prove this, Camden drew on the arguments from Burghley's *Summary of Certain Reasons*, justifying coinage reforms on the grounds that they would bring an end to fraudulent practices 'at home and abroad', and help to abate the high prices of commodities, a move of particular value to those on fixed incomes.[66] Given its importance, therefore, Elizabeth's re-coinage constituted 'a great and memorable Act', which, Camden argued, turned to Elizabeth's 'greater, yea greatest, Glory'.[67]

Through presenting the Queen's management of commerce and finance as a product of her identification with the interests of the public, and associating her achievements in these fields with ideas of 'honour' and 'glory', Camden was able to show how economic affairs could form part of a Livian type of exemplary history. And like other exponents of this mode of writing, Vergil and Hall among them, Camden emphasised that virtuous actions, as well as being 'good' in themselves, could expect to achieve this-worldly recompense. On occasion, this recompense emerged from God's personal intervention. For example, when at the start of her reign, Elizabeth 'found her Treasure exhausted [...] God (as if he favoured what she undertook)' helped her furnish her armoury by discovering 'a most rich Vein of pure and native Brass [...] near *Keswick* in *Cumberland*'.[68] This both satisfied native demands for the metal and generated exports. Elsewhere, the Almighty's involvement was less direct, and events were simply shown to work to the advantage of the virtuous statesman. Thus Camden contrasted Elizabeth's willingness to take in Protestant refugees with the behaviour of Alva, who 'breathed nothing but Slaughter and Bloud against them'.[69] Alva's actions gained him and his people nothing; Elizabeth's, however, worked 'to the great Benefit and Advantage of the *English*: for they were the first that brought into *England* the Art of making those slight Stuffs which are called *Bays* and *Says*, and other such like Stuffs of Linen and Woollen weaving'.[70] Such comments, when viewed alongside the *Annales*' discussions of Elizabeth's other achievements, imply the existence of a providentially ordered world in which virtuous, public-spirited actions would be rewarded. Camden's point, however, was that both the acts that were worthy of reward, and the rewards themselves, could be economic in character.

2. Dishonourable commerce: luxury, avarice and the free trade debate

Ideas of honourable and, on occasion, glorious economic statecraft underpin much of Camden's discussion of economic affairs. Equally significantly, however, his association of honour with public interest, on the one hand, and dishonour with self-interest, on the other, led him to adopt a critical attitude towards those aspects of commercial life that he saw as dominated by prodigality and avarice. In discussing such issues, Camden is rather less reliant on Burghley than in the examples considered thus far. However, his approach remains rooted in the broad humanist framework he inherited from his patron, and, as we shall see, on one occasion at least his analysis worked to protect the reputation of the former Lord Treasurer.

Camden's discussion of prodigality was primarily concerned with new approaches to luxury goods, particularly clothing. Reflecting on this issue in his record for 1574 he observed:

> In these days a wonderous Excess in Apparel had spread it self all over *England*, and the Habit of our own Countrey, through a peculiar Vice incident to our Apish Nation, grew into such Contempt, that men by their new-fashioned Garments, and too gaudy Apparel discovered a certain Deformity and Arrogancy of Mind, whilst they jetted up and down in their Silks glittering with Gold and Silver, either imbroidered or laced.[71]

Elizabeth objected to such practices on economic grounds. Not only did expenditure on these items cause the nobility to 'waste their

Estates' and acquire debts, it also, through taking large quantities of money out of the kingdom, led to the 'impoverishing of the Commonwealth'.[72] At the same time, the growth of an 'excess of Pride' was said to have been accompanied by the emergence of 'riotous Banquetting and prodigal Bravery in Building'.[73] While the latter development worked to 'the great Ornament of the Kingdom', it also caused, Camden concluded, the 'Decay of the glorious Hospitality of the Nation'.[74] Fashionable Elizabethans were, therefore, prioritising their own vain and selfish interests over the needs of the state and its people.

Similar accusations of selfishness were levelled at tradesmen. Negotiations aimed at restoring goods taken from English traders by pirates from Zeeland, for example, failed 'by reason of the Avarice of the English Merchants, and the Insolency of the Zelanders', thereby resulting in 'Loss to both Nations'.[75] Avarice was also blamed for the breakdown of trading relations between England and Portugal in the 1570s and the decision by certain English merchants, despite the ongoing military engagements between England and Spain, to furnish the Spanish with ordnance in the early 1590s.[76] Elizabeth herself meanwhile, in one of her letters responding to accusations from the Hans Towns that England had violated ancient commercial agreements, is shown to defend the right of the English to suspend trading privileges by distinguishing between 'the Case of Kingdoms' and 'the Case of Cities'.[77] In relation to the former, she argued, trading privileges may be revoked for the good of the commonwealth as 'it concerneth Kings to maintain and support their Royal Dignity, rather than to encourage the Avarice of Merchants, lest they grow too insolent and high for Kings'.[78] The implication of Elizabeth's remarks, therefore, was that although trading cities might be entirely beholden to the lowly desires of merchants, kingdoms had higher and more honourable concerns.

Such comments appear to place Camden very close to a contradiction. On the one hand, he condemned a ruler such as Ivan for his contemptuous attitude towards merchants. On the other, both Camden and the Queen whose life he celebrated were suspicious of the low, avaricious desires of those engaged in trade. Camden's point, however, was not that trade was fundamentally dishonourable, but rather that to advance a nation's interests, its government needed to regulate commercial affairs carefully. This was an area in which

Elizabeth was shown to have excelled. Thus she abruptly dismissed the claims of the Hans Towns and, despite the distrust generated by her merchants, successfully negotiated a peace treaty with the Portuguese monarch. This agreement proposed 'a perfect Amity and free Commerce on both sides', and allowed the English to trade in 'the Azores, Madera, and the Coast of Barbary'.[79] Actions were also taken against over-elaborate forms of dress and the Spanish traders. With regard to the former, the Queen issued a series of proclamations, which demanded that 'every man should within fourteen days conform himself for Apparel to a certain prescribed Fashion'.[80] In relation to the latter, 'as soon as the Queen found out' about her merchants' illegal trade, she 'prohibited the same by a strict Proclamation, under such Penalties as are due to those who aid the Enemies of their Countrey'.[81]

Elizabeth's greatest regulatory success, however, occurred in relation to monopolies. From the mid-sixteenth century onwards government had begun to grant exclusive royal patents to manufacturers. Although these were initially introduced to protect innovation in manufacture, they quickly became subject to abuses as patents were passed on to and exploited by royal creditors and favourites.[82] In discussing this issue, Camden used ideas regarding the public interest both to attack monopolistic practices and to defend Elizabeth's conduct in relation to them. His first mention of the issue came in his account of the Parliament of 1601, the final session of the Queen's reign.[83] After briefly outlining some of the 'wholsome laws' passed, he noted that, considering the complaints 'brought in' to the lower house concerning monopolies, the Queen 'to be beforehand with them, put forth a Proclamation, whereby she partly declared those Grants to be void, and partly left them to be tried by the Laws'.[84] Camden approved of this action, observing in parentheses that 'under a specious Pretence of the Publick good, but indeed to the great Prejudice of the Commonwealth', some individuals had gained letters patent from the Queen granting them 'sole Privilege and Leave of selling certain Merchandizes'.[85] His discussion concluded with a transcript of a section of the so-called 'Golden Speech' which Elizabeth gave to Parliament. In it, she thanked the lower house and, for recalling her from errors, proclaimed her affection for the nation and emphasised her awareness that the commonwealth should be governed for the 'Good and Advantage' of its people, not its monarch.[86] Responsibility for recent 'Misdemeanours and Miscarriages', meanwhile, was placed firmly at the feet of her courtiers.[87] The servants of princes, Elizabeth noted, are 'oftentimes too much set upon their own private advantage', a truth frequently concealed from princes whose shoulders are burdened 'by the Weight of the greatest and important Affairs'.[88]

Two features of Camden's analysis are of particular significance here. First, the organisation of his account of monopolies is unusual. The lion's share of the word count is devoted to the incident's resolution, while the 'problem' that Elizabeth solves is dealt with only very briefly. As a result, questions regarding how the Queen had allowed such a system to develop or the extent to which she profited from it are entirely ignored. The reasons for such a move are unclear. However, given that it was Burghley who played a key part in establishing the system of monopolies, such an approach certainly enabled Camden to avoid further censure of his former patron.[89] Moreover, as monopolies remained a contentious issue for James, it is understandable that Camden, generally a highly cautious commentator when it came to controversial topics, sought to avoid delving too deeply into their operation.[90] Second, underpinning Camden's comments on monopolies, and his account of the monarchical regulation of commerce more generally, was the same distinction between 'good' and 'bad' forms of commerce that had been key to Bacon's *History*. Thus, like Bacon, Camden assumed that there was a difference between 'lawful and royal trading' which brought real benefits to the commonwealth, and bastardised forms of commerce that enriched particular avaricious individuals but compromised the nation's wider interests. Moreover, both Bacon and Camden thought that it was the monarch's role to legislate against the latter type of trade and promote the former, thereby ensuring that commerce contributed to, rather than undermined, the kingdom's prosperity and security. Where the two writers differed, however, was in their application of these ideas. Bacon presented Henry, on occasions at least, as using the rhetoric of public interest to advance his private, avaricious desires. Camden, in contrast, as we have seen, had little desire to trace the psychological roots of Elizabeth's behaviour, and treated her publicly stated aims as the key forces shaping her actions.

Generally speaking, therefore, Camden maintained that while certain individuals had sought selfishly to advance their own interests during the Queen's reign, her careful regulation had worked to curb such activities.[91] Nevertheless, on a couple of occasions Camden used the same ideas of public interest with which he had defended the Queen's economic statecraft to question aspects of English policy. The key issues here concerned the organisation of trading companies. While England's trading bodies were not run directly by government in the manner of the Dutch East India Company, they drew their 'very existence from Royal Prerogative'.[92] Indeed, each of them was reliant on a Royal Charter through which they were granted exclusive rights to trade with a particular territory. This practice had been utilised by Mary, who chartered the Muscovy Company (1555), and Elizabeth, who helped to establish the Barbary (1585), East India (1600) and Levant Companies (1592). James then extended it, augmenting the East India Company's privileges in 1609, and granting new charters to, among others, the Spanish Company (1605), the Virginia Company (1606) and the Newfoundland Company (1610). What was unique to James's reign, however, was the level of opposition such measures received.[93] Two Bills seeking to abolish the exclusive rights held by trading companies passed through the House of Commons in 1604.[94] As part of their progress, a committee, chaired by Sir Edwin Sandys and containing a number of notable critics of James, investigated the issue. Its subsequent report, authored by Sandys, judged the trading companies to be 'monopolies' – a claim rejected by their supporters – and called them violations 'against the natural Right and Liberty of the Subjects of *England*'.[95] Sandys' 'Free Trade' Bills eventually foundered in the Lords, but the Commons achieved a notable victory in 1606 when it was able to end the monopoly held by the Spanish Company.[96]

To an extent, the East India Company was able to escape the ire of the free trade campaigners. While the criticism of other trading bodies, particularly the Muscovy Company, was savage, the expense involved in trading with the East meant that even a critic of monopolies such as Sandys acknowledged that 'a joint stock company' was required.[97] This is not to say, however, that the East India trade lacked opponents. The difficulties involved in selling English goods in the East meant that the Company was reliant on the export of bullion, particularly silver, to support its trade.[98] Such procedures led a range of writers, among them Robert Kayll, Thomas Milles and, later, Gerard Malynes, to blame England's shortage of precious metals, and with it the nation's other economic woes, on the East India merchants. Indeed, the most famous work of mercantilist literature of the period, Thomas Mun's *England's Treasure by Forraign Trade* (1664), was written specifically to defend the East India Company from popular accusations about its practices with regard to bullion.[99]

Given such a context, it is noteworthy that Camden himself showed a degree of sympathy with the trading companies' critics. Despite his praise for the achievements of the East India Company, his account of its activities ends on a distinctly cautious note: 'whether to the Good of the Commonwealth, so great a Mass of Silver being still exported out of *England*, and such a Multitude of Sea-men consumed every Year in the Voyage, let Wise men speak and Posterity judge'.[100] Even more significant is the *Annales*' discussion of commerce with Muscovy. In his record for 1569 Camden had noted the extreme dissatisfaction that German merchants and non-company English merchants had expressed towards the Muscovy Company's 'monopoly' on trade with Russia. Further criticism, he showed, was to come from Feodor I, Ivan IV's successor as Tsar. Feodor, Camden observed,

> granted to all Merchants of what Nation soever free Access into *Russia*: and being oftentimes solicited by the Queen to confirm the Privileges granted by his Father to the *Moscovia* Company of English Merchants, to wit, that onely English-men of that Company should come into or trade in the North parts of *Russia*, and that Customer-free, in regard they were the first that discovered the Passage thither by Sea; he thereupon desired her to give Liberty to all the *English* to trade into *Russia*; for to permit some, and deny others, was Injustice. Princes, he said, must carry an indifferent hand betwixt their Subjects, and not convert Trade (which by the Law of Nations ought to be common to all) into a Monopoly to the private Gain of a few.[101]

This passage is, perhaps, one of the most interesting in the *Annales*, not least because the core arguments that the Tsar utilised against Elizabeth are very similar to the sort of claims the Queen makes elsewhere in the text. Indeed, both the English and Russian rulers are shown to criticise monopolies and private gain, while calling for monarchs to treat their subjects in an even-handed manner. Also noteworthy here is Camden's use of sources. His account appears to be based on the English translation of Feodor's letter by the diplomat and traveller Jerome Horsey, a copy of which is preserved in the state papers. In this document, Feodor asserted that Elizabeth should 'license or make open the trade' without any restriction in favour of 'those five, six, or ten men which hath from long time so traded into our countries'.[102] However, neither Horsey's translation, nor the original Russian letter on which it was based, contained any direct mention of 'private gain' or the politically charged term 'monopoly'. Moreover, no reference is made in the source documents to 'the laws of nations'. The precise reasons for Camden's uncharacteristically 'free' approach to archival material here are difficult to fathom. However, the effect of his reformulation was to put into the Tsar's mouth a forceful critique of a key plank of English commercial policy. Moreover, this critique was in line with both the broader economic logic of the *Annales* and the scathing critique of government practices developed by Sandys. As a result, while it cannot be claimed that Camden specifically endorsed the arguments of the trading companies' critics – he makes, after all, no direct comment on Feodor's letter – he certainly allowed an eloquent distillation of their core claims to be expressed in his work.

Conclusion

The *Annales* is a key text in the history of economic statecraft. Its principal contribution was to use conventional humanist criteria of the Livian, exemplary variety to judge the worth of financial and commercial actions. With regard to finance, this was a relatively straightforward task, and one made easier by the accounts of Elizabeth's reign that Camden received from Burghley. At her accession to the throne, Camden emphasised, as Burghley had done, that Elizabeth's situation was an unpropitious one. England in 1558

> lay […] most afflicted, imbroiled on the one side with the Scottish, on the other side with the French War; overcharged with Debt incurred by *Henry* the Eighth and *Edward* the Sixth; the Treasure exhausted; *Calice* and the Country of *Oye*, with great Provision for the Wars, lost, to the great Dishonour of the English Nation; the people distracted with different Opinions in Religion; the Queen bare of potent Friends, and strengthened with no Alliance of foreign Princes.[103]

The Queen's success in dealing with these problems lay in her absolute identification with the commonwealth's interests. This enabled her to limit personal spending, provide liberal funds for the defence of the nation, and take firm actions against those who sought to enrich themselves through co-opting state revenues or debasing the currency. As a result, Camden was able to link the effective management of revenue to the pursuit of the public good, and then use discussion of these issues as part of a narrative of national recovery and renewal. This ensured, in turn, that finance was presented as an aspect of statecraft, which had the capacity, like military and other political achievements, to bring a statesman honour and glory.

Commerce, however, was rather more complicated. The public-spirited forms of behaviour that the *Annales* sought to defend were, in one sense, directly opposed to the self-interested, profit-seeking activities involved in trade. Indeed, Camden used their departure from the 'common good' as a means of criticising what he saw as some of the defining features of Elizabethan commercial life: mercantile avarice, extravagant forms of dress and housing, and monopolies. Underlying his comments on these issues was a Machiavellian suspicion of the ethical value of mercantile life. As J. G. A. Pocock has noted, 'if there was a morality for the trading man, exchanging one commodity for its equivalent value in another, that morality was conspicuously not linked to the virtue of the citizen – the only secular virtue yet known to Western Man'.[104] However, while these issues undoubtedly linger on the edge of the *Annales*, Camden's key concern, like Botero's, was not so much with trade itself but its management by government. And here it was much easier to link the Queen's activity with ideas of public service. In promoting English trading companies, Elizabeth was not enriching herself, Camden showed, but rather promoting the wealth and honour of the nation. Her role in defending merchants from attacks by foreigners, meanwhile, was conceived of as part of her larger duty of care towards her subjects. Finally, the frequent disjunction between the interests of tradesmen and the interests of the commonwealth was shown to provide opportunities for the statesman. Through legislating against corrupt, avaricious practices, Camden demonstrated, it was possible to develop the sort of 'lawful and royal trading' that advanced the common good. Indeed, while commerce was frequently viewed as ethically dubious, economic statecraft was shown to bring a monarch virtuous forms of honour and glory.

3

Chronology and commerce: Edmund Howes's *Annales*

Bacon's *History* and Camden's *Annales* exerted a prolonged influence over the reputations of Henry VII and Elizabeth I. Indeed, as will be explored in Part II of this book, the eighteenth-century debate concerning the financial and commercial management of these monarchs was structured around a series of attempts to adapt and update Bacon's and Camden's narratives. The situation with regard to James I was a good deal more complicated. No account of a similar stature emerged and the historiography of the first English Stuart king is characterised by its diversity, and, particularly in the years following the Civil War, its vituperative debates and disagreements.[1] Perhaps the most influential 'early' analysis of commercial and financial practices during James's reign, however, was that contained in Edmund Howes's *Annales*, the principal subject of this chapter. At one level, this influence was direct; the *Annales* continued to be read into the eighteenth century, and, as will be shown in Chapter 9, was both utilised and praised by David Hume. Howes's sway was also increased by the work of Richard Baker, whose commentary on James in his hugely popular *Chronicle* (1643) was based around a series of pithy summaries of the *Annales*. A brief discussion of Baker's *Chronicle* follows my account of Howes.

1. Edmund Howes's *Annales*

Edmund Howes, like Bacon and Camden, was interested in commerce. His relationship with the subject, however, was different to that of his more renowned contemporaries. Both Bacon's *History* and Camden's *Annales* were, in some sense, products of Jacobean Court culture, and drew mainly on government sources to provide narratives of high politics. This helped to ensure that, while both writers were happy to deal with issues relating to trade, the focus of their accounts was the state's management of commercial affairs. Howes, as we shall see, shared this concern with economic statecraft. His analysis, however, was also shaped by his links with the workshops, warehouses and offices of the City. And it was through describing the activities of individuals attached to these locales, both in England and across the world, that he was able to develop a highly innovative account of English commercial history. In dealing with Howes's writing, I begin by looking briefly at his life and approach to historical writing. I then explore his interrelated accounts of immigration, manufacture and trading companies, before outlining his analysis of the role that James had played in augmenting national prosperity.

Howes commenced his historical research in around 1602, when he gained employment as an assistant to the chronicler John Stow.[2] On Stow's death in 1605, Howes took on the task of updating his various works, publishing new and expanded editions of his *Abridgement or Summarie of the English Chronicle* in 1607, 1611 and 1618, and of the *Annales* in 1615 and 1632.[3] This latter work revised Stow's account, as well as adding new prefatory material and a section on James I.[4] In the dedication to the 1615 edition of the text, Howes attributed his work on the *Annales* to a personal promise made to Archbishop Whitgift, and his list of acknowledgements included six bishops – three of them Archbishops of Canterbury – the Lord Chancellor, the Lord High Treasurer and the Captain of the King's Guard.[5] Thanks were also extended to Camden and Cotton.[6] What Howes failed to acknowledge, however, at least in his printed works, were his close financial links with the City's trading companies. From 1605 onwards he received an annual pension of £10 from the Merchant Taylors' Company.[7] This was supplemented by a further 5 marks seven years later when he presented the Company with a copy of the *Annales* – a work containing a lavish description of the visit the King paid to the Merchant Taylors in July 1607.[8] Howes's discussions of the Virginia and East India Companies were seemingly a result of similar connections. The court minutes of the Virginia Company for 20 May 1622 noted that:

> Mr Howe the Chronicler makinge a request for 12*li* of Tobacco, which he pretends was promised him yearely in consideration of his paines

> and willingenes to doe the Companie service in his Booke relating [to] the Passages concerninge Virginia, The Court was pleased to graunt his request for this yeare, givinge order that somuch should be delivered him of the Companies Tobacco which he thankfully accepted of.[9]

A comparable, if perhaps more informal, arrangement existed with the East India Company. The Company's minutes for 3–5 June 1629 contain the following account:

> Petition of Mr. Howe, the chronicler, that he had in his labours past set down many things of importance concerning the affairs of the Company, which will remain upon record to posterity for their honour, so in his works not yet divulged he intends to make some further relation, and therefore he desired the Court to consider his zeal, and in regard he is now grown old and hath lost his sight that they would bestow upon him some gratuity. The Court although they remembered at present nothing in this kind in any work of his, yet were pleased in charity to confer upon him 5*l*., to be paid by Mr. Mountney in respect there was not so much in the poor box.[10]

Four years later, Howes was still involved with the Company, although his financial situation seems to have dramatically improved. The minute book for 9 January 1633 contains a request from Howes that he be allowed to reinvest back into the Company the £12 10*s*. dividend he was to receive, and through adding some of his own money, make the investment up to the sum of £50.[11] These appeals for monetary support, it should be emphasised, took place after Howes had completed the majority of his contribution to the *Annales*. Consequently, it is possible that he exaggerated his previous links with commercial organisations in order to extract himself from financial difficulties. However, the detail with which he treated Company affairs, and the fact that his applications were accepted, gives credence to the idea that he was officially or semi-officially employed. There were also a number of precedents for such arrangements. From 1579 onwards Stow himself had received patronage from the Merchant Taylors' Company, in the form of a £4 annuity; from 1592 this income was supplemented by a pension, initially worth £4 and later rising to £6.[12] Indeed, it was Stow's pension that Howes appears to have inherited.[13] Also noteworthy were the dedicatees of Stow's various volumes. His initial patron had been the Earl of Leicester, one of Elizabeth's key advisors. However, in the later part of his career he increasingly identified his works with the City of London. *A Summarie of the Chronicles* from 1590 was dedicated to Sir John Hart, a merchant tailor and Lord Mayor of London, while *A Survay of London* from 1603 and the 1604 edition of *A Summarie* were both dedicated to later Lord Mayors. Howes's own interactions with London's trading companies, therefore, can be seen as symptomatic of an increasingly close relationship between England's merchants and its historical writers.

As well as moving in a different social milieu to Bacon and Camden, Howes also wrote a different type of history to them. The *Annales* was explicitly conceived of as an English 'chronology', a genre of writing that Howes defined by distinguishing its stylistic conventions from those employed in humanist histories. Chronology avoided the 'phantastique speaches' and the 'superfluous curiosity, lofty stile, and needlesse Eloquence, such as our fore-fathers never knew or heard of'; instead it was written in 'good plaine English, without affectation'.[14] References to Graeco-Roman ideas of character and causation were entirely absent and it was chronological order, rather than any causal or thematic links, that determined the arrangement of material. As a consequence, Howes's discussion, like that of other chroniclers, had a fragmented feel, with his detailed – at times day-by-day – account of James's activities frequently being interrupted by the staple fare of chronicle literature: transcribed documents and tales of violent crime, unusual animals and bizarre weather. Through offering such information, the *Annales* sought both to capture the specific details of past events and to provide a series of moral *exempla*. 'The Originall and true purpose of Chronology', it was argued, 'was to shew Successors, the Actions good and bad of their Ancestors, and to remaine as documents to pursue the good, and eschew the bad.'[15] Like other practitioners of exemplary history, however, Howes did not present a random assortment of moralistic fables. Rather, he maintained that underpinning the movement between 'good' and 'bad' actions was a divinely ordained plan. Over time, God's 'mercy and benefits have haply encreased more and more', thereby ensuring that human beings had been able to achieve a series of ever greater feats, and that history itself formed a narrative of progress.[16] While the matter was never fully theorised, the *Annales* implied that divine support came in concentrated bursts, which served to create rapid and highly advantageous transformations in particular locales. During the previous fifty years, England had experienced one such burst and had seen a 'universall encrease of Commerce, and traffique throughout the kingdome, great building of royall ships, by private merchants, the repeopling of Cities, Townes, and Villages, besides the undiscernible, and sudden encrease of fayre and costly buildings'.[17] Developments had been particularly rapid in London. And, showing none of the scruples about the corruptive capacities of luxury found in Camden's writing, Howes celebrated the city as

> one of the best governed, most richest, and flourishing Citties in Europe, plenteously abounding in Free Trade and Commerce with all nations, richly stored with gold, silver, pearle, spice, peper & many other strange commodities, from both Indies; Oples from Candy, Cyprus, and other places under the Turkes dominion; strong wines, sweete fruits, Suger, and spice from Grecia, Venice, Spayn, Barbary, the Islands, and other places lately discovered and knowne.[18]

God's 'ineffable goodnesse', Howes emphasised, was the ultimate cause of modern forms of prosperity.[19] However, while the key function of chronology was to pay tribute to the almighty's achievements, this necessarily involved reflection on the secondary (worldly) causes that God had employed to generate change. In developing an account of these secondary factors, Howes looked at developments that had occurred both inside and outside England. With regard to the former, the nation's recent advancements were traced back to a single source: immigration. 'Civill dissension' in Flanders, and the 'great factions, and brawles' in France had led many Protestant families to flee their homelands.[20] Such individuals, Howes argued, had increased the population, and through marrying into the local population, raised the birth-rate. These changes had, in turn, created a property boom as the large numbers of previously empty houses were filled, rents were raised, and the building of new properties was encouraged. Importantly, therefore, the smart new districts of London which the *Annales* celebrated were a direct consequence of England's adept handling of a refugee crisis.

An increasingly cosmopolitan society also led to important innovations in manufacturing. To demonstrate this the *Annales* provided short accounts – usually a paragraph or two long – of changes in a diverse range of production processes including those relating to printed material, silk stockings, knitted worsted stockings, coaches, cambric, starching, ruffs, taffeta, dyes, silk production, Spanish felts, alum, Venetian glass, the cutting of iron bars, copper-plate and paper-making.[21] For each item, the nature of the advancement was explained and, where the information was available, the names and nationalities of those involved were listed. The vast majority of these innovators were shown to be foreigners. Coaches, it was noted, were introduced into England by a Dutchman, Guilliam Boonen, in 1564.[22] Another Dutchman made the country's first dyes.[23] The production of alum was achieved with the help of manufacturers from Germany, while starching was pioneered by a Mistris Dinghen van den plasse of Flanders.[24] Foreigners also helped to create beneficial patterns of emulation. The apprentice William Rider, for example, 'chanced to see a paire of knit Wosted stockings, in the lodging of an Italian Merchant, that came from Mantua'.[25] He borrowed the stockings, and was able to reproduce a similar product; 'these', Howes concluded, 'were the first worsted stockings made in England'.[26] The success of Mistress Dinghen's starching business, meanwhile, was partially attributed to 'the best and most curious [English] wives of that time, observing the neatnesse, and delicacy of the Dutch for whitenesse, and fine wearing of linnen' and desiring something similar for themselves.[27] English innovation had also played a role, albeit a limited one, in shaping continental practices. 'The Art of Knitting, or weaving silke stockings, Wastecoates, and divers other things, by Engines, or steele Loomes' was 'devised and perfected' by William Lee, 'Master of Arts, of Saint Johns Colledge, in Cambridge'.[28] Lee took this innovation to France, 'where hee obtained a pattent of the King', and his servants then 'taught the secret of their Art' in 'Spayne, Venice, and in Ireland'.[29] Importantly, Howes does not present such practices as in any way unpatriotic. Rather his account is premised on the ideas that advancements in knowledge, specifically practical manufacturing knowledge, were a key source of England's transformation into a successful, affluent state, and that it was the role of an English chronicler to celebrate English achievement – understood in the broadest possible sense.

While Howes appeared sure that his narratives of innovation were a useful and original addition to his chronicle, he was rather less confident when dealing with overseas affairs. This, he acknowledged, was a crowded field in the literary marketplace, and it was impossible for a general work of English history to match the detailed accounts collected and published by Richard Hakluyt. Equally, however, he was aware that trading companies had played a vital role in advancing 'traffique' and saw them as a key feature of modern English history. Such beliefs necessitated a degree of historiographical innovation, as events taking place thousands of miles from England, and beyond the immediate control of its statesmen, needed to be integrated into an Anglocentric narrative. Indeed, there is a sense in which the re-evaluation of ideas regarding England's political and national identity necessitated by colonial expansion reverberated into historical writing as a question of historiographical form.[30] Put simply: where should one place discussion of the colonies? Howes's 'solution' was a relatively straightforward one. At various points in his account he abandoned basic chronology, and provided narratives of the development of individual trading companies, primarily the East India Company,[31] the Virginia Company,[32] the Muscovy Company[33] and the New Foundland Company.[34] The source material for these sections was the period's travel writing, and like the mariners and traders who produced these works, Howes combined business and colonial history with tales of nautical adventure and geographical and anthropological analysis.

Howes's discussion of such material served both to legitimate and support the specific actions of England's trading companies, and to provide a more general justification for colonial, commercial endeavours. The former aspect of Howes's agenda can be seen particularly clearly in relation to discussions of Bermuda. His account of the island, initially a territory of the Virginia Company, was drawn principally from material contained in the published work of the Lyme Regis merchant Silvester Jourdain. Jourdain had been a passenger on the Virginia-bound *Sea Adventure* when it sank off the coast of the island in 1609, the event that led to the territory's colonisation. Howes opened his discussion by paraphrasing Jourdain's dramatic account of the ill-fated voyage, before offering a brief narrative concerning the development of the colony. The text then concluded with some remarks on its government and a vivid description of the island's resources, again drawn from details provided by Jourdain:

> And when the said new company was truely informed of the wholesomenesse of the Aire and pleasantnesse of the soyle, and the aptnesse thereof, of it selfe in all respects to maintaine a Collony, the ground

> being so fertile that it will yield two harvests in one yeere: great plentie of woods, and lofty Ceaders: well stored with fowle, and, great plenty of good fish: and that besides the fertilitie of the soyle, which they had tryed, would beare with great encrease, all kind of English graine, fruits, trees, hearbes and vines, besides the great store of Abergreece [i.e. ambergris], and some pearle, which is found there they sent yeerely supplies thither of men, and some women, with all things necessary for so worthy a plantation, so as at this time there are six hundred persons well fortified, with plenty of great ordinance.[35]

This already lengthy description was further expanded in 1632, when an extra paragraph was added dismissing the claim that Bermuda was a series of floating islands, and attributing such suggestions to excuses made by navigators who had failed to locate the settlement.[36] What the *Annales* demonstrated, therefore, was that the Company's territories were extravagantly fertile, well-armed and firmly fixed to the ocean's floor. As such, they were in no more danger of being invaded by foreign powers than they were of drifting away in the wind, and represented a potentially appealing prospect for any would-be investor or colonist.

Howes provided further support for the trading companies through his discussions of the diligence and industry that characterised their endeavours. His approach here echoed that of Richard Hakluyt. Hakluyt conceived of the *Principall Navigations* (1589) as a way to 'recommend to the world' the previously unheralded 'industrious labors, and painefull travels of our countrey men'.[37] In continuing this project, Howes offered numerous new examples of English endurance. At Nycobar, the discovery of 'great kingdomes' by the English ships was attributed to 'their painefull and industrious travaile'.[38] The ultimate success of the Virginia colony was described through an account of its attitude to work; thus Sir Thomas Dale, the Marshal of Virginia, Howes notes, wrote to the Company's governors declaring that 'the English were now become laborious and industrious'.[39] Similar qualities characterised the activities of the key figures involved in colonisation. Sir George Somers, the admiral of Virginia, and Robert Harcourt, the planter of a colony in the south of Guyana, were described in identical terms as 'very industrious and forward'.[40] Iohn Gwy, the 'Generall' of the colony in the south-eastern parts of Virginia, was 'a man very industrious and of good experience'.[41] The Lord De La Warr, the Lord Governor and Captain General of all the English Colonies of Virginia, used so much of 'his best diligence and industrie' that he became ill and was forced to return to England.[42] England's colonial activity, therefore, was not based on the violence and duplicitousness that Elizabethan accounts had frequently associated with Spanish endeavours. Rather, the expansion of territories and markets constituted a respectable form of labour, which enabled individuals to do their duty both to the commonwealth and God.

These arguments were developed further through a general vindication of European and English commercial and colonial endeavour. The 'Westerne Christian Princes', Howes argued, had received the particular 'blessings of Almighty God' in the form of 'free possession, of [God's] divine Gospell' and 'the most use, and best practice of all excellent Artes, and Sciences, as well for warre as peace, especially in building of Shippes, and profoundnesse in the Admirable Art of Navigation'.[43] This had enabled them to defeat the 'tyrannous oppressions' of the 'Turke', and become 'great masters of the Ocean'.[44] As was demonstrated through a short but celebratory series of accounts of the feats of Columbus, Magellan and Cortes, the first nations to master navigation were the Spanish and Portuguese. In contrast, England's geographical position ensured that it had lagged behind other countries. Thus while it was a 'truely auncient, and right worthily renowned' nation, the fact that it was 'divided by the Ocean from the maine land' isolated it from intellectual developments in Europe. In recent years, however, 'the providence of her Princes, together with the diligence and industry of the people' had enabled England to overcome this handicap. As a result, it was 'now possest with as full measure of knowledge in all things, as any kingdome in the World, especially in navigation and discovery of remote Nations'.[45] This, in turn, raised the already high estimation in which the English were held, advancing their 'Wealth and Traffique'.[46] For Howes, therefore, the expansion of commercial markets, like developments in manufacturing, was the product of recent advancements in knowledge. Moreover, as had been the case with manufacturing, providing a narrative of English commercial development involved tracing the various ways in which the nation had emulated other countries and, in doing so, matched and, on occasions, surpassed their achievements. The ultimate effect of such arguments, however, was to emphasise that the origin of the knowledge on which commerce depended lay with God, and that, as a consequence, England's commercial ascendency had its roots in God's providential order.

What role had the monarchy played in England's divinely ordained commercial success? Howes's assumption that new forms of technical knowledge were the key worldly drivers of development led him to present mariners, merchants and manufacturers, rather than statesmen, as the principal instigators of England's recent transformation. Equally though, innovation was shown to be dependent on support and encouragement from government. To demonstrate this argument, Howes reflected on James's involvement in both domestic manufacturing and overseas trade. With regard to the former, the King's key function had been to provide backing for emerging industries. In relation to silk, for example, James, 'well knowing' the benefits the manufacture of the fabric had brought to Spain and Italy, and 'being desirous by all laudable meanes to imploy his poorest Subjects', made several experiments in cultivating silk worms.[47] When these proved effective, 'according to the Kings expresse order', mulberry trees, the principal food for silk worms, were obtained from France.[48] After this, it was the 'industrious gentlemen that kept worms', foremost among them William Staledge, the 'Comptroller of the Custome house', whose endeavours enabled silk manufacture to expand.[49] The King, however, offered continued and useful encouragement through granting a patent to 'bring in' mulberry seed, and an order allowing trees to be planted across the country.

Royal support had also brought about the development of England's alum industry. Production of the chemical, a key element in dyeing processes, had been pioneered by John Bourcher, with assistance from Yorkshire landowners and skilled workmen from Germany.[50] To aid their work, the King granted Bourcher and his associates a thirty-one-year patent for the 'sole making' of alum, prohibited alum from bring imported, provided storehouses and gave 'very gracious respect and Princely remuneration' to those who had taken pains in the manufacture of the product.[51] James later went on to take 'the whole traffique [of alum] to himselfe'.[52]

In relation to international trade, Howes stressed that James's pacifistic foreign policy and the peace it brought had opened up the enticing prospect of 'free trade with all nations'.[53] At the same time, the King had made a series of specific interventions on behalf of the corporations, most notably the East India Company. Although the territories discovered by the Company were rich, the 'long and chargeable' nature of their voyages, their great wages and other expenses 'discouraged them to persist, except their Charter were greater'.[54] Such issues were, however, swiftly and wisely resolved by James who, for the 'enriching, and better strengthening of this Kingdome', granted them 'an enlargement of their first Letters Pattents, and gave them a Charter to continue for ever' and banned all other tradesmen from engaging in the importation of pepper.[55] In describing the companies and schemes for which James provided support, Howes avoided the highly loaded term 'monopoly'. Nevertheless, his key point was that through restricting competition, the King had enabled fledgling manufacturing and commercial endeavours to survive and prosper. This, in turn, had enriched the nation as a whole.

To further emphasise the importance of the relationship between monarch and merchants, Howes provided lengthy accounts of James's visits to two companies: the Merchant Taylors' Company and the East India Company. With regard to the former, Howes observed that on 16 July 1607:

> his Majestie, and Prince Henry being accompanied and attended with very many of the Nobilitie, and other Honourable Personages, came in private manner to Merchant taylors Hall to Dynner (the Queene being also expected) where they were very Royally and joyfully feasted and entertained, with great and pleasant variety of Musique, of voyces and Instruments, and ingenious speeches, being the feast day of the Merchant taylors for the election of the Master and Wardens.[56]

An elaborate description of the proceedings followed, focusing on the lavish gifts the Company presented to the King, principally a purse of gold and a 'role' containing the names of the various royal and noble individuals who had previously been 'freemen' of the Company. Howes then went on to discuss the entertainments the Company put on – lute music and song from a series of individuals concealed in a large model ship – and the ceremony through which Prince Henry was made a freeman of the Company. He concluded his account by observing that

> the bountie of this feast and plenty of all things as well for pleasant Princely entertainments of the King, the Prince, the Nobilitie, and the rest, where were very many brave Courtiers and other Gallants, [...] was most rare and excellent.[57]

A similar description is provided of a visit the King made to the East India Company in 1609:

> [On] the thirtieth of December, the King, and Prince, with divers of the chiefe Nobilitie, went to Debtford to see the great Shippe [*Trade's Encrease*] Launched, and when they had seene every roome in the Shippe, they were royally Banqueted in the chiefe Cabin: and their followers were Banqueted at a long Table in the halfe decke, plenteously furnished with delicates served in fine China Dishes, all which were freely permitted to be carried away by all persons. The King shewed many favours unto the Merchants of the company and gave unto Sir Thomas Smith, Governor of that Society, a very fayre Chayne of Golde, with a Jewell wherein was the Kings picture, and commended his sundry good endeavours, for the Company and common wealth: the Chiefe Elders of the Company kissed the Kings Hand.[58]

Such accounts fulfilled two principal functions. First, they allowed the Companies to display their wealth and good taste; they are presented here not as associations of avaricious merchants of the sort described by Camden, but rather as refined courtiers, capable of putting on elegant forms of entertainment. Second, they celebrated the close relationship between the Companies and the King, and, as such, served to enhance the credibility of both. The former, it was emphasised, had received royal sanction for their endeavours, the latter had supported and contributed to the honourable activities of the nation's leading tradesmen. The key implication of Howes's accounts, therefore, was that the interests of 'Company' and 'Commonwealth' were firmly aligned.

2. Richard Baker's *Chronicle*

Howes's ideas were to be repackaged and popularised by the work of the chronicler Richard Baker.[59] In the early part of his life Baker had enjoyed a good deal of success. A descendant of Henry VIII's Chancellor of the Exchequer, Sir John Baker, he held land in Essex, Gloucestershire, Kent and Oxfordshire, served as an MP, and later went on to become a JP for Middlesex and High Sheriff of Oxfordshire. However, his decision to act as guarantor for his father-in-law's debts proved a disastrous one. He lost his properties, and, from 1635 onwards, was incarcerated in the Fleet Prison. It was while he was a prisoner that Baker began his literary career, initially focusing on devotional and moralistic themes. In the final part of his life, his attention turned towards history. He completed *Discourses upon Cornelius Tacitus*, a translation of a study by Virgilio Malvezzi, in 1642, and the following year published his *Chronicle*, an account 'of the Kings of England from the time of the Romans Government, to the Raigne of King Charles'.

Baker's principal innovation, as he openly acknowledged in 'An Epistle to the Reader' that prefaced his account, was its organisation. His own position, he noted, resembled that of the Roman historian Suetonius. Before Suetonius came to write his *Lives of the Caesars*, 'many excellent men had [already] written the Story of the Roman Emperours, both accurately and eloquently'.[60] However, Suetonius was able to gain 'Commendation' not by adding to the 'matter' or 'substance' of history, but rather through altering its 'forme and disposition' and by 'distinguishing [...] into Classes and Chapters' that which had formerly been 'delivered in one continued Narration'.[61] A similar sort of innovation, Baker contended, would improve chronicle writing, enabling it to extend beyond 'matters of State' to cover the matters of 'meaner Accidents' which it had failed to address and which were 'proper' for the genre.[62] Consequently, although his chronicle contained 'whole passages, as they are already set downe by others', it distinguished itself from these works by combining a brief chronological narrative of each of England's monarchs with thematic essays concerning their reigns. These latter sections dealt with a wide range of matters, among them 'Lawes and Ordinances', 'Works of Piety' and 'Casualties'. The work was a popular success. By the end of the seventeenth century Baker's *Chronicle* had run to nine editions in England, and had been translated into Dutch.

Both the narrative and essay sections of Baker's account of James I discussed financial and commercial affairs at length. The narrative material is dominated by a series of paraphrased accounts of Howes's work; indeed, Baker's comments on the manufacture of alum,[63] the role played by the King in the extension of the East India Company's charter,[64] and his attendances at the launch of the *Trade's Encrease*[65] and the Merchant Taylors' dinner[66] are all summaries of the *Annales*. More interesting, however, were the two 'essays' on economic themes. The first of these concerned taxation, an area dealt with only briefly by Howes. Baker's discussion took the form of a list of the various levies that James had imposed, among them parliamentary subsidies, fines, customs and benevolences. His central argument was that the King was not guilty of 'covetousnesse to gather wealth'.[67] Instead, his taxes and impositions were a product of the need to maintain many ambassadors, show 'bounty' to his followers and fund several courts. None of these expenses, Baker emphasised, 'hee could avoyd', and, consequently, any 'grudging' against his measures was without 'just cause'.[68]

Further support for James was offered in Baker's other economic essay: 'Of the English Plantation in the Indies, that were in King James his time'. The content of his analysis closely resembled that of Howes's discussions and, like his predecessor, Baker provided brief narratives of the development of colonies in Virginia and Bermuda, supplementing this material with a description of New England. Baker's main source was John Smith's *The Generall Historie of Virginia, New-England, and the Summer Isles* (1624).[69] This work had not been published when Howes completed the section of the *Annales* dealing with North America, but, in compiling it, Smith made extensive use of two works that Howes had drawn upon: his own earlier account, *A Map of Virginia* (1612), and Silvester Jourdain's *A Plaine Description of the Barmudas* (1613).[70] Baker's key move with regard to this material was to emphasise the role played by James in the development of the North American settlements. Introducing his account, Baker noted that James's feats with regard to the acquisition of colonies came 'very neare' to those of Augustus Caesar.[71] However, rather than acquiring an empire 'by the violent ways of Armes, King *James* did it by the civill way of Plantations'; indeed, these plantations constituted 'the proper effect of his Peaceable government'.[72] Baker returned to this theme in the essay's conclusion. The extensive treatment of the Indies by other authors, he noted, made it unnecessary to provide a detailed analysis of such matters. It was 'sufficient to have shewed, that King *James* had the honour, to have settled [the plantations] in His time, and under the Influence of His peaceable Government'.[73]

It is difficult to imagine that Howes could have taken issue with any of Baker's comments. Much of his analysis, after all, either drew out conclusions that were implicit in the *Annales* or simply summarised Howes's account. Nevertheless, Baker's selection of material is significant. In relation to manufacturing he included only those sections of Howes's account that had ascribed a significant role to the King. With regard to the plantations, meanwhile, he ignored

Howes's discussion of a Europe-wide advancement in knowledge, and presented English success less as a consequence of the industry of the colonists, and more as a product of the wise government of the monarch. To an extent, such an approach served to reverse Howes's partial separation of political and economic analysis; in this respect Baker's account resembled the narratives of royal achievement authored by Bacon and Camden. What distinguished Baker's account from other works, however, was not just its unconventional structure, but its more polemical tone. Baker used each of the essays to provide a defence of a particular aspect of James's government. Thus, just as the taxation essay pointedly rejects claims of monarchical extravagance, so the plantations essay provides a defence of the King's highly controversial pacifism. In taking such an approach, Baker's work seeks not just to describe the King's actions, in the manner of Howes, but to vindicate him in the face of his critics. This more disputative approach, as we shall see, was a harbinger of future developments in the historiography of economic statecraft.

Conclusion

I would like to conclude Part I of this book with a few general observations. The 'modern' historical writing of the Jacobean and Caroline periods was characterised by its unprecedentedly detailed engagement with commercial and financial themes. In discussing such matters, historians employed a variety of 'new' types of source material, including legal records, state papers and narratives compiled by colonialists and merchants. The decision to turn to such documents was a consequence of the widely accepted assumption that economic affairs constituted an aspect of statecraft. As such, they were a worthy subject for the historian to address, and one that could be treated alongside discussions of military, political and ecclesiastical issues.

However, while there was a broad consensus regarding the importance of finance and commerce, there were also considerable divergences in the ways that writers dealt with such matters. Success in economic management could, in the manner of Bacon's *History*, be presented in a 'realist', Tacitean manner, and be seen as emerging from a monarch's amoral – and sometimes immoral – desires and interests. Equally, Camden showed that it was possible to conceive of good commercial statecraft as an exemplary Livian virtue, a product of the statesman's willingness to subordinate private interests to the welfare of the commonwealth. There were also distinct differences between the way in which historians viewed the relationship between power and plenty. None of the writers discussed here went as far as Machiavelli and conceived of these two categories as fundamentally incompatible. Nevertheless, both Camden and Bacon saw plenty as a potential threat to the nation's welfare and suggested a series of measures to ensure that commercial interests were reconciled to the national interest. Howes and Baker, in contrast, like Botero, assumed that plenty and power were concomitants; for both, what was advantageous to a state's merchants was necessarily advantageous to the state itself. Howes's interests are also, in a sense, broader than those of the other writers considered. Bacon, Camden and Baker were writing histories of particular monarchs; as a consequence, commercial and financial issues were dealt with only when they had an impact on Westminster and Whitehall. While Howes fully acknowledged the importance of the monarchical management of commerce, he was also interested in tracing the role that individuals outside of government had played in shaping commercial developments. As a consequence, his account was able to acknowledge the achievements of someone like Mistress Dinghen in a way that would not have been possible in the 'high' political history of his contemporaries.

It is also important to emphasise that modern history was by no means the only genre of writing which sought to analyse developments in commerce and finance. The early 1620s were years of economic depression, as exports in cloth declined, producing high unemployment and social unrest.[74] Attempts to understand the origins of these problems led to a wide-ranging debate, conducted first in a series of government committees, and later in print. From these discussions two broad groups emerged. The first, headed by Gerard Malynes, saw this as a monetary crisis; through the corrupt dealings of usurers, bankers and foreign exchange-dealers, it was argued, England's currency had become undervalued.[75] This had led to a shortage of money, as foreign investors bought up currency, forcing England's merchants to offer ever greater quantities of goods at ever lower prices to preserve their profits. To solve the crisis, Malynes and his supporters argued, it was necessary to raise the value of currency through direct government regulation. The second group, containing Thomas Mun and (in his later work) Edward Misselden, saw England's problems as the product of a trade crisis.[76] Consequently, while Mun and Misselden agreed with Malynes that there was a shortage of money, they attributed this to problems with the balance of trade. As Misselden observed: 'If the Native Commodities exported doe waigh downe and exceed in value the forraine Commodities imported; it is a rule that never faile's, that then the Kingdome growe's rich, and prosper's in estate and stocke: because the over plus thereof must needs come in, in treasure.'[77] Underlying such comments was the notion that it was the forces of supply and demand that determined the value of goods and currencies, not government regulation. Consequently, as Lars Magnusson has argued, Mun's and Misselden's analyses are premised on 'the existence of an independent economic sphere outside polity and state'.[78]

To an extent, these debates are completely detached from the historical narratives with which this discussion has been concerned. The historians do not engage with or quote from the political economists and vice versa; indeed, although it was written in the 1620s, Mun's key work, *England's Treasure by Forraign Trade*, was not published until 1664. There are, however, some important points of congruence between the approaches of works of political economy and works of history. The two discourses dealt with the same cluster of commercial and financial issues, foremost among them the role of monopolies, free trade, reforms to coinage, the dangers of luxury, the relationship between war and commerce, and the benefits of technological innovation. Even more significantly, historians and political economists were united in their conception of the role that could be played by the monarch with regard to trade. Thus, while Magnusson is correct to note that Mun opposed direct interference from government in relation to exchange rates, he did not hold a similar view about commerce. Indeed, for Mun, it was through government involvement that a positive balance of trade could be produced. As was noted in *England's Treasure by Forraign Trade*:

> So that a King who desires to lay up much mony must endeavour by all good means to maintain and encrease his forraign trade, because it is the sole way not only to lead him to his own ends, but also to enrich his Subjects to his farther benefit: for a Prince is esteemed no less powerful by having many rich and well affected Subjects, than by possessing much treasure in his Coffers.[79]

Malynes broadly endorsed this view, arguing that:

> Traffique [...] may properly be called, *The Preheminent studie of Princes*; the rather, because the Sacred wisdome hath approved this *Axiom*: That a King is miserable (how rich soeuer he be) if he Raignes over a poore people.[80]

While history was concerned with a broader range of issues than political economy, both discourses accepted that the success of a state was dependent on the soundness of its finances, and both maintained that it was the task of the monarch to manage a nation's commercial interests. Moreover, both sought to establish the principles through which kings and queens might succeed in this task. At the same time, in tracing these principles, political economists and historians, on occasion, saw the need to look to the successes of other nations for inspiration. Just as Howes saw the imitation of the Dutch, Italians and Germans as the key reason for modern developments in manufacturing, Mun argued that similar practices were required with regard to trade. As he noted, the strength and wealth of England would be matchless 'if we should (but in part) apply our selves to such policies and endeavours as are very commonly used in some other Countreys of *Europe*'.[81] The key example of good practice here was the Dutch. Indeed, for Mun, as for many subsequent writers on economic affairs, the Dutch were both a commercial rival and, perhaps more importantly, world leaders in economic statecraft. As a consequence, while Dutch successes posed a threat to English interests, they also provided England with opportunities to acquire useful forms of economic knowledge.

These close connections between history and political economy imply that the ingredients were in place by the second quarter of the seventeenth century for new, sophisticated and detailed treatments of the history of economic statecraft in England. A Baconian historian might, for instance, have provided a complete history of economic legislation. Howes's work could have led to the development of further case studies regarding innovation in manufacture. More analysis might have been provided of immigration's impact and the role played by emulation. Ultimately, however, such forms of writing did not come to fruition in English historiography. Rather, as will be discussed in the next chapter, it was the political events of the 1640s which were to determine history's future direction.

Part II

4

The English Civil War and the politics of economic statecraft

The relationship between historical writing and the political and religious conflicts of the 1640s was a complex one.[1] Historians of the period generally emphasised that their loyalty was to the 'truth' rather than to any particular faction or party. Hamon L'Estrange, for example, used the frontispiece to his *The Reign of King Charles* (1655) to claim that this was a work 'Faithfully and Impartially delivered'.[2] Similarly, in the preface to his *Observations* (1656), a detailed critique of L'Estrange's *History*, Peter Heylyn claimed to be writing 'with a minde free from love, or hatred, or any of those other affections, which pre-ingagements in a party doe possesse men with'.[3] Thomas Fuller, meanwhile, defended his *Church-History of Britain* (1655) by observing that the work 'was so far from *prostituting* her Self to *Mercenary Embraces*, She did not at all Espouse any *Particular Interest*, but kept her self a *Virgin*'.[4] In making such comments, authors were emphasising their adherence to a series of well-established ideas about the importance of impartiality in historical writing. Indeed, before stating his own commitment to 'Truth', the parliamentarian historian Thomas May noted that 'the use of History, and the just Rules for composure of it [had] been so well and fully described heretofore' that it was 'lost labour and a needlesse extention of the present work' to discuss them further.[5]

Authors were also aware, however, that writing in a time of conflict presented certain challenges. Civil wars served not only to divide people, but also historical source material and, as May observed, his own position in Parliament meant that his knowledge of Parliamentarian 'Councels' was better than that of Royalist ones. Moreover, May acknowledged that the nature of the subject he was to discuss made it difficult to avoid partiality and impossible 'to escape the suspition or censure of it'.[6] A similar point was made by Fuller, who gave the first chapter of his *Appeal of Iniured Innocence* (1659) the title: 'That it is impossible for the *Pen* of any *Historians* writing in (as our's) a divided Age, to please all Parties'.[7] The politically charged atmosphere in which history was written and read was also affected by the role that historical argument played in the period's ideological conflicts. As J. G. A. Pocock has argued:

> what occurred was that belief in the antiquity of the common law encouraged belief in the existence of an ancient constitution, reference to which was constantly made, precedents, maxims and principles from which were constantly alleged [...]; and discussion in these terms formed one of the century's chief modes of political argument. Parliamentary debates and pamphlet controversies involving the law or the constitution were almost invariably carried on either wholly or partially in terms of an appeal to the past made in this way.[8]

This ensured that history and politics became intertwined to the point where, in the words of David Norbrook, it was 'very hard to separate political debate [...] from debates about the true meaning of English history'.[9] To write history, therefore, was to enter into a public discussion concerning the relative rights of king, Parliament and people, and the position of the Church of England within English society.

From the 1640s onwards, historical accounts of James I came to be shaped by these considerations. The key issue to be decided was the relationship between the King's approach to government and established English constitutional practices. For historians critical of the Stuarts, James had rejected the constitution and instigated the chain of events that led to the Civil War. Those more sympathetic to the Scottish King argued that his conduct was broadly in line with that of his predecessors; the unrest that had occurred in the period was a product of the malign Puritan and republican factions who were later to dismantle the constitution and execute their monarch. Writers were, of course, acutely aware that a complex blend of political, legal and confessional concerns had been at stake in the various confrontations between Charles and his critics. Nevertheless, they saw that debate had frequently coalesced around issues concerning revenue, most significantly disagreements regarding the King's right to 'Tonnage and Poundage', his attempts to raise money through the forced loan of 1626 and 'Ship Money', and his various efforts to secure parliamentary subsidies. The origin of these conflicts, it was agreed, was to be found in the reign of James, whose struggles to raise money in the face of a recalcitrant Parliament prefigured those of his son. As a consequence, James's management of revenue became a highly politicised and divisive issue, which received detailed commentary from the period's historians. Indeed, Michael Sparke's *The Narrative History of King James, for the first fourteen Years* was published with 'An abstract or Brief Declaration of the Present State of his Majesties Revenew', a seventy-two-page list of 'all monies [James] brought into his [...] coffers'.[10] Commerce occupied a more complex position in the period. Discussions of James lack the detailed engagement with the commercial aspects of economic statecraft that, as we have seen, had been a feature of Jacobean writing. Equally, however, references to trade and tradesmen are frequent, and England's moral decay – a theme as important to Royalist writers anxious to 'explain' the Regicide, as it was to Parliamentarian authors seeking to condemn Stuart practices – was frequently presented as a process of commercialisation.

The main body of this chapter explores how these ideas were treated by the Civil War era historians Anthony Weldon, Arthur Wilson and William Sanderson.[11] Each of the writers, it will be argued, despite their political differences, developed a moralistic analysis of James's financial management rooted in Livian ideas of exemplary virtue and honour. The final section of the discussion shows how these ideas were developed by the historian and political economist Roger Coke in the 1690s.

1. Parliamentarian history: Anthony Weldon's *Court and Character of King James*

Anthony Weldon's writing was shaped by his personal relationship with the King.[12] In the first part of his career Weldon had served in James's Court, acting as both clerk of the green cloth and clerk of the kitchen. At some point during the later years of the King's reign, however, he lost these positions; some accounts have claimed that this was a result of a scurrilous description of Scotland that he wrote in 1617, while others have seen Weldon as a victim of reforms to the royal household introduced by Lionel Cranfield in the 1620s.

What is clear, however, is that by the time of the Civil War, Weldon was an avowed opponent of the King. He served as the head of the parliamentary committee for Kent, and acquired a reputation – albeit possibly an undeserved one – for his autocratic and tyrannical management of the county.

Weldon died in 1648, and his *The Court and Character of King James* was published posthumously in 1650. The image of James that it presented was not a flattering one. Attention was drawn to the King's cowardice, his over-large tongue and his poor personal hygiene, and he emerges from the text as both a ludicrous figure and a repulsive one.[13] Running alongside these highly personal attacks, however, was a more general narrative regarding the effects of Stuart government. For Weldon, James's reign had seen the emergence of a new and pernicious obsession with money. The origins of this development lay in the King's poor financial management and, more specifically, his violation of the core precepts of conventional Aristotelian ideas about liberality. Aristotle had argued that the liberal man was one who 'will both give and spend the right amounts and on the right objects, alike in small things and in great, and that with pleasure; he will also take the right amounts and from the right sources'.[14] While James could not be called mean, he had, in Weldon's view, spent both excessively and unwisely, wasting huge amounts of money on enriching unworthy individuals, primarily the 'beggarly' Scots and a series of undeserving favourites.[15] Equally, the King had erred in his approach to the taking of money, drawing excessively on the purses of his subjects, and spending resources that were not his own. As Weldon observed, James would 'rather part with 100*li.* hee never had in his keeping, then [*sic*] one twenty shillings peece within his owne custody'.[16]

The ultimate consequence of the King's failings was that financial concerns came to be prioritised over all other matters. As Weldon noted, 'ever since Queene *Elizabeths* death, the raysing money hath been the only way to raise men, as being held the essential property of a wise man, to know how to bring in money (*per fas aut nefas*)'.[17] This idea was further emphasised by Weldon's attempt to associate the actions of James's primary political advisors and ministers with low and corrupt forms of mercantile activity. Thus Weldon described the struggle between Salisbury and Suffolk for the King's favour as a confrontation to decide 'who should ingrosse him, and make him their Monopoly'.[18] Particularly vehement, meanwhile, were the attacks launched on the courtiers Lionel Cranfield and Sir Arthur Ingram. The former was the holder of a series of Court posts and, from 1621 to 1624, Lord Treasurer. The latter served as 'cofferer' of the king's household in 1615. Weldon described them as

> two meane fellowes grand Projectors, the one, *Ingram*, an ordinary Waiter of the Customes, the other, *Cranfield*, an Apprentice, who had served three broken Citizens, and it is probable by his wit and honesty he might thrive by the all, and lay that for his first a foundation of his future projecting.[19]

Such backgrounds, it was argued, rendered them fundamentally unsuitable for high office. As was observed in relation to Cranfield: '[he was an individual] whose minde was ever so base, as never to discerne what Honour was, nor ever had hee any other inherent Honour then what in his Apprenticeship he raked out of the Kennel'.[20] Similar themes are also present in Weldon's discussion of the selling of honours. Salisbury, Weldon argued, had bought himself a position of power in the early days of James's reign. He then went on not only to teach the King 'how to enhance his [James's] Prerogative so above the Lawes, that he might inslave the Nation', but also successfully instigated a scheme for selling new 'Baronets'.[21] Defending this idea to the King, Salisbury observed:

> he [James] should finde his *English* Subjects like Asses, on whom he might lay any burthen, and should need neither Bit, nor Bridle, but their Asses eares; And when the King said, It would discontent the generality of the Gentry: He replyed, Tush Sir, you want the money, that will doe you good, the Honour will doe them very little; And by these courses he raised himselfe, friends, and family, to Offices, Honours, and great Possessions.[22]

The key implication of such comments was that 'honours', in becoming a commercial object freely available for purchase on the open market, had lost their fundamental honourableness. More generally, the corruption that England underwent during James's reign is imagined by Weldon as a process through which both statesmen and honour itself became commoditised and, as a consequence, morally compromised.

In making such comments Weldon employed a highly conventional anti-commercial rhetoric, which had received its most famous formulations in Aristotle's *Politics* and the work of Machiavelli. His position, however, is complicated by his claim that it was James's poor financial management that had brought about the decay of honour. Indeed, the effect of the King's dishonourable conduct is measured, in part, in financial terms. Thus, when discussing James's pacifism, Weldon noted that he 'had rather spend 100,000*li.* on Embassies, or to keep or procure peace with dishonour, then 10,000*li.* on an Army that would have forced peace with honour'.[23] As a result, his decisions were 'no less chargeable then dishonourable and unprofitable to him and his whole Kingdome'.[24] The key consequence of the King's approach to finance, meanwhile, was to have 'enriched many in particular, as *Salisbury*, *Suffolke*, *Northampton*, *Worcester*, *Lake* &c. yet [to have beggared] himself and the Nation in generall'.[25] For Weldon, therefore, if the King had behaved in a more honourable manner, prioritising national interests over individual ones, both he and England would have benefited in financial terms.

2. Parliamentarian history: Arthur Wilson's *The History of Great Britain*

A more detailed and scholarly account of James's reign was to emerge in Arthur Wilson's *The History of Great Britain* (1653).[26] Before turning to history in the latter part of his life, Wilson had enjoyed a rich and varied career.[27] Born in around 1595, he spent two years of his youth in France as the guest of wine merchant relatives. On his return to England, he eventually trained as an exchequer clerk, before entering the service of Robert Devereux, third Earl of Essex. He accompanied Essex to the Palatinate in 1620 and later saw military action as part of the campaign to restore Frederick V, the territory's deposed ruler, to his former throne. After leaving Essex's service in 1631, Wilson studied medicine at Trinity College, Oxford, and authored a series of plays, three of which found their way on to the London stage. Later he gained employment with Henry Rich, the Earl of Warwick, and both served under him in the wars in the Low Countries and acted as the steward of his estates when Warwick was fighting for Parliament. Wilson continued to write during this period, penning both his history and an autobiography, a work which, in line with Presbyterian beliefs, sought to trace the role played by 'Divine Goodnes' in shaping 'the many occurences of [...] life'.[28]

The *History of Great Britain* opened with a 'Proeme' in which Wilson confidently proclaimed his own impartiality. This work would, he noted, occupy a middle passage between the 'Scylla' of Weldon's angry attack on James and the 'Charybdis' of William Sanderson's hagiographic *Aulicus Coquinariæ* (1651). However, while Wilson largely avoided the *Court and Character*'s scurrility, his approach had a good deal more in common with Weldon's than Sanderson's. Indeed, the bulk of his introductory remarks were concerned with defending the right of the historian to criticise a monarch. This point, like many others in Weldon's ornately written account, was made through an extended metaphor. '*Histories*', he argued, 'are like *Anatomies*, especially when they reflect on *Persons*.'[29] Crude attempts to 'hack, hew or bespatter' were to be avoided; rather a 'gentle hand' was required, which could work with '*Authority* and *Knowledge*'.[30] However, while neither history nor anatomy should 'cauterise, and slash with *Malice*', they both needed to be truthful in order to be useful.[31] When tracing the ways and passages of the body in dissection, therefore, it was necessary to note 'where *Obstructions* have been, where Diseases have bred, and by this *Pattern* learn to remove the accrecion of bad *Humours*'.[32] Similarly, in history, '*Examples* of basenesse, and unworthinesse, if truly and genuinely related, may deterr and hinder the violent *Career* of such as mind no other *happinesse* than what this *vapour* of *vain-glory* can contribute; and esteem a good *Name* more among *men*, than acceptance with *God*.'[33] Such an approach to history had been widely endorsed in the past; Tacitus, for example, Wilson argued, was never blamed for 'personating *Tiberius* Dissimulation, *Nero's* Cruelty, *Seianus* Pride, [nor] *Livia's* and *Messalina's* Adulteries'.[34] 'These times', however, were 'full of perplexed and disastrous Divisions', which ensured that any impartial work, his own included, was likely to face a series of impassioned criticisms.[35]

The key aim of the *History of Great Britain* was to explain the origins of such divisions. Its general argument was that in Jacobean England the '*sensitive* faculties' had gained 'predominance over the Reasond', thereby producing an age of excess and vanity.[36] James was in large part responsible for this state of affairs. His excessive generosity to favourites had fomented luxury and debauchery, and these, in turn, had undermined the dignity, popularity and financial security of the monarchy. Such developments were frequently presented as either literal or metaphorical processes of commercialisation. A particularly useful example of the latter approach comes in his general analysis of the role of the monarch. Wilson began by thinking about the movement of heavenly objects, noting that 'We see all the *Motions* of *Superiour Bodies*, in what excellent *Order* and *Perfection* they move.'[37] He went on to contrast two types of bodies. On the one hand, there are comets which, emitting 'grosse and putrid *Matter*', follow an unpredictable course, are auguries of 'Prodigious Calamities', and, after blazing a little, extinguish themselves.[38] On the other hand, there are celestial bodies that 'beget no *wonder* […] but keep a constant *Course* in their own *Spheres*, and are not contaminated with *things* below them, yet they retain a *Powerfull Influence* over them'.[39] This latter type of body provides a good model, Wilson notes, for Princes who should 'shine in *Glory*'.[40] However, he continued, when Princes

> grovell here for trash and trumpery, and trade away that gallant stock of *Love* housed in their *Peoples Hearts*, for some false *Coin*, minted by *Passion*, mutable *Affection*, or mis-led *Reason*, they doe degrade themselves. And then the onely difference betwixt a *King*, and a mean *Man*, is, That the one, by his Trade, cosens a few; the other a great many, but himself most.[41]

A monarch's failure to perform his duties, therefore, is viewed – in metaphorical terms at least – as transforming him from a celestial object into a corrupt tradesman. Similar associations are at play in the *History*'s main narrative. The disastrous state of James's revenue, it is noted, meant that he came to see Parliament not as a source of counsel, but rather of money. Consequently, he sought to make '*Merchandize* of the Common-wealth' by conceiving of them as 'his *Banke*, his *Merchants*'.[42] This attempt to treat politicians as tradesmen was based on a fundamental misunderstanding: '*Merchants* looke for their money againe with advantage, and therefore their *Counsell* in disposing it may be well spared'.[43] Parliament, however, 'if they raise money from the *People* (which is never to be repayed) there is good reason they should know not onely to what purpose it is levied, but how prudently and fitly laid out'.[44] The logic of commerce, therefore, was not the logic of the constitution. Equally, those engaged in commercial and financial activities were not, at least in a well-run polity, statesmen. Indeed, Cranfield's tenure as Lord Chancellor was evidence of the Court's failings. This individual,

> who had been a Citizen of *London*, bred up in the *Custome-house*, and knowing the *secret contrivances* of those Officers, was thought fittest to manage the King's Revenue: For in expensive and wanting *Courts*, those great Officers are most acceptable, that by their *finesses* and *projects*, can bring in that, which with *riot* and *prodigality* goes out.[45]

For Wilson, therefore, poor financial management had helped to create an age of projects and projectors.

Such comments have a good deal in common with the analysis developed in Weldon's *Court and Character*. What separates Wilson from Weldon, however, is his account of the consequences of James's government. As we have seen, Weldon argued that James's gratuitous expenditure had served to impoverish the people of England, while his pacifism had sacrificed the interests of the nation in order to enrich a small group of corrupt courtiers. For Wilson, by contrast, peace had brought universal plenty, albeit a form of plenty that had undermined England's moral and political fabric. These ideas were developed through yet another analogy, this time between political and natural bodies. If a body is inactive and overfed, he argued, it will contract 'gross humors, which will have vent'.[46] To maintain a healthy body, therefore, 'Exercise' is required to 'keep the *spirits* active, [...] digest the grosser and sulginous matter' and strengthen 'the *Nervs* of a Kingdom or *Republique*'.[47] Such exercise could only be achieved through 'Warre', which, he argued, 'is *necessary* as *Physicke* for unsound *Bodies*'.[48] These assumptions led Wilson to present the King's pacifist foreign policy as a contagious, enervating force. It had, he observed, ensured that the Germans had 'swelled into a Dropsie of *Voluptuousness*, by *Plenty*, and the *sweets of Peace*', while France 'wanting *Exercise*' had become 'surfetted with diseases at home, which by fits broke out into *Tumors* among themselves'.[49] In England 'bravery and feasting, the *Parents* of *Debaucherie* and *Riot*, flourished'.[50] Such behaviour not only served to corrupt the populace, but also made the writing of history difficult. 'There is', Wilson contended,

> no *Theam* for *History* when men spill more *drink* than *blood*; when *plots* and *contrivances* for *Lust*, acted in dark corners, are more practiced than *Strategems* in *War*; and when the *Stages* with silken *Pageants* and *Poppets*, that slacken the *sinews*, are more frequented than those *Theaters* of *Honor*, where *Industry* brawns and hardens the *Armes*.[51]

Perhaps more worryingly, peace also had the potential to breed civil discontent. 'Some', Wilson noted, compared James to Tiberius 'for *Dissimulation*'; however,

> *Peace* was maintained by him as in the Time of *Augustus*; And Peace begot *Plenty*, and *Plenty* begot *Ease* and *Wantonness*, and *Ease* and *Wantonnesse* begot *Poetry*, and *Poetry* swelled to that *bulk* in his time, that it begot strange *Monstrous Satyrs*, against the King own person, that hauntrd [*sic*] both *Court* and *Country*.[52]

Wilson was unwilling to provide details of these 'satyrs', but switching to a horticultural metaphor, noted that the 'tongues' of those times

> made every little *miscarriage* (being not able to discover their true operations, like smal *seeds* hid in earthy *Darknesse*) grow up, and spread into such exuberant *branches*, that evil *Report* did often pearch upon them. So dangerous it is for *Princes* by a *Remisse Comportment*, to give growth to the least *Error*; for it often proves as *fruitful* as *Malice* can make it.[53]

These events, it was emphasised, had been avoidable. If the King's 'spirit' had 'raised' him up to war when 'the voice of God (the voice of the people) called him to it, happily it might have hindred the great *Effusion* of *Bloud* amongst our *Selves*, that happened after in his Sonnes time'.[54] What the King had failed to understand was that '*Peace* is a great *Blessing*, if it bring not a *Curse* with it; but *War* is more Happy in its effects than it, especially if it takes away the *distemper* that grows by long surfets, without destroying the *Body*.'[55]

To an extent, such comments simply constitute a rejection of economic statecraft. Wilson showed little interest in discussing James's day-to-day management of commerce, and presented England's colonial successes as achievements of its oppressed people rather than its absolutist monarch. Moreover, there is no sense in the *History of Great Britain* that commerce might contribute to a nation's military greatness. Rather, wealth is conceived of as a sensuous, feminine form of sickness, and war as its harder, more masculine cure. Despite this, Wilson continued to see the management of finances as critically important. Indeed, the King's inadequacies were, in a sense, economic in character. He had, with disastrous consequences, failed to administer the nation's revenues adequately, and the key event of his reign had been the growth of a new, pernicious form of plenty.

3. Royalist history: the writings of William Sanderson

Direct responses to Weldon's and Wilson's accounts are to be found in the work of the Royalist historian William Sanderson.[56] Born in 1586, Sanderson was the son of a merchant, also called William. The elder Sanderson enjoyed a highly successful career in trade, acquiring property in England and Ireland, providing funding for the voyages of Martin Frobisher and Walter Raleigh, and becoming a well-known figure in the Elizabethan Court. His son also claimed exalted connections, noting that he had lived a '*long time in Court*' and adding, with a nautical flourish, that while he did not '*have any hand to the Helm*, [he] *cabin'd neer the Steerage*'.[57] His precise activities during the conflicts of the 1640s are not known, but the inscription on his memorial in Westminster Abbey observed that he was famed for 'his family, learning, untainted fidelity to his prince' and noted the 'great hardships [he] sustained under the late tyranny of rebels'.[58] His reputation, such as it is, rests primarily on his work as a historian. In 1651 he published *Aulicus Coquinariæ*, a point-by-point denunciation of Weldon's *Court and Character*. He later expanded this pamphlet-length piece into a larger, descriptively titled narrative work: *A Compleat History of the lives and reigns of, Mary Queen of Scotland, and of Her Son and Successor, James the Sixth, King of Scotland, and (After Queen Elizabeth) King of Great Britain, France and Ireland* (1656).[59] This account repeated many of his previous comments on Weldon, often copying directly from his earlier discussion, and developed a detailed critique of Wilson's *History*.

Sanderson's principal argument was that James's reign had been characterised by 'peace and plenty'.[60] These conditions had brought England considerable advantages: enriching the King's subjects, increasing revenues and raising the nation's reputation internationally.[61] Moreover, 'trade increased [mightily] by the wise Government of this King'.[62] Such claims constitute a direct rejection of Weldon's arguments about the poverty of Jacobean England. Equally, however, Sanderson sought to counter the arguments about luxury that had been central to Wilson's work, arguing that

> The splendor of the *King*, *Queen*, *Prince* and *Princess* with the rest of the royall yssue, the concourse of strangers hither from forein Nations, the multitude of our own people from all parts of our three

> Kingdoms gave a wonderfull glory to the Court, at this time, the only Theatre of Majesty; Not any way inferiour to the most Magnificent in *Christendom*; Prince and people increasing in honor and wealth.[63]

Setting forth this wealth in state, Sanderson continued, with 'all moderate additions of *Feasts*, *Masks*, *Comedies*, *Balls* and such like' was a 'prudentiall' move.[64] Such spectacles acted as 'necessary *Mirrors*, wherein mens Actions are reflected to their own view'.[65] The objections of Wilson – or as Sanderson labels him, the 'squeazie stomacht Historian' – were a product of his own historical ignorance, and consequent lack of awareness that such practices were 'politickly used in the *Romane-Common-wealth* and *Monarchy*' and were judged 'tollerable' in Christian kingdoms and states.[66] Attention is also drawn to Wilson's own literary background. He was 'bred up a Poet, frequently, a Rymer and Composer of playes', Sanderson observed, and had only turned to history when 'his trade fell to decay' and he was forced to 'trot any way to get money'.[67] A comparison, therefore, is implied between the wealth and glory of the Jacobean Court and the poverty, hypocritical spite and jealousy of its Puritan historian. While such comments constitute a complete rejection of the account of luxury developed in the *History of Great Britain*, elsewhere in his discussion Sanderson sought to use Wilson's argument about modern corruption against him. In the 'Proeme', which prefaces his account, for example, Sanderson argued that in James's time the kingdom had grown '*aged in happinesse*' to the point that

> *The very excess seemed to abate the pleasure: Or as the hot sent of Musk to some Savors seems to stink. Repetitions of our Blessings then, did not so much affect our Nations as dull them. Peace made us wanton; Plenty intemperate; Mercies secure; Our Benefits then became our Weapons to rebell against his* [James's] *fame now; The whole Land being sowred by the Peoples Sins; too much felicity introduced Luxury, and Correllaries of Vices, Pride, Ambition, Contempt of things Divine and Human. This Nation in short time sick of a surfeit of Health; afterwards broke with two* [sic] *much wealth; and now it comes to amendment. Ryot begins to grow thirsty, made so, to go plain; Gluttons to fast; Wantonness, starved into Soberness.*[68]

The illness that Sanderson diagnoses here is not, as had been the case in Wilson's account, one of the Court: rather it is one of the people. Indeed, the primary symptom of the nation's sickness, for Sanderson, was the emergence of the sort of gratuitous criticism of the monarchy found in the work of Weldon and Wilson. Such claims allowed James to be exonerated of any real crime; he was, in a sense, a victim of his own good government. Equally, however, they ensured that Sanderson was distinctly ambivalent with regard to the 'peace and plenty' which are presented as both James's primary achievement and the causes of the Stuart dynasty's demise.

Ambivalence also characterises Sanderson's attitude to the growing mercantile presence at Court, as can be seen most clearly in his discussions of Ingram and Cranfield. As noted previously, James's critics had made much of these individuals' backgrounds in trade, and portrayed them as lowly and dishonest projectors. In response, Sanderson drew attention to Cranfield's 'antient Family in Gloucestershire' – as demonstrated by 'their bearing of Arms in the Heralds office' – and sought to defend his career in trade.[69] His rise from merchant adventurer to minister of state was evidence of 'his extraordinary qualities' and the 'blessing of God upon his indeavours'.[70] Moreover, his skills as a merchant were highly useful to the state, giving him 'great understanding in the affairs of the *Customes*'.[71] As a result, Sanderson asked rhetorically, 'who [was] more fit [...] than this man of *experience*, in Stating the *Accompts*, for the *Revenues* of the *State*, which [...] he improved, and not unlikely *thereby*, purchased *Envy* for his *Eminency*'.[72] A similar defence is provided of Ingram. At the time of his appointment to the King's household, the '*Customers*' [the tax farmers] at the Treasury 'had cozened the King, engrossing by that means, the wealth of *Trading*'. Because of his own knowledge of trade, however, Ingram could 'and honestly might, discover the cunning craft of the cosening *Merchant*'.[73] This was of particular importance, Sanderson noted, at a time when royal expenditure was rising and revenue was falling.

However, while Sanderson defended Cranfield and Ingram personally, his general assumptions regarding merchants were highly unflattering. These individuals are characterised by their desire to 'cozen' both fellow traders and the nation, and they 'never want will [...] to abuse each other, and [acquire] gain to themselves'.[74] Mercantile expertise was useful to government because only a merchant could understand and uncover the fundamentally deceitful practices of his fellow tradesmen. James's decision to appoint such individuals, meanwhile, was a product of the dire state of the nation's finances. As Sanderson observed:

> indeed was in this Kings life, the last of that Office [Lord Treasurer], and the meanest of birth, lately altered from the Trust of *Nobly-born* persons. The Treasury of antient Spring-tides was of late sunck into neap-ebbs of *Revenue*, and enforced a necessity of providence in collecting, and judgement and practice in disposing: Neither of these could be found by experience suitable to our latern Lord like-breeding, ignorant and careless.[75]

Such comments are used to emphasise the appropriateness of the King's actions for the situation in which he found himself. Equally, however, the fact that individuals such as Cranfield and Ingram were required in government was, for Sanderson, evidence of fundamental problems in the Jacobean Court and Jacobean society more generally.

4. The Civil War, history and economic statecraft

At the heart of Civil War era debates concerning James's economic statecraft lay a paradox. Discussions were characterised by new, more combative forms of argumentation. Historians sought not just to represent the people and events of the past, but to actively discredit rival interpretations. The result was a shift not just in the tone of history, but also in its form. Writers either needed to balance chronological narrative with polemic, or reject chronology entirely in favour of a point-by-point denunciation of alternative accounts. Ironically, however, despite the increasingly vituperative nature of such confrontations, the historiographical differences between historians actually narrowed during this period, and a consensus emerged, albeit a broad one, regarding what constituted good economic statecraft. The task of historians, commentators agreed, was to act as judges of the statesmen whose lives they narrated, and to assess whether a particular monarch provided a good or a bad example to posterity. The criteria used to make such assessments were Livian in character. A good monarch, it was assumed, was necessarily a virtuous monarch; a bad monarch was either personally sinful, or lacked the moral authority to counter the influence of his nefarious courtiers. Given the focus on praising or discrediting specific individuals, there was no room for Baconian-style analysis of the relationship between private virtue and vice on the one hand, and the public's interests on the other. Nor was there a place for the broader engagement with issues relating to economic and social change found in the work of Howes.

With regard to financial issues, the framework was straightforwardly Aristotelian. It was the specific duty of the monarch to manage the nation's financial resources in a manner that demonstrated his liberality. This involved both collecting the right amount of revenue from the right sort of people in the right way, and distributing that revenue in a similarly judicious manner. Commerce, meanwhile, and England's increasing commercialisation were treated with a good deal of suspicion. Indeed, while the accounts of Weldon, Wilson and Sanderson drew on the ideas of honour and dishonour that had underpinned Camden's *Annales*, their primary concern was not with celebrating honourable trade, but condemning its dishonourable forms. Given such views, the key questions for historians concerned blame. Their task, after making the conventional claims regarding the need for impartiality, was to identify who had caused England's problems and what they had done wrong. While no consensus was to emerge on this issue, it was widely accepted that the nation's difficulties were, in part, financial and commercial in character.

5. Whig history and political economy: Roger Coke's *A Detection of the Court and State of England*

To conclude this chapter, I would like to look at a final account, which in part moves away from the approaches discussed above: Roger Coke's *A Detection of the Court and State of England* (1694).[76] After a successful career as a writer on commerce and trade, and a rather less successful career as a businessman, Coke turned to historical writing in the final years of his life. The move appears to have been a profitable one. The *Detection*, a narrative account of the four Stuart kings and the Protectorate, ran to four editions, the last of which was published in 1719. Coke's conception of historical writing was, in many ways, a conventional one for the period. 'To compose Histories', he noted, paraphrasing the Venetian historian Giovan Battista Nani, 'is sacred, and not to be undertaken but with an upright Mind, and undefiled Hands'.[77] The sacred quality of history writing, he continued, was a product of the historian's immense power:

> taking to himself an absolute Dictatorship, nay an Authority more than Human, over Times, Persons and Actions, governs Fame, measures Deserts, penetrates Intentions, discloses Secrets; is with an

> undistinguished Arbitriment over Kings and People, the Judg of Ages past, and Master of those to come; Absolves or Punishes, Deceives or Instructs.[78]

In exercising this quasi-judicial function, Coke sought to evaluate the achievements of England and its monarchs against a series of Whiggish criteria. His key concern, therefore, was with the degree to which the King and the people, particularly the former, had conformed to the '*Constitutions and Laws of the* English *Monarchy*'. These institutions, Coke observed, '*have continued for near Nine hundred Years, viz. since King Egbert*'.[79] At their heart was the notion that kings could not '*abrogate old Laws, or impose new, or raise Monies from the Subject above the Revenues of the Crown, without Consent in Parliament*'.[80] When monarchs conformed to the constitution, popular resistance to them is 'High Treason *in this World and Damnation in that to come*'.[81] However, if kings failed to abide by England's laws and constitutions, then the will of the king and the will of the people came into conflict with one another.[82] This served to '*distract the Allegiance*' of the king's subjects, and give '*Life and Motion to the ambitious Humour of Male-contents*'.[83] The aim of the *Detection*, Coke asserted, was to show the consequences of the emergence of just such a divided will in '*the Reigns of the Kings of the Scottish Race*'.[84]

These ideas directly informed Coke's treatment of James I. His key claim was that the King's violations of the constitution and poor management of the nation's economic interests were interconnected products of his flawed character. James, Coke argued, was an incompetent, lazy and prodigal individual, who showed an unhealthy regard for a series of highly pernicious favourites. To an extent, these traits meant that he neglected his kingly duties. And while he did so, the Dutch 'still grew more powerful at Sea' and Henry IV of France 'was accumulating incredible Treasure at Home, and laying the Foundation of vast Designs Abroad'.[85] James's crime, however, was not simply inaction. Rather, his incompetence in economic management and his extravagant, debauched lifestyle had led him to adopt a series of unconstitutional approaches to revenue, among them payments for knighthoods, the selling of honours, benevolences and monopolies.

Such ideas are entirely in line with the accounts of Weldon and Wilson. Coke, however, was to develop his analysis a good deal further than his predecessors by drawing on the principles that had underpinned the pamphlets on trade that he published in the 1670s, foremost among them *A Discourse of Trade* (1670) and *England's Improvements* (1675).[86] His key claims in these works had been that three particular factors determined the wealth of a nation: convenience of place, numbers of people and free trade.[87] While England had the best natural resources of any nation, Coke argued, it had failed to increase its population and had introduced a series of measures that restricted commerce, notably monopolies, the apprentice system and the Navigation Acts. In the *Discourse* and *England's Improvements* Coke had offered a systematic analysis of England's errors with regard to economic policy based around a series of theorems and propositions. The *Detection* essentially transformed this material into a chronological narrative, outlining the specific actions that England's monarchs had performed with regard to commerce and finance, and assessing their effectiveness.

In relation to James I, Coke's most detailed discussion of commercial affairs concerned monopolies, a theme he returned to repeatedly. His approach to the issue is distinctive. He is not so much concerned with the reasons why James set up monopolistic trading companies or the events and debates surrounding their establishment. Rather, as can be seen particularly clearly in his discussion of the monopoly on Spanish trade established in 1604, his account departs from conventional historical analysis entirely and provides a long list of arguments in favour of free trade, derived in part from the *Discourse on Trade*. Coke's assertion was that people's subsistence is naturally dependent on the assistance of others and their own labour. Monopolies, he contended, by excluding individuals from certain trades, deprive people of the assistance and labour they naturally require to live and, therefore, violate the law of nature. This violation, Coke continued, was worse than the tyranny that the Pharaohs exercised over the Israelites; whereas the Egyptians imposed 'a greater Hardship how to live' by compelling the Israelites to make bricks yet denying them straw, monopolies deny 'poor Men their Means of living'.[88] In addition to this, monopolies, by restraining the 'Labours and Industry of Men in any Profession, Art or Mystery', not only hinder their improvement in a particular country, but provide a way for rival nations to enlarge their own manufactures.[89] After outlining these issues at length, Coke concluded by noting that 'we have thought fit to premise this, that a better View may be had of what follows'.[90]

The discussion that follows is essentially a brief account of the end of the monopoly, by means of a 'memorable Law' passed by Parliament.[91] To an extent, Coke's account here is conventionally Whiggish in its desire to attribute any positive developments that took place in Jacobean England to Parliament rather than the King. What is noteworthy, however, is that his argument marks a substantial departure from those of James's other critics. As we have seen, Weldon conceived of James's reign as a time of poverty, while Wilson saw it as dominated by a corrupt and debauched form of plenty. Coke disagreed, arguing that 'tho the King was never poorer than at this time', free trade with Spain ensured that 'the Nation was far richer than in all the long Reign of Queen *Elizabeth*'.[92] Such comments, coupled with Coke's opposition – on commercial grounds – to war with Spain, provide an important hint as to his priorities. He was, it would seem, rather more interested in defending what he conceived of as England's trading interests than he was in advancing conventional pro-Whiggish or anti-Stuart arguments.

To an extent, Coke's account provides a demonstration of the difficulties of blending political economy with narrative history. In showing how James had failed to understand the basic principles of commerce, Coke was obliged to offer lengthy summaries of those principles himself. As a result, the narrative tended to stop at the point where the economic analysis began. At the end of the *Detection*, meanwhile, Coke abandoned narrative altogether, and expressed his argument in a numbered list of twenty-three commercial policy recommendations. Consequently, his work functions as a useful example of a historical account that puts commerce at its heart; indeed, the *Detection* is built on the idea that 'the Riches of *England*' and its 'Strength and Glory' are 'derived from our Foreign Trades'.[93] In this sense, therefore, concerns regarding commercialisation, which had been a key feature of the work of Civil War era historians, are entirely absent from the *Detection*. When discussing economic issues, however, Coke does not reject conventional assumptions regarding history's didactic function. His account of the Act that ended the Spanish monopoly, for example, concluded by noting that 'the Reasons in this Act extend to all other Beneficial Trades, as to *Turkey*, the *East-Country* and *Hamburgh* Trades, and to *Africa* and the *East-Indies*'.[94] Implicit in this statement was the suggestion that action against monopolies was required from modern statesmen. Coke also stressed that his motivation for writing the *Detection* was rooted in his concern for England's economic interests. He had taken up his pen to convince the various orders of society – listed as nobility, gentry, clergy and merchants – that 'the Employment of People, and the Freedom of Trade, be the two great Principles of the flourishing and happy State of any Country'.[95]

Writing in the conclusion to the *Detection*, Coke observed that 'I have done, and I do not know but I am the first that ever begun a Work of this Nature.'[96] This claim, while a bold one, is entirely justified; no other history of the period had attempted to blend political economy with history in quite this manner. It might be added that no other work was ever to attempt it again, and there is undoubtedly a sense in which Coke's approach represents a historiographical dead end. Nevertheless, as we shall see in the next chapter, his ideas helped, in part, to set the agenda for the most successful historian of the first half of the eighteenth century: Paul de Rapin de Thoyras.

5

Whig history: Paul de Rapin de Thoyras's *Histoire*

The latter years of the seventeenth century saw a series of calls for a complete account of England's history from the Roman invasion to the present, which would be able to rival both in quality and scale the work of Livy.[1] Initial attempts at such an endeavour were made by, among others, John Milton, William Temple and Jonathan Swift, while more substantial accounts emerged from Robert Brady and James Tyrrell, both of whom reached Richard II.[2] A success, of sorts, was achieved in 1706 with the publication of *A Complete History of England*, a two-volume compilation of material from authors such as Bacon, Camden and Wilson, supplemented with a new volume covering the period from Charles I onwards authored by White Kennet.[3] Laurence Echard, meanwhile, produced the first single-authored 'general' account, the *History of England* (1707, 1718).[4]

A more popular and, ultimately, more influential work, however, was to emerge a few years later with the publication of Paul de Rapin de Thoyras's *Histoire d'Angleterre* (1724–27), the subject of this chapter.[5] In the thirty years following its publication, Rapin's *Histoire* received three separate English translations,[6] sold around 18,000 copies,[7] and spawned a range of derivative texts.[8] It also contained, as Hugh Trevor-Roper has argued, 'the classic exposition of the Whig – the "old Whig" – interpretation of history'.[9] From this perspective, England's past was the story of the ongoing survival of the nation's Saxon constitution in the face of a series of threats from innovating monarchs and their proto-Tory supporters. Such an account, Trevor-Roper noted, was rooted in a 'philosophy of idealist conservatism' and contained 'no suggestion [...] that change has occurred or should occur in history, no reference to economic life or ideas'.[10] While other historians writing both before and after Trevor-Roper have maintained that institutional political development did play a key part in the *Histoire*,[11] the absence of an engagement with economic ideas continues to be seen as a distinguishing feature of Rapin's work. Laird Okie, for example, has argued that Rapin was a 'transitional' figure between the early modern compilation chroniclers and the more enlightened approaches of Hume, Robertson and Gibbon.[12] His modernity lay in his innovative use of sources, his concern with causation, and his desire to explain the emergence of the party system rather than simply vindicate one or other faction. Rapin remained, however, a traditionalist in the sense that he wrote 'political history pure and simple, unleavened by any significant discussion of the economy or cultural history'.[13]

Such claims usefully highlight the political focus of the *Histoire*, but they require, I believe, further clarification. Rapin's account emphasised not just the constitution's ancient origins, but also its capacity to bring prosperity and, with it, felicity to the nation's populace. And in developing an analysis of the material foundations of happiness, Rapin sought to show that trading and financial interests were promoted by constitutional government and damaged by arbitrary rule. This argument led him to utilise and develop earlier accounts of economic statecraft, provide some important commentary on trade and taxation, and, consequently, to engage with economic ideas. The result of this engagement, it will be argued, was the development of a Whiggish form of exemplary history, which frequently drew upon commercial and financial material.

1. Rapin and Leclerc

Born into a Protestant Savoyard family and trained as an advocate, Rapin was forced to leave France by the revocation of the Edict of Nantes in 1685.[14] After residing for a time in London, he enlisted with a group of French Huguenot volunteers, a move that ultimately led to his joining William of Orange's invasion force of England in 1688. Rapin continued his military career until 1693, when he accepted, possibly at William's bidding, a position as tutor to the son of the Earl of Portland. Over the next ten years he moved frequently between England and the United Provinces, before the marriage of Portland's son provided him with an opportunity to settle down and devote himself to full-time historical study. Initially he took up residence in The Hague but, seemingly in an attempt to economise, he moved to the small town of Wesel in 1707. Here Rapin kept in touch with the wider Republic of Letters through a correspondence with Jean Leclerc, the editor of the erudite periodical *Bibliothèque choisie*.[15] It was Leclerc who presented Rapin with his key source, Thomas Rymer's *Foedera*, a collection of England's various alliances and treaties, which Rapin both abridged for publication in *Bibliothèque choisie* and employed extensively within his own narrative.[16]

Rapin's approach to historiography also had much in common with that of Leclerc. The Dutch Huguenot circles in which both writers moved had close connections to Whig politics in England.[17] Huguenots had helped to provide refuge and companionship for those fleeing Stuart England in the 1670s and 1680s, enthusiastic backing for the Revolution of 1688, and military support for the new state that emerged under William. At the same time, the attack on absolutist forms of government that underlay much exclusion-era Whig thought meant that it enjoyed considerable popularity and influence among exiled Protestants, who were anxious to find ways of theorising their opposition to Bourbon cultural practices.[18] Leclerc was among the most significant of these exiles; he corresponded with Locke, played an instrumental role in translating and publicising the Englishman's work and, in his 1699 work *Parrhasiana*, developed a distinctively Whiggish analysis of historiography.[19]

Leclerc's primary aims in the historical sections of *Parrhasiana* were to establish the sort of skills historians required to produce good history and to measure the successes and failures of various classical and contemporary writers in acquiring those skills. After looking at the importance of a knowledge of one's subject, impartiality and a clear and concise style, he went on to defend, as Wilson and Coke had done, the right of historians to pass judgement on the individuals and events they described. His discussion of historical judgement, however, drew not on the ideas of Wilson, but rather on those of the Dutch jurist Hugo Grotius. In his legal work, Grotius had sought to demonstrate the existence of a natural law that was 'manifest and self-evident' to all, regardless of the society they lived in or the religion to which they adhered.[20] Thus, for Grotius, all individuals had the right to defend their own lives, and 'to retain, those things which are useful for life'.[21] At the same time, they could neither inflict injury upon their fellows, nor seize their possessions.[22] Despite the absence, therefore, of a shared civil code of regulations, a universal natural law made it possible to judge the justice or injustice of the often mutually antipathetic claims made by different states. Leclerc's innovation was to apply this basic approach to historical writing. The historian, he showed, whose craft was also concerned with providing judgements in the face of a series of competing, hostile claims, could identify a series of universally accepted criteria through which to assess the merits of individual historical actions.[23] Praise or censure for individuals should be given to those who conform to 'the Principles of Humanity' – 'that we ought not to do that to another, which we should call Injustice if they did to us' – while governments should be assessed on their capacity to ensure the happiness of those committed to their charge.[24] This happiness was conceived of in typically Whiggish terms as a product of the state's ability to protect the liberty and property of its populace. It consisted of three things:

> 1) In being only obliged to obey the Laws, which are approved by a long Use, or enacted according to the usual manner;
> 2) In enjoying quietly one's Estate, and the Fruit of one's Labour, as long as one obeys the Laws, without being under the apprehension of being deprived of it by any violent Means.
> 3) In contributing to the publick Charges, as much as the Subjects can bear, without being over-burthened.[25]

The final point is developed elsewhere in *Parrhasiana*, where Leclerc argued that if 'exorbitant' levies are extracted from a nation's subjects, 'there is not Money enough among Trading-men' and 'Industry ceases'.[26] Affordable taxes, therefore, are a vital factor in determining whether a state is 'Flourishing' or 'must necessarily fall to Decay'.[27]

Leclerc went on to compare the successes of ancient and modern historians in employing such ideas in their work. Ultimately, he concluded, despite the weaknesses of other aspects of their historical writing, it was the Greeks and Romans who had understood politics best. Whereas the 'Heathen Historians' had adhered to the principles of justice, modern historians sought to flatter their princes by embracing a brand of Machiavellianism which maintained 'that a State cannot be Happy and Quiet, unless People blindly submit to the Will of a Prince'.[28] It was this 'Spirit of Slavery' that had led historians to label the English 'a wild and inconstant Nation, for no other reason, but because they obey their Kings, when they do not incroach upon their Priviledges; and oppose their Designs, when they go about to destroy them'.[29] Indeed, for Leclerc, what England's neighbours labelled 'Wildness and Inconstancy [...] a *Greek* or *Roman* Historian would call [...] *Constancy* and *Love of Liberty*'.[30]

Rapin accepted these basic principles and employed them in two distinctive ways in the *Histoire*. First, he approved of the idea that a historian should act as a judge over the individuals he described and, as Leclerc had done, he used the people's happiness, and the extent to which they prospered in material terms, as the key criteria for assessing the success or failure of particular political leaders. Underlying such an approach was a belief that the people are, in a sense, always right; that which pleases them is praiseworthy, that which troubles them, blameworthy. Second, in his account of England's system of government, Rapin endorsed Leclerc's commentary on the measures that produced popular happiness and offered some additional analysis of the constitutional and political practices through which such happiness could be achieved. Thus, for Rapin, although English kings were entrusted with a substantial income and 'some *Privileges* approaching *Absolute Power*', there were two things over which they were denied jurisdiction: '*The Power of changing the Laws that had been enacted by Consent of King and People*; and *the Power of raising Taxes by* [their] *own Will and Pleasure*'.[31] At one level, by making such comments, Rapin is offering a contribution to the ongoing debate concerning the pedigree of English liberties. In his *A Complete History of England* (1685–1700), Brady, drawing on the analysis forwarded by Henry Spelman, had argued that the Norman invasion, and the subsequent introduction of feudalism, constituted a fundamental rupture in English government and law. This ensured that Englishmen did not have the ancient rights claimed by Whiggish writers and that English liberty was a modern innovation. Such claims were rigorously opposed by a number of writers, foremost among them James Tyrrell, whose *General History* (1696–1704) sought to demonstrate both that the ancient form of English government was a limited monarchy, not an absolutist one, as Brady had claimed, and that England's constitution had remained fundamentally unaltered since Saxon times.[32] Rapin, while willing to acknowledge the presence of beneficial constitutional innovation, clearly sided with the Whiggish Tyrrell over the Tory Brady. What is perhaps most significant, however, is that the emphasis of Rapin's account, like Leclerc's, is less on *de jure* historical rights, and more on the *de facto* benefits that good government could provide. Thus for Rapin, England's constitution was successful because it aligned the interests of the king with those of his people. Through securing liberty and property from any monarchical incursions, it allowed individuals to enjoy 'the Fruits of their own Labour and Industry', and this, in turn, generated the wealth among the populace required to uphold the monarch's income.[33] 'It can't be denied', Rapin concluded, 'but such a Government is extremely well calculated to render both Prince and People Happy.'[34]

The key task for government was to maintain this happiness. English liberties, as Rapin conceived of them, were dependent on 'an *Intimate* Union between the Prince and People, like that between the Head and Body'.[35] Communication and cooperation between these parties was vital; if conflict or mistrust arose, their union was threatened. Indeed, for Rapin, parliaments, and their predecessors, the Saxon 'Wittena-Gemots', acted as '*Representatives* of the whole Nation' whose function was to facilitate conversation – and with it understanding – between the king and his people.[36] This emphasis on cooperation also shaped Rapin's analysis of war. To wage war with other nations, monarchs required the backing and funding of Parliament. As a result, wars were a product of the sort of parliamentary and monarchical cooperation on which the constitution relied, and they could only be fought with any conviction if advancing popular and, therefore, for Rapin, legitimate aims. In contrast, those monarchs who avoided international conflicts were less dependent on Parliament for money and prone to following their own rather than the nation's interests.

2. Rapin's James I

Such arguments placed considerable emphasis on financial issues and, in developing them, Rapin scoured a broad range of histories for information about money and taxation, adapting material where necessary. With regard to James I, only a limited amount of adaptation was required. The profligate lifestyle and absolutism of England's first Stuart king, Rapin argued, meant that he was a highly unsuccessful manager of the nation's economy. Such a view was a seventeenth-century commonplace and, in developing an analysis in this vein, Rapin drew on a range of sources including the works of Weldon, Wilson and Coke.[37] Like his predecessors, Rapin emphasised James's extravagance and repeated anecdotes from Wilson and Coke concerning the liberal gifts he presented to his courtiers,[38] and copied out in full Coke's list of the fortunes amassed by such individuals.[39] He also referenced, albeit in more negative terms than the original, Baker's accounts of the lavish entertainments that James organised for foreign dignitaries,[40] and provided a fully itemised balance sheet – copied from the work of the antiquary Thomas Frankland – to show how the King had spent £93,294 – including a £7,680 bill for fireworks – on the marriage between his daughter and Frederick V, Elector Palatine.[41]

This excessive expenditure, Rapin argued, served to undermine political cooperation. Aware of the King's profligacy, and opposed to his views on monarchical prerogative, the Commons were unwilling to provide James with additional money. As a result, he was forced to find new, unconstitutional ways of raising income both at home and abroad. Extensive details are provided of these innovations and the opposition with which they met. The domestic programme, Rapin noted, included a series of measures, 'not all *legal*', among them '*Monopolies*, *Benevolences*, and *Loans*', as well as various attempts to sell honours and titles.[42] Particular attention is paid to James's monopolies, and Rapin paraphrased accounts from Coke, Baker and Wilson to discuss the selling of patents on cloth,[43] alum,[44] inns, ale houses, and gold and silver thread.[45] Such measures were perceived by the populace as a threat to their rights, and were rigorously opposed by Parliament, which argued that they worked 'to the great Prejudice of Trade'.[46] Criticism is also made of James's dealings with England's neighbours and, employing material from Coke, Rapin drew attention to the King's mismanagement of Spanish and Italian commerce through the creation of a monopolistic trading company,[47] his misguided attempt to sell fishing rights to the Dutch,[48] and his decision to cancel part of the debt owed to England by the United Provinces in return for quick payment.[49] For Rapin, therefore, the King prioritised his own short-term need for money over the long-term political and economic welfare of the nation.

While he was deeply reliant upon the work of other historians, Rapin's economic analysis also had a degree of originality. A central theme of Wilson's work had been the ways in which James's pacifist statesmanship had corrupted his subjects. As he observed in the conclusion to the *History of Great Britain*: '*Peace* was maintained by him as in the Time of *Augustus*; And Peace begot *Plenty*, and *Plenty* begot *Ease* and *Wantonness*.'[50] Coke, as we saw in the previous chapter, did not see 'plenty' as an enervating force in this manner, but agreed with Wilson that James's reign had increased national wealth. Rapin pointedly rejected both interpretations; rather than being morally defiled by James's policy, the people in his analysis consistently act as the voice of the constitution, emitting critical 'Murmurs' whenever the King's actions impinged upon popular rights.[51] Moreover, for Rapin, the peace that James brought had led not to commercial gain but rather to humiliation, as England became the subject of Europe-wide ridicule for its failure to defend itself in the face of affronts from the Spanish and Dutch.[52] While acknowledging that weakness was an ingrained feature of the King's character, Rapin maintained that it had been exacerbated by his wider political interests. The King's reluctance to defend Protestantism through a war with Spain stemmed both from his half-hearted adherence to the reformed religion and his desire to secure a marriage between his son and the Spanish Infanta and with it a massive dowry for the English crown.[53] Despite, therefore, the high-flown rhetoric with which he defended it, the origins of James's pacifism lay in 'Fear, Carelessness, [and an] excessive Love of Ease and Repose'.[54] Even when James did, finally, agree to enter into battle, the money he secured from Parliament was largely taken up with servicing his debts. Indeed, for the King, war, or the prospect of war, functioned simply as 'a good Pretence to get Money, which he wanted very much'.[55] Rapin's conclusion, therefore, was unequivocal; as a result of the various financial burdens placed on the populace and the lack of support for trade ''tis certain *England* never flourished less than in [James's] Reign'.[56]

Rapin's ideas concerning James and his immediate successors profoundly shaped his analysis of English history. Indeed, he generally presented the nation's monarchs either as proto-Stuarts who disregarded the people and followed their own desires – with disastrous political, military and economic consequences – or as more constitutional rulers who, like Alfred the Great and Edward III, aligned their own interests with those of the populace.[57] This approach permeates the whole of the *Histoire*, but can be seen particularly clearly in its discussions of the reigns of Elizabeth I and Henry VII. The Frenchman's commentary on these rulers is based on earlier accounts. However, it adapts the Stuart-friendly analyses of writers such as Camden and Bacon to produce a more Whiggish narrative that emphasises the importance of popular government and the virtues of liberty and low taxes.

3. Rapin's Elizabeth I

'Let a Man turn over the whole History of *England*', Rapin proclaims in relation to Elizabeth's government, 'and he will find no Reign wherein [...] the Kingdom was more flourishing.'[58] The Queen's key achievement was to have 'caused the *English* to enjoy a State of Felicity unknown to their Ancestors under the most part of the Kings her Predecessors'.[59] 'This', Rapin continued, 'is the *Touchstone* by which all those are to be tried whom God has set over Nations and Kingdoms.'[60] To support such a thesis and to situate Elizabeth's actions within a European context, Rapin utilised a number of other works of history, most notably George Buchanan's and James Melville's accounts of Scotland, Mézeray's *Histoire de France*, and Grotius's *Annales et Historiæ de rebus Belgicus*.[61] His discussion of domestic policy and the circumstances that had caused England to flourish, however, was entirely based on material taken from Camden. So, as Camden had done, Rapin presented Elizabeth as a defender of the merchant interest, and utilised material from the *Annales* concerning the Queen's moves to protect English trade with the Hans Towns,[62] her attempt to persuade the Danish king to reduce the customs imposed on English merchants,[63] and her commercially beneficial decision to allow Huguenot refugees to settle in England.[64] He also followed Camden in emphasising the importance of Elizabeth's frugality.[65] By keeping expenditure to a minimum and assiduously rooting out financial abuses such as monopolies, the Queen won the goodwill and trust of the nation.[66] As a consequence, when extraordinary occasions demanded it – such as the threat posed to European stability and English sovereignty by the Spanish – the people and Parliament were able and willing to provide her with extensive revenue. Both writers agreed, therefore, that Elizabeth's successful management of the nation's finances helped to produce contentment at home, and allowed England to achieve a series of military and diplomatic successes against its European rivals.

To adapt the *Annales*' account of Elizabeth's management for a Whig audience, however, Rapin employed two principal strategies. First, when information in Camden's work threatened to undermine Elizabeth's Whiggish credentials, Rapin simply ignored it. Thus, while Rapin had sharply criticised James's use of a trading monopoly with regard to the Spanish and Italian trades, he chose not to refer to Camden's account of Elizabeth's role in the establishment of the equally monopolistic companies of Turkey, Barbary and East India merchants.[67] Similarly, when Rapin came to discuss the successes of the Muscovy Company, he based his account entirely on Camden's work, but carefully edited out the Englishman's references to the exclusive privileges that the Company had been awarded. For Rapin, it would seem, monopolies were a characteristic of absolutist governments and, therefore, not a feature of the reign of a successful monarch such as Elizabeth. Second, Rapin developed an original account of Elizabeth's motivations. Camden's discussion, as we have seen, focused on Elizabeth's wisdom and skill, which she directed towards her 'cares': defending the Protestant Church, preserving her people's safety and winning 'Love amongst her Subjects, amongst her Enemies Fear, and Glory amongst all Men'.[68] Although he accepted that such 'cares' were significant, Rapin argued that they were themselves a product of the Queen's self-interest. The secret to understanding her reign lay in the precariousness of her position when she ascended the throne; she had France, Scotland, the Pope and all the Catholic powers for enemies, and could put little faith in the Irish or the greater part of her English subjects.[69] On occasion, particularly with regard to her treatment of Mary, Queen of Scots, Elizabeth's concern for her own safety had led her to act in a cruel and duplicitous manner. Moreover, throughout her reign she had prioritised self-preservation – the desire to keep her ever 'tottering' crown 'firm upon her Head'[70] – over 'Generosity', 'Justice' and 'Equity'.[71] With regard to domestic policy, however, Elizabeth's fragile power base had been central to her success. The Queen's weakness meant that she needed to secure the goodwill of her subjects, and to this end she was obliged to follow a populist programme of measures, of which low taxes and Protestantism formed a key part. As a result, her actions were entirely shaped and regulated by the will of the people, and the successes of her reign demonstrated both the value of restricting a monarch's powers and the wisdom of the populace's political judgement.

4. Rapin's Henry VII

Further adaptation was also required in relation to Henry VII. Rapin's account is based on material taken from two works: Rymer's *Foedera* and Bacon's *History of the Reign of King Henry VII*. The former provided Rapin with details concerning the various treaties that Henry negotiated with the monarchs of France, Brittany, Spain, Flanders and the Holy Roman Empire, many of which were translated and transcribed for inclusion in the *Histoire*.[72] Such extracts allowed Rapin to develop a much more detailed account of England's diplomatic relations with other powers than that contained in any previous general history, and to show the central role which commercial negotiations had played within international relations. However, this material was interpreted through the lens of one of Bacon's central arguments, namely that Henry's avarice had shaped all aspects of his relationships with foreign powers. Thus, before transcribing from Rymer the 1489 treaty between Henry and Anne of Brittany, Rapin noted that Henry's actions were determined by a desire to counter the French and 'to make Money of the Succours he sent the Dutchess, the Expences whereof he was willing to advance, in order to be re-paid with Usury'.[73] Similarly, the peace treaty negotiated with France in 1492 is interpreted as a straightforward product of Henry's desire to augment his income.[74] Underlying such analysis is the idea that for Henry, as for James I, war, or the threat of war, was simply a justification for levying taxes on England's ever-bellicose population. The profits from such impositions could then be siphoned into the royal coffers if conflict could be minimised or avoided altogether.

In advancing this argument, Rapin stays very close indeed to Bacon. For example, in his account of the war with France during 1491, Bacon noted that Henry sought to make profit from war in 'two ways': 'upon his subjects for the war, and upon his enemies for the peace'.[75] Rapin simply translated Bacon's statement and expanded it: 'In this [Henry] had a double View of *Profit*, upon his *Subjects* by means of a *Subsidy* for the War, and upon his *Enemies* for a *Peace*, which would secure him the Payment of what was due to him.'[76] Rapin was also dependent on Bacon when dealing with domestic affairs. Particular attention is paid in the *Histoire* to the way in which Henry raised money, and detailed accounts are provided of the various taxes, fines and benevolences he levied. Again, all of this material is derived directly from Bacon's *History*. Rapin paraphrases its account of the revival of 'benevolences' as a means of raising money,[77] repeats the lengthy account of the impositions and fines levied by Henry's notorious tax-collectors, Empson and Dudley,[78] and utilises a number of anecdotes from Bacon concerning Henry's punctiliousness with regard to financial affairs.[79] More generally, Rapin assumes, as Bacon had done, a direct causal relationship between monarchical financial policy and popular political action. For both writers, it was the high levels of taxation under Henry that had created 'murmurs' of discontent among the people, and, ultimately, fomented a series of angry, if unsuccessful, rebellions.

While Rapin's debt to Bacon was large, he was, as he had been with Camden, highly selective in his appropriations. Bacon, as noted in Chapter 1, tempered criticism of Henry's approach to monarchical revenue with accounts of, and praise for, his skills as a legislator and manager of the nation's commercial interests. Rapin, however, ignored such concessions, passing over the list of good statutes that punctuate Bacon's narrative and, in spite of his extensive borrowings from it, maintaining a generally critical view of Bacon's work. Inaccuracies in Bacon's account of a truce with France, for example, are attributed to the fact that Bacon was 'prepossessed no doubt in [the King's] Favour',[80] and later, when discussing Bacon's fall from power, Rapin accused him of making 'his Court to [James I], by setting up [Henry VII] as a Pattern of Wisdom and Virtue'.[81]

Perhaps even more significantly, Rapin, as he had done in relation to James, developed his own analysis of the nation's economic health. In Bacon's view, Henry's desire to heap up riches had itself helped to promote commerce; as 'a King that loved wealth and treasure he could not endure to have trade sick'.[82] For Rapin, however, violations of popular liberties of the sort carried out by Henry were inevitably damaging both to individual wealth and national commerce. As he observed, Henry had 'doubly ruined his Subjects; first by draining their Purses, and secondly by hindering the Coin, of which he had great Quantities in his Treasury, from circulating in Trade'.[83] Rapin's verdict on Henry was, ultimately, a damning one. It could not be denied that the King had 'great Abilities', perhaps most notably as an '*Oeconomist*'.[84] However, 'these Abilities had no Object but himself'.[85] Moreover, while Rapin insisted that it was not always conquerors who were the greatest kings, the peace that Henry eventually instigated proved to be more 'more fatal' to the people than war.[86] It was the 'insatiable Avarice of the King [that] hurried him continually to devise Means to accumulate Riches, the which must be done at [the People's] Expence'.[87] Such practices rendered Henry highly unpopular, and this, coupled with the King's doubts concerning the legitimacy of his claim to the throne, 'filled his Soul with Fears and Suspicions'.[88] Henry's reign, therefore, could not 'be said to be happy, either for himself or for *England*'.[89]

Conclusion

Rapin's approach in the *Histoire*, therefore, was to draw on economic discussions from earlier accounts, but to adapt this material in order to demonstrate that a moderate form of Whig constitutionalism had a greater capacity to promote wealth and happiness than any absolutist alternative. Underlying this analysis were a number of basic principles: that monopolistic trading companies are detrimental to commerce; that taxation is a zero-sum imposition in which the financial gains secured for the monarch exactly match the losses received by the people; and, more generally, that the character and conduct of a nation's monarch determine the level of prosperity enjoyed by its people. To an extent such ideas are in line with those of Camden and other writers of exemplary history. What distinguished Rapin's work from that of his predecessors, however, were both the Whiggish criteria he employed to measure monarchical achievement, and his comparative approach to historiography. As noted in the dedication to George I, which prefaces the *Histoire*, the task Rapin set himself was to 'instruct foreigners of the origin and progress of the English Monarchy'. Through doing so, he believed he had

> furnished [his] readers with an easy means of comparing the reign of your Majesty [George I] with the preceding reigns, and the opportunity to observe how attentive Your Majesty is to follow in the footsteps of the Kings of England, who were most distinguished by their virtues, and by their sincere love for their People, and with what care he

distances himself from the false paths, where some have unfortunately misled themselves.[90]

Rapin's account, therefore, employed a form of exemplary history, which encouraged its readers to think about the relationships between past and present monarchs. While he was aware that the institutional structure of the monarchy had changed over time, by proceeding in such a manner Rapin assumed that the essential 'true' and 'false' paths available to kings and queens remained a constant. As a result, for Rapin, as for Leclerc and Coke, there were fixed criteria available to historians through which they could judge and contrast the effectiveness of individual rulers.

Somewhat surprisingly, the first writer to question this comparative analysis was Rapin's English translator, Nicholas Tindal. Although Tindal accepted and endorsed much of the general historiographical framework of the *Histoire*, through the use of footnotes and marginal notes his translation modified Rapin's analysis in two ways. First, Tindal went back to Rapin's sources and provided a detailed series of elaborations and clarifications. As part of this process he rewrote the majority of the marginal notes through which Rapin had acknowledged his debts to other scholars, adding numerous 'new' attributions. For example, whereas the original French edition included thirteen references to Bacon in its account of Henry VII, the fourth edition of Tindal's translation had 182, as well as numerous footnotes that presented material from Bacon and other sources to correct 'mistakes' in Rapin's analysis.[91] At times, the employment of such information worked to undermine the Whiggish assumptions on which Rapin had based his account. To return to Henry VII, the English notes contain legal records and data from Bacon concerning the King's economic reforms, and Tindal comments at one point, with reference to Hall's *Chronicles*, that Henry 'lent merchants a great deal of money, without gain or profit, in order to encourage trade'.[92] Such ideas are in direct opposition to Rapin's primary economic argument and challenge his assumption that an avaricious and absolutist monarch such as Henry would necessarily be a poor manager of the economy. Similar issues are at play in relation to monopolies. Rapin, as noted above, had avoided any mention of Elizabeth's role in the establishment of monopolistic trading companies. Tindal, however, utilised material from Camden to provide full details of the part she played in setting up monopolies for the Turkey, Barbary and East India Companies, and emphasised that the Muscovy Company, whose interests the Queen vociferously defended, had an exclusive right to trade in Russia.[93]

Second, Tindal supplemented Rapin's coverage of economic matters with a range of antiquarian material.[94] From the second edition onwards, when dealing with post-Conquest monarchs, Tindal placed a footnote after the king or queen's 'character' containing illustrations of the coins used during his or her reign, and substantial information on the denominations employed and their design and metallic composition.[95] In the period from William Rufus to Edward II, these 'coin-notes', as Tindal referred to them, were expanded still further by detailed analyses of medieval systems of revenue and revenue collection. Tindal's primary source here is Thomas Madox's 1711 work, *The History and Antiquities of the Exchequer of the Kings of England.* He not only extensively paraphrases and quotes from Madox, but he also ensures that his work copies its organisation, and adheres to its principal thesis that the history of revenue can be divided into two distinct periods: the first – from William's accession to the Magna Carta – marking the Court of Exchequer's period of 'Ancient grandeur'; the second – from Magna Carta to Edward II's death – showing its gradual demise into a state of decline.[96] At one level, these additions can be seen as a product of a growing desire among commentators to provide arithmetical and numerical support for political forms of analysis.[97] More generally, the result of such appropriations is the inclusion alongside Rapin's work of a rather different mode of history. Rapin assumes that the monarch's 'character' is the principal determinant of taxation policy. Madox, in contrast, presents revenue gathering as a system which, while it is shaped by individual monarchs, maintains its own customs and practices across different reigns. As a result, it became possible to trace medium and long-term advancements within the management of revenue and commerce. Such ideas regarding long-term economic change, as we shall see in the following chapters, were to be developed substantially by later historians.

6

Tory history: Thomas Salmon's *Modern History*

The popularity of Rapin's *Histoire* ensured that it generated a large number of responses from other historians. Indeed, both Thomas Salmon's *Modern History* (1724–38), the subject of this chapter, and Thomas Carte's *General History* (1747–55), the subject of the next, provided direct attacks on Rapin's account. However, whereas Rapin had shown little interest in contemporary debates about public credit, Salmon's and Carte's analyses were structured around criticisms of the system of government borrowing developed under William III. In dealing with these issues, both writers drew on the economic statecraft tradition. Indeed, through some careful deployment of material, they were able to use the work of Bacon and Camden to provide commentaries on recent innovations in financial practice. At the same time, however, Salmon and Carte were concerned that modern governments had – with disastrous consequences for national welfare – lost control of England's economic institutions. Such claims led to the development of what might be labelled an anti-economic statecraft analysis; Salmon's and Carte's point was not so much that finance and commerce were being badly managed by monarchs, but that they were not being managed at all. Equally, however, the effect of such commentary was to vindicate established ideas; the modern era was conceived of as retrograde, and the monarchical administration of, and responsibility for, economic activity were presented as the desirable norm. My discussion in this chapter opens with an outline of the period's principal financial innovations, before looking at how 'Court Whig' and 'Patriot' writers dealt with these developments in their historical commentaries. I then proceed to explore the main elements of Salmon's narrative.

1. The financial revolution and historical debate

England underwent a financial revolution in the 1690s, as attempts by its Whig governments to raise money for the nation's war efforts led to a series of changes in the management of government revenue. The most important development was the establishment in 1694 of the Bank of England. Its loans allowed government borrowing to increase from around £1 million in 1688 to £16.7 million in 1697, and £54 million in 1720, and its collaboration with the Treasury ensured that interest rates declined from 14 per cent in the early 1690s to between 6 and 8 per cent in the late 1690s, and 3 per cent by the 1730s.[1] Such successes were a product of the state-backed guarantees that the bank provided, its pioneering use of paper money as a mechanism for releasing credit into the economy, and the diverse range of investment opportunities it provided.[2] Indeed, not only could individuals deposit money in the bank itself, but the tickets and tallies it issued became tradable commodities. This ensured that existing lenders could quickly cash in their loans, and there were ready opportunities for new investors. As a result, the Bank of England solved many of the government's financial problems through ensuring that, in the words of P. G. M. Dickson, 'debts that were permanent for the state [became] liquid for the individual; subject only to the risk of capital loss if market prices fell'.[3]

These changes in England's financial infrastructure had a number of political consequences. Partnered with improvements in the collection of tax revenue, the expansion of borrowing caused a substantial increase in annual government expenditure, which climbed from £1.8 million in 1688 to £6.2 million in 1695, and after 1710 remained consistently over £5 million.[4] Access to such financial resources played a vital part in securing British successes in the Wars of the Grand Alliance and Spanish Succession, and enabled the English and, later, British state to fund larger and more permanent bureaucracies and armies. This, in turn, helped to protect the state from threats both at home and abroad. At the same time, the transferability of government bonds, and the market this created, produced a shift in the relationship between the populace and the state. As Karl Wennerlind has argued, whereas the government's credit had previously been 'dictated by the interactions between the monarch and a small number of powerful financiers', it became increasingly reliant on the public's perception of the state's 'current capacity to service the interest payments and its imaginary ability to repay the debt in some distant, theoretical future'.[5] Public opinion, as a consequence, started to function as 'the arbiter of public credit', and polemicists responded with a series of attempts either to support or undermine confidence in the government's financial management.[6]

Such patterns of argument did much to shape political debate in the Walpolean era. For the Court Whigs, the key task was to demonstrate the ways in which, under their management, England's new financial infrastructure had contributed both to the political and economic strength of the nation.[7] With regard to the former issue, writers emphasised the support that the culture of borrowing had given to English liberties. As one writer noted, the '*national Debt* was contracted [...] for the Preservation of our most excellent *Constitution* from *Popery* and *Slavery*. This encouraged the best *Subjects* at the *Revolution* to venture their *Lives* and *Fortunes* in maintaining a long and expensive *War*.'[8] In relation to economic matters, Court propagandists maintained that it was financial reforms that had helped to transform England into a wealthy nation. Thus the *London Journal* argued that bank notes and South Sea bonds had served usefully as money, that getting into debt had become a 'business itself', and that banks supported the circulation of wealth by 'enabling dead money to be gathered into stocks'.[9] These arguments were given further strength by another strand of Court Whig discourse which emphasised that England's much-celebrated liberties were a relatively modern innovation. Lord Hervey, for example, writing in his *Ancient and Modern Liberty Stated and Compared* (1734), argued that

> 'Till the *Restoration* there was no such thing as Liberty; *That* after the *Restoration* was nothing compared to the Strength it gain'd at the *Revolution*; and the Strength it then acquired, is so far, in my Opinion of Things, from being now impair'd, that it never flourish'd in such full Vigor as in the happy and prosperous *Reign* of his *present Majesty*.[10]

In making such claims, writers drew on the ideas of Spelman and Brady, as well as James Harrington's Baconian account in *Oceana* (1656) of the changes instigated by Henry VII in patterns of property ownership.[11] Thus the *London Journal* rejected Whiggish glorifications of Old England, maintaining instead that the 'Ancient Constitution' was the product of an '*Over-balance of Lands,* vested in the *King*, the

Nobility and the *Church*'. This ensured that the commons lived the lives of '*Beggars and Slaves*'.[12] Such a state of affairs had only been ameliorated through the actions of Henry VII who, by allowing the lords to alienate their land, had started the process whereby the balance of property shifted to the people. In the present, the author estimated, this latter group held above 17 parts in 20 of the land 'besides their vast Wealth in Money, Stock &c.' and, as a result, 'by the *Modern Constitution the People* are strong' and England was a nation of '*Rich Men* and *Freemen*'.[13] Hervey, meanwhile, offered a similar view of the modern era: '[England's] Possessions abroad are unattack'd, and her Commerce so unrival'd, so unobstructed, and so flourishing, that the Imports and Exports were never higher, nor our Credit in greater Prosperity.'[14] The age of public debt for such writers, therefore, was also the age of liberty and wealth.

The most prominent critique of this sort of analysis was that developed by Lord Bolingbroke. From the mid-1720s onwards, Bolingbroke was engaged in a campaign to unite dissident Whigs and Tories into an anti-Walpolean Patriot party.[15] This was no easy task. The sympathy shown by many opposition Whigs for Dissent, coupled with the anti-clericalism and Erastian tendencies of some Whig propagandists, was anathema for staunchly Church of England Tories and made combined action on religious issues impractical.[16] Cooperation was possible, however, in relation to Court financial practices, and Bolingbroke developed a series of stinging attacks on the national debt, stockjobbing and the nation's trading companies, arguing that these institutions were undermining both the constitution and England's commercial interests. Historical analysis played a key part in this commentary, most notably through Bolingbroke's *Remarks on the History of England* (1743), a work assembled from a series of essays first published in the opposition journal the *Craftsman* between September 1730 and May 1731.[17] For Bolingbroke, England's history was structured around an ongoing conflict between the '*Spirit of Liberty*', which sought to advance the nation's interests, and a '*Spirit of Faction*', that expressed only '*personal* and *private Interests*'.[18] To develop this theme, he drew both on Rapin's analysis of the 'ancient constitution' and Harrington's discussion of the balance of property. His debt to Harrington is most apparent in his account of Henry VII. Here, despite emphasising that the Tudor king's actions were shaped by the '*Spirit of Faction*', he endorsed the Harringtonian claim that Henry's reforms had caused the balance of property to pass from the nobility to the commons. To an extent, such a position distanced Bolingbroke from Rapin. Indeed, whereas the Frenchman viewed Henry's influence as entirely pernicious, Bolingbroke not only emphasised the long-term benefits of his actions, but repeated Bacon's Tacitean assertion that Henry's avarice made him a highly successful promoter of 'Husbandry, Manufactures [and] general Commerce'.[19] Bolingbroke's key point, however, was that reforms enacted by Henry served to re-establish the basic '*Principles of Government*, which had prevail'd amongst our *Saxon* Ancestors' and which had been at the heart of Rapin's analysis.[20]

Once this argument was formulated, the reigns of Elizabeth and James could be dealt with in a relatively straightforward manner. Thus, as Harrington had done, Bolingbroke maintained that Elizabeth's awareness of the people's newfound power led her to court their affections, and he went on to demonstrate this through an analysis that owed much to Rapin. Ideas of economic statecraft were key to his argument, and he emphasised that the Queen's popularity was, in part, a product of her success in promoting commerce, and, through eliminating the debts amassed by her predecessors, '*restoring the* Credit *of the* Crown'.[21] However, while Elizabeth's sensitivity to the balance of property led to a victory for the '*Spirit of Liberty*' and national affluence, James failed to follow her example. This explained a number of Stuart England's key features, also discussed by Rapin: the rise of government debts; the decline of commerce; the return of the '*Spirit of Faction*'; and, as a result, the emergence of the political crisis that eventually led to the collapse of the monarchy in the 1640s.

For Bolingbroke, both Elizabeth's successes and James's failures had important consequences for modern politics. English history, he argued, produced numerous examples of '*Causes* of the same Kind laid again, and producing *Effects* of the same Nature'.[22] Walpole's regime, like James's, he maintained, was driven by the 'spirit of faction'. Indeed, the *Remarks* explicitly presented the 'Spirit of Stockjobbing' that had come to characterise the modern age as a form of faction, noting that both worked 'to advance the Interest of a few worthless Individuals, at the Expence of the whole Community', and that both threatened trade and liberty.[23] Britain, therefore, was not experiencing new forms of wealth and freedom as the Court Whigs maintained, but rather old varieties of poverty and corruption. Moreover, Jacobean history provided a good guide as to what was likely to happen when a self-interested and factious government ruled over a nation where the balance of property lay with the people: '*Jealousy, Discontent, Tumult*' and, potentially, '*open Resistance,* and [the] *Deposition of the Prince*'.[24]

2. A Tory history

Thomas Salmon's *Modern History* drew on and, in part, synthesised elements from the Court Whig and Patriot analyses of England's recent past. Born in 1679 in Meppershall, Bedfordshire, Salmon spent the first part of his career as a soldier, serving in both India and, during the War of the Spanish Succession, Flanders.[25] On his return to England he briefly ran a Cambridge coffeehouse, before moving to London and gaining employment with the printer John Darby as the editor of the volumes eventually published in 1719 as *A Compleat Collection of State-Tryals*.[26] A series of historical works with a marked Tory bias followed. These included a laudatory history of Queen Anne (1721),[27] an abridgement and angry critique of the work of the Whig historian Bishop Burnet (1724)[28] and *The History of Great Britain and Ireland* (1725), a collection of historical excerpts concerning pre-Norman history.[29] The most controversial of Salmon's publications, however, was *A Review of the History of England* (vol. 1, 1722; vol. 2, 1724), his account of the titles to the throne claimed by England's various post-Norman monarchs. In January 1724, just in advance of the planned publication of the second volume, the dissenting orator John Henley wrote to Lord Carteret, the Minister for the Southern Department, warning him that Salmon's work contained an attack on 'ye Ministry and ye Succession'.[30] Carteret took these claims seriously, and on 1 February copies of the *Review* were seized by the King's messengers and the printer and bookseller taken into custody.[31] In the following weeks, seemingly with Carteret's support, Henley went on to produce lists of what he considered the *Review*'s most 'offensive' passages. These collections of quotations drew attention to its attacks on Whiggish causes – Dissenters, the Dutch and the government's management of the Treaty of Ryswick – and its use of a series of inflammatory parallels. Thus Henley transcribed Salmon's comments that King Stephen 'was not so harden'd in Wickedness as some of his Successors, he cd not under a mock shew of justice, put men to death in cold blood, only for doing their duty to their lawfull sovereign'.[32] To this he added in brackets: 'This points very plainly at ye late [Jacobite] Rebellion.'[33] Ultimately, it appears, some sort of deal was done; the printer and publisher of the *Review* appeared in recognisances in May 1724, and the volume itself was published shortly afterwards.[34]

His run-in with the government did nothing to dampen Salmon's historical enthusiasm and later in 1724 he embarked upon *Modern History*, a monthly publication which ran from 1724 to 1738 and, when completed, filled thirty-one octavo volumes.[35] Its remit was an ambitious one. Beginning with the 'Kingdoms in the East' and travelling 'Westward with the Sun', Salmon provided an account of all the kingdoms of the known world.[36] As the preface explained, for each territory referred to he sought to include discussion of a wide range of issues: 'Situations, Persons, Habits, Buildings, Manners, Laws and Customs, Religion, Policy, Arts and Sciences, Trades, Manufactures and Husbandry, Plants, Animals and Minerals'.[37] While such an approach gave Salmon's work a wide geographical scope, he did not ignore domestic issues. Thirteen of his volumes were concerned with England, and eleven of these were used to provide a detailed, politically oriented history of the country from the invasion of the Romans to the death of Queen Anne.

Salmon conceived of these English sections of his account as a Tory history of England, and, as such, an explicit attack on the ruling Court Whig government. The uncompromising nature of his Toryism, however, also served to distance him from much other opposition writing of the period. Indeed, whereas Bolingbroke maintained that since the Revolution of 1688 there had been no real difference in opinion between honest Whigs and honest Tories, Salmon launched an aggressive attack on all types of Whiggism, drawing particular attention to the dangers it posed to the Church of England. He also entirely rejected Rapin's analysis, and used a series of newspaper advertisements to market the English volumes of *Modern History* as being 'intended chiefly to set such Transactions in a true Light as are misrepresented by Rapin, and to point out the Fanatical and Republican Notions advanced in [his] Work'.[38] Five of the Frenchman's mistakes were highlighted:

1. That the Kings of England do not derive their Authority from the People, as Rapin pretends they do.

> 2. That their Subjects have no Right to call them to an Account, or to dethrone them, on pretence of Male-Administration, as is suggested in Rapin's History.
> 3. That several of our Kings have carried the Prerogative higher than either King James I or King Charles I.
> 4. That neither of those Kings were the Authors of the Troubles that happen'd in theirs or the succeeding Reigns, but the Fanaticks and Republicans.
> 5. That Queen Anne was a glorious Princess, and ever studied and contributed to the Happiness of her People, notwithstanding Rapin hath taken the Liberty to Libel her Administration.[39]

Underlying such comments was a broader critique of Rapin's approach to historiography, the outlines of which Salmon had first formulated in his introduction to the *History of Great Britain*. For Salmon, Rapin's principal crime was to use 'ancient history', particularly Saxon history, as an artifice to vindicate modern ideas about republican government and Presbyterianism.[40] Such an approach was fundamentally flawed; given that the Saxons were the '*most stupid Generation that ever this Island knew*', there was no reason to suppose that they would happen upon '*so beautiful a Form of Government, as that we enjoy at this Day*'.[41] At the same time, Salmon accepted the Court Whig claim that there was no essential continuity between the political institutions of the past and those of the present. English government, Salmon argued, had never continued '*thro' any one Century the same; sometimes the Regal Power has approach'd to Absolute, sometimes the Barons, and at other times the Commons, have depress'd, and even depos'd their Princes*'.[42] The '*Liberties and Properties*' of the present, therefore, were not the product of ancient precedent, but the ratifications provided by a '*Thousand Acts and Concessions of our Princes*'.[43] Such ideas directly informed *Modern History*, and helped to ensure that Salmon's approach to prerogative was fundamentally at odds with Rapin's and Bolingbroke's. For Rapin, while its legitimate limits were set by the Saxon constitution, monarchical prerogative, in *de facto* terms, constituted an unstable element, which periodically threatened to undermine the constitutional order. Salmon, in contrast, argued that the constitutional order had been created and maintained by royal prerogative. England's history, therefore, was the story both of the creation of that order and of the series of highly pernicious attempts by 'republican' elements to undermine it.

Running alongside such arguments in *Modern History*, and frequently in tension with them, was a Patriot-style attack – albeit one with a marked Tory bias – on the financial institutions that had emerged in the wake of the Revolution of 1688. Thus, for Salmon, the national debt had its origins in the approach to finance developed by the Whigs in the 1690s. Working on the assumptions that '*The more you borrow, the more Friends you make*' and '*Interest is a stronger Tie than Principle*', ministers had borrowed at very high interest rates – 'thirty, forty, and sometimes fifty *per Cent*' – to ensure that moneyed men 'became [...] Friends to the Government'.[44] In doing so, the Whigs had sacrificed the financial security of the nation in order to enrich their friends and selfishly maintain their own position in power. The debt was expanded still further as a result of the pernicious influence of the Dutch. Whig governments of the 1690s and 1700s, he argued, drawing on a standard theme in Tory polemics, had been entirely governed by the Dutch to the point where, during the reign of Anne, they had sought to 'interpose and assume an Authority to direct the Queen in the Distribution of her Favours'.[45] Moreover, as a result of the Dutch influence:

> We were obliged to take the Burthen of the *Low Country* War upon us, and throw away our People against stone Walls at a vast Expense, chiefly to enlarge the Territories of our Allies, and gratify the Ambition and Avarice of some of their Friends, without stipulating for a single Town we should conquer, or to receive any Benefit from the Revenues of the conquer'd Countries; while we engaged much beyond our annual Revenues, and contracted more Debts in the Quarrel, than all our Allies put together.[46]

Rather than functioning as a true sovereign state, therefore, England had become a cipher for Dutch territorial and commercial ambitions. This situation was only rectified when the Tories entered into government in 1710. During their four years in office they had defended Britain's trading interests, extricated the nation from the war with France and begun the process of paying off the national debt. As a result, and despite dire Whig warnings regarding the effect of a change in government on the nation's financial security, 'the Publick Credit was never higher than when the Alteration of the Ministry was made'.[47]

3. Salmon, Elizabeth I and Henry VII

Salmon's attacks on both Rapin and the Court Whigs did much to shape his analysis of Queen Elizabeth. In relation to the former, Salmon drew attention to the unreliable and partisan nature of the Frenchman's account. Rapin, Salmon noted, had drawn extensively on Camden's *Annales* when discussing Elizabeth. However, in doing so, he had deliberately ignored Camden's detailed accounts of the plots of the Presbyterians – referred to by Salmon as Rapin's 'Brethren of the *Geneva* Stamp' – to reduce 'the whole Kingdom under their Tyranny'.[48] *Modern History* responded by putting these plots centre stage and, through a series of borrowings from Camden and the Church historian John Strype, provided full details of the Puritans' pernicious activities and Elizabeth's courageous and successful attacks upon them.[49] Such a move then enabled Salmon to emphasise the political distance between Rapin and the Queen. Indeed, as Salmon presents matters, Elizabeth was the key Tory bulwark against the selfish Whiggish sect whose interests Rapin sought to advance.[50] Underpinning this analysis was a rejection of the *Histoire*'s analysis of Elizabeth's motivations. Rapin, as we have seen, sought to show that Elizabeth's achievements in domestic policy were a product of her weak position; it was her need for popular support to maintain her 'tottering' crown that led her to follow a frugal, low-tax approach.[51] Salmon, while acknowledging the Queen's popularity, rejected these claims entirely. The Queen was not led by the people, but rather ruled over them. Indeed, the successes she enjoyed were a product of the care she took to keep 'a due Distance between the Subject and the Soveraign' and the fact she 'never suffer'd her People, either without Doors or within, to grow upon the Prerogative'.[52] Her actions, meanwhile, were in no sense the products of self-interest, but emerged, as Camden had argued, from a genuinely virtuous desire to protect Protestant and English interests.

Ideas about self-interest, of the sort that characterised much exemplary history, also directly influenced Salmon's approach to economic affairs. Connecting together the various strands of *Modern History* was an account of the rise and subsequent decline of English national greatness. In the preface to the first volume, Salmon, in a manner which mirrors Bolingbroke's analysis, noted that the 'Genius of the People [...] for maritime Affairs, new Discoveries, and a Zeal to

Extend their Commerce through every part of the habitable World' had ensured that England reached the zenith of its success in the reign of 'the glorious Queen ELIZABETH'.[53] Nevertheless, in subsequent years, as a result of the pernicious influence exerted by the interconnected activities of Republicans, Presbyterians and the Dutch, the 'publick Spirit', which had upheld England's imperial and commercial greatness, had vanished.[54] As a result,

> Private Interest, inglorious Sloth and Ease, and a fond Care of our worthless selves are now deem'd Marks of the most consummate Wisdom; and the Man would be accounted frantick who should hazard his Person or his Fortune abroad in the Advancement of Trade, or gaining new Acquisitions to the *British* Empire.[55]

Salmon's treatment of Elizabethan trade and finance was shaped by this narrative. In relation to the former, he sought to present Elizabeth's reign as a period of nationally beneficial commercial endeavour. This was partly a product of the Queen's own measures which, Salmon argued, drawing heavily on Camden, included the running of the Muscovy Company, the commercially beneficial decision to allow Huguenot refugees to settle in England, and the successful establishment of sumptuary laws.[56] Equally significantly, however, she had been supported by the selfless actions of her people. Thus attention was drawn to England's Elizabethan adventurers, among them Captain James Lancaster and Sir Thomas Randolph. The former navigated the Cape of Good Hope and, despite finding his ship 'miserably shatter'd in a Tempest of Thunder and Lightning', proceeded on to Sumatra, 'from whence the Ship return'd very richly laden to *England*, but with only seven Hands on Board'.[57] The latter, as is noted in an account drawn from Camden, journeyed from Archangel to the Caspian Sea, 'traded with the *Persians* and *Indians*', and 'propos'd to have open'd a Trade with *China* that way'.[58] Ultimately, Randolph's plans came to nothing, but they demonstrated, Salmon argued, this time moving beyond the arguments made in the *Annales*, 'the Genius of our Ancestors in that Age for making new Discoveries, and extending their Commerce'.[59]

Selfless action was also key to Salmon's analysis of Elizabethan finance. Following Camden closely, he argued that the root of Elizabeth's success lay in her frugality, which had ensured that the money 'other Princes lavish'd away upon Favourites and greedy

Courtiers, and in Shews and Festivals, [Elizabeth] apply'd to the Support of the Government'.[60] Such practices enabled the Queen to repay the debts acquired by her ancestors, which Salmon estimated were worth four million pounds, and to rearm the nation. Moreover:

> Though she had, great part of her Reign, all the Powers of *Europe* to contend with, and a Party of Catholics and Puritans ever preaching up Sedition and Rebellion at home, it does not appear that her Majesty ever contracted a Debt that was not paid off in a Year or two, or left the Nation burthen'd with one extraordinary Tax; for which, Posterity must ever celebrate her Memory.[61]

The Queen's achievement, therefore, was to have protected the nation's domestic and financial interests without imposing any financial burdens on its people.

This image of Elizabeth had a good deal of polemical value. On occasion, Salmon explicitly used Elizabethan achievements to highlight the magnitude of Whig failures. In his discussion of the events of 1702, for example, he argued that the Whigs had massively increased the levels of debt in order to fund wars that wasted English lives and did nothing to advance English interests. This conduct, his commentary concluded scathingly, was 'very different from that observ'd in the Reign of Queen *Elizabeth*'.[62] Elsewhere, Salmon used 'positive' assessments of Elizabeth to develop a series of polemically useful contrasts between the Queen's reign and those of her various predecessors and successors. With regard to Henry VII, this was a relatively straightforward task. Henry, for Salmon, simply provided further evidence of the 'long observ'd' political dictum 'that nothing can be more destructive to *England* than for the King and his Ministers to entertain private selfish Views, opposite to the true Interest of the Nation'.[63] In expanding on this theme, Salmon sought to show how the avarice that shaped the first Tudor king's reign, and the equally self-interested profligacy that characterised that of his son, both contrasted with the selfless actions of Elizabeth and had caused the financial problems from which she had rescued the nation.

Such an analysis had a good deal in common with that of Rapin and, as the Frenchman had done, Salmon constructed his account by paraphrasing those sections of Bacon's *History* that were most critical of Henry. In doing so, however, Salmon developed not just a general critique of pernicious forms of statesmanship, but also a specific commentary on contemporary political events. This can be seen particularly clearly in *Modern History*'s account of Henry's use of taxation. At the time Salmon published his account – February 1733 – the standard theme of opposition writers was the corruption of the ministry. Specifically, polemicists sought to demonstrate that Walpole was using places and pensions to bribe Members of Parliament, in a move that threatened the constitution and the liberties it upheld. The key issue of the day, meanwhile, was the Excise Bill announced by Walpole at the very end of 1732.[64] Under the terms of the proposed reform, duties on wine and tobacco would be switched from customs duties, which were paid at import, to excise duties which were paid when goods were released from a warehouse on to the domestic market.[65] These measures were vigorously and, ultimately, successfully resisted by the opposition, in part through a series of attempts to demonise excise officers.[66] Such individuals, it was argued, were pernicious hirelings whose powers to act as 'Prosecutors, Evidence and Judges in their own Cause' undermined the right to trial by jury and made it possible for 'unjust Sentences' to be given against 'particular Men, in Order to gratify the Malice, or Avarice, of a *corrupt Minister*'.[67] The power officers had 'of *entering* into a Person's House [...] as often as they please' and whenever they please, meanwhile, constituted a threat to the liberty and property of merchants, especially as officers stood to benefit in financial terms from any seizures they made.[68] Even more worryingly, the influence that the Crown would gain from an increase in its income and a rise in the number of officers it had at its disposal would shift the balance of power away from the people, and undermine their liberties.

Salmon clearly had such issues on his mind when composing his account of the events of 1504. The first part of his discussion stayed close to his source material. He began by paraphrasing Bacon's list of the various extortions through which the King had enriched himself that year, before noting that Henry's successes meant that, as 'says the Lord *Bacon*', 'Golden Showers [...] pour'd down upon the King's Treasury all at once'.[69] From here, however, Salmon proceeded to conjure up a series of images that owed more to contemporary accounts of excise officers than to any work of Tudor history. Thus the people's misery was a consequence of their being 'perpetually pilfer'd and prosecuted by an Army of Tax-gatherers and Informers'.[70] As a result, 'no Man enjoy'd his Fortune in quiet, it was well if he could redeem his Person from Prison, by sacrificing his Estate'.[71] Henry's relationship with Parliament was also described in distinctly 'modern' terms. Any hope of relief for the people from the King's exactions was eliminated, 'as the Parliament were either aw'd or brib'd into a Compliance with the Court'.[72] The phrasing here is key. The idea that Parliament were 'aw'd' to support the King is broadly in line with Bacon's claim that, by this point in his reign, the King enjoyed 'absolute' power over his Parliament. However, the suggestion that Henry might bribe individuals at Westminster makes no sense at all in relation to Bacon's analysis; why would a king as powerful and avaricious as Henry seek to pay money to his own Parliament? Hinting at such practices, however, enabled Salmon to conflate Henry's actions with Walpole's and, by doing so, to use Bacon's critique of Henry's selfishness and avarice to attack Walpolean corruption.

4. Salmon and James I

Salmon's account of James I is a good deal more complex. On the one hand, as was conventional in Tory writing of the period, he sought to defend James from the various accusations that had been levelled at him by Whiggish commentators. Thus he denied suggestions that James had attempted to subvert the political and religious status quo,[73] emphasised the continuities between Elizabeth's reign and her successor's, and argued that James's financial problems were a product of debts acquired by Elizabeth rather than personal extravagance. The economic achievements of the period, meanwhile, as they had been in earlier pro-Stuart accounts, were seen as evidence of James's success as a monarch. Brief descriptions, derived from Howes's account, were provided of a number of economic innovations, including the commencement of alum manufacture, improvements in shipping and the establishment of the plantations in America. These developments, particularly the latter, ensured that 'our foreign Trade [...] was vastly extended and enlarged in most Parts of the World, especially in *America*'.[74] As a consequence, and contrary to Rapin's suggestions, it was not James's failures that were responsible for the unrest of the period. Indeed the King was only blameworthy in the sense that, having 'slacken'd the Reigns of Government on his Accession', he 'suffer'd the People to dispute against the Constitution in Church and State (which Queen

Elizabeth would never bear) and thereby encourag'd the Puritans and Republicans to encroach upon him'.[75]

Running alongside and, on occasion, working in direct tension with these arguments was an attempt to develop a series of parallels between James's reign and modern Britain. Two issues were of particular significance here. First, Salmon sought to emphasise the similarities between the situation that James found himself in, as a Scot ruling over an English kingdom, and the position of the Hanoverian monarchs. James might, Salmon noted, 'have enjoy'd a perpetual Calm during his Reign' had his 'Favours' not 'been so unbounded towards his Countrymen, the *Scots*'.[76] Through 'squandering away his Money upon that People, [he] also brought his Treasury low' and this 'with the Perverseness of the Puritans, were the Sources of most of the Misfortunes that happen'd afterwards'.[77] The King's actions were a product, Salmon emphasised, of the differences between the relative prosperity of the two kingdoms. James came

> from a poor barren Country, to a Kingdom where Wealth abounded more at that time than in any Nation in *Europe* perhaps, and he met with a People whose Professions of Loyalty and Submission, accompanied with Offers of their Lives and Fortunes, were as unlimited as his Expences and Gratuities to his Countrymen are said to have been.[78]

In case any of his readers had missed the association that he was seeking to develop, Salmon concluded with some general comments on non-native monarchs. 'Allowances', he argued, 'are to be made for his [James] being a Foreigner and a Stranger to the Constitution; such Princes always lie under great Disadvantages.'[79] 'Nor', Salmon continued, 'wou'd I pass over his too great Indulgence to his Favourites and Prime Ministers, which was certainly very prejudicial to the Kingdom and himself.'[80] Ultimately, however, such practices demonstrated not so much the failings of James/George, but the hypocrisy of the Whigs. As Salmon noted: 'I can't help observing, that Princes who have been guilty of the same Failing, have met with much better Quarter from the Party who charge King *James* with this Weakness.'[81]

Second, Salmon sought to emphasise that James's reign had seen the emergence of the sinister Dutch conspiracy which currently threatened English interests. The aims of the Hollanders, he argued, were twofold: 'the Encouragement of their Sect, and the ingrossing the Trade of the World'.[82] This led them to embark on a series of attempts to 'ruin the Trade of their Benefactors [the English] in all Parts of the World; drive them from their Settlements; murder their Merchants and Factors, and deprive them of their Fisheries'.[83] In the international sections of Salmon's analysis, these ideas were used to develop a comparison between English and Dutch approaches to trade and empire. The Dutch's insatiable desire for power had led them to acquire an empire through force. English settlements, in contrast, were 'fairly purchased, or voluntarily transferred to them'.[84] Indeed, the English had never 'attempted to encroach on the natives, or enlarge their territories by force in any one instance; and those who live under their governments, enjoy greater privileges than they did under their former princes'.[85] There was, however, one area where the Dutch were superior to the English: the state management of commerce. Thus, whereas the Dutch had made their East Indian and African trades 'a national concern' and had 'supported them by the power of the states', 'ours is under the care of a few merchants, who have seldom any views beyond their present gain, and scarce ever consider the general interest of their country'.[86] That the Dutch had been allowed to develop connections in these areas, however, was presented as a result of James's inadequacies as a monarch. Indeed, describing the expansion of Portuguese and Dutch influence in India the 1610s, Salmon observed:

> Thus were the subjects of *Britain*, the greatest maritime power then in being, insulted and interrupted in the most valuable part of their commerce, by two [*sic*] the most despicable nations in *Europe*. Heavens! what a soul must that Prince be endued with who then sat upon the *British* throne: or how exceeding mercenary must his ministers be? those who pretend to account for this stupid conduct say, that the *Dutch* actually purchas'd our leading men, who sold the nation, and voluntarily suffer'd the *Dutch* to run away with all the valuable branches of our trade. When they could not effect their ends this way, their good friends, the presbyterians, were incited to create a civil war amongst us, and take off our attention to trade by our pretences of further reformation.[87]

These ideas were repeated and developed in Salmon's account of English history. During James's reign, it was argued, 'the *Dutch* were endeavouring to beat us out of the Trade of the fine Spices; which they accomplished [...], our Merchants not being protected by the Government as they ought to have been'.[88] In making such claims,

Salmon sought both to emphasise the parallels between James's reign and contemporary practices – when once again a failure to stand up to the Dutch had proved catastrophic – and to develop a causal connection between past and present. From Jacobean times onwards, it was argued, the Dutch had supported a 'Faction in our Bowels' that 'bids Defiance to our Constitution'.[89] This group, as Salmon presented matters, was responsible for many of England's problems; indeed, the failings of English commerce, the national debt and the Civil War were all products of a malign Dutch interference. As a consequence, the pro-Dutch Whiggish faction had a substantial history of its own, and had already done much to undermine monarchical power and cripple England's financial and commercial interests.

Taken in sum, such comments ensured that a fundamental tension ran through *Modern History*'s discussion of James. On the one hand, as part of his attack on Rapin, Salmon provided a conventional Tory account, which celebrated James's achievements as a manager of the nation's economic interests and praised him for continuing the work of Elizabeth. On the other hand, however, Salmon's desire to develop a critique of Walpole's ministry made it strategic for him, on occasion, to present James as a bad foreigner whose actions, or rather inaction, paralleled that of George II and helped to bring about the culture of borrowing on which the Whig regime relied. Indeed, James's failures are seen as a symptom and a cause of a wider process of long-term decline in which debt, foreign influences and increasingly self-interested forms of behaviour had undermined England's commercial and financial fortunes. Ironically, both the celebratory and critical elements of Salmon's account of James were the product of a consistent adherence to the Tory cause. Salmon, an opponent of all forms of Whiggism, was attempting a narrative critique of Court *and* Patriot forms of Whig history. As the ambivalences that characterise *Modern History* testify, this was no easy task.

7

Jacobite history: Thomas Carte's *General History*

A more far-reaching critique both of Rapin's *History* and Whiggish ideas of credit was developed by the Oxford historian Thomas Carte in the 1740s and 1750s.[1] Carte was a diligent and able scholar, and the author of a series of well-documented historical works including a three-volume *History and Life of James Duke of Ormonde* (1735–36) and the four-volume *General History of England* (1747–55).[2] He was also a Non-Juror and an active Jacobite conspirator. In the 1720s he worked as an agent for the Court of the Pretender and was secretary to Francis Atterbury at the time of his unsuccessful 1722 'plot'.[3] Following this, a warrant was issued for Carte's arrest and he fled to France, only returning after a pardon from Queen Caroline in 1728. Once back in England, Carte continued to act as a go-between for various Jacobite groups, wrote a series of polemical pamphlets and authored a scheme to coordinate Tory party action in elections. In 1739 he personally passed a letter from the Pretender to Walpole, after being persuaded that the latter might be sympathetic to the former's restoration.[4] The scheme was not a success. Walpole showed no interest in the letter, threatened Carte with arrest, and proceeded to interrogate him on his knowledge of Jacobite plans. Although Carte avoided prosecution, he remained an object of interest to the authorities, and was briefly incarcerated in 1744 on suspicion of concealing arms.

Carte's Jacobitism also contributed to the commercial failure of the *General History*. The project had begun promisingly. In 1737 Carte published a proposal calling for a new history of England and emphasising the inadequacies of Rapin's account; the Frenchman, Carte claimed, had simply not had the knowledge of the constitution or the relevant primary material to produce a competent work. To ensure the success of his own attempt, Carte advocated the establishment of a society '*to encourage the writing of an History of England*' which through subscriptions would be able to fund the procurement of the requisite archival material.[5] This suggestion was greeted with enthusiasm, and by the end of the year Carte had achieved pledges for £600 per annum.[6] Subscribers were to include Oxford colleges, the Church, City Companies and the Corporation of London, as well as both Jacobite grandees and senior Whigs.[7] On its publication in 1747, however, Carte's history gained immediate notoriety as a result of a footnote in its first volume, which repeated the story of Christopher Lovell, a Bristol labourer who, in 1716, had supposedly been cured of scrofula by the touch of the Pretender. Such claims were widely derided and Carte was attacked by a distinguished cast of critics including Josiah Tucker, Edward Gibbon, Horace Walpole and Henry Fielding. Indeed, Fielding, writing in the *Jacobite's Journal*, conducted a mock 'trial' of Carte's work, ultimately convicting its author of 'a very high Offence; no less than that of perverting the Intent of History, and applying it to the sordid and paltry Use of a Party'.[8] Although Carte continued to work on the history until his death in 1754, he never recovered either his public credibility or the interest of the reading public.

Modern historians of historiography have been rather more generous. Laird Okie praised the *General History* for its use of archival sources and observed that, at its publication, Carte's work constituted the 'most ambitious attempt to date to produce a definitive history of England'.[9] More recently, Paul Kléber Monod has labelled it one of the 'great neglected texts of the eighteenth century', and argued that its account of the druids of ancient Britain provided a significant example of a Jacobite vision of British nationalism.[10] Of equal importance to Carte's notion of Britishness, however, was his understanding of European feudalism. Indeed, through an analysis of Europe's shared feudal origins Carte developed an account that both rejected the analyses of finance and commerce that underpinned the works of Rapin and provided a distinctive critique of modern ideas of credit.

1. A Jacobite polemic: Carte's critique of Corbyn Morris

The origins of Carte's analysis of economic affairs are to be found in his work as a Tory/Jacobite pamphleteer in the early 1740s. A key task for government polemicists was to show that the system of public credit and the military and political innovations of the period worked in partnership to secure liberty and prosperity. The version of this argument which attracted Carte's ire was that developed by the Court Whig propagandist Corbyn Morris in *A Letter from a Bystander to a Member of Parliament* (1742).[11] Morris's pamphlet sought to defend Walpole's use of a standing army by emphasising its importance not just to England's military, but also to its financial security. Underlying this latter claim was a conception of public credit as 'the Pulse of the Nation': a force that was difficult to restore to health when upset and uniquely sensitive to rumours of foreign invasion.[12] The fickle qualities of credit could, however, be offset by the army which, through allaying fears regarding the security of the Hanoverian regime, served 'to keep our Properties from continually fluctuating, to preserve our Trade, and to give Strength and Stability to the Government'.[13] Given, therefore, that England was a nation awash with 'Riches and Plenty', and that the terror and confusion caused by a run on the Bank of England had the capacity to lose 'forty or fifty Millions of [pounds of] Property' from government securities, it made sense to maintain the existing force.[14] Morris was also careful to emphasise that the modern military did not pose a direct threat to liberty. While a standing army undoubtedly augmented the power of the Crown, the constitutional innovations secured by the Revolution of 1688 meant that the balance of power lay with the people. Prior to William III's accession monarchs had possessed 'an absolute *uncontrollable Power*' over the standing revenue, a state of affairs that had been particularly abused by the Stuart kings.[15] Now, however, the King's private revenue had been restricted to the Civil List and the public revenues were 'entirely under the Command of the Parliament'.[16] Such control, coupled with the increase in trade that had enriched the wider population, meant that the income of the Crown had, in relative terms, decreased, and 'our *Tendency at present*, unless it be rightly *moderated*, lies much stronger to *Democracy*, than to *absolute Monarchy*'.[17]

Carte responded to these claims with *A Full Answer to the Letter from a By-Stander* (1742), a point-by-point rejection of Morris's argument and a direct attack on the Whigs' management of England's economic interests. For Carte: 'A Man must be an utter Stranger to this City, that does not know the Decay of Trade, and to the Kingdom, if he does not see an universal Face of Poverty upon the common People.'[18] Morris's claims about the dangers to public securities, meanwhile, were nonsensical; Carte confessed himself unable to 'conceive how the Nation in general could be a loser by one *Englishman's* selling and another's buying Stock at lower Rates than usual'.[19] Equally fallacious was the Bystander's account of taxation. As Carte demonstrated through a brief narrative account of the history of revenue, until the Revolution of 1688 the spending of the Crown had been closely monitored by Parliament and its income had been relatively small. Key to this had been the system of feudal military tenure, whereby vassals were given land in exchange for performing predetermined duties to a lord or king. Often, Carte argued, these duties took the form of 'knight-service' rather than a pecuniary payment.[20] Where 'Scutage' – a payment in lieu of knight's service – had been required, the amounts demanded were low. In recent years, however, military tenures had been abolished and taxation had been transformed.[21] Charles II, for example, had received, Carte argued, an average of £1,353,000 a year during a reign dominated by a series of expensive wars.[22] In contrast, over the twenty-eight years preceding the publication of Carte's *Answer*, a period 'in which we have had no Foreign War', the average rate of taxes was 'above *Four Millions* a Year'.[23] Even this sum, however, had been insufficient to meet government spending, as shown by the nation continually labouring under a debt 'of about *Fifty Millions*'.[24] Such high levels of debt and taxation, Carte contended, did much to explain the woeful state of commerce and manufacture, and provided stark evidence that, contrary to Morris's claims, the power of the Crown had increased since the Revolution. Indeed, whereas military tenures had created

> Leaders that understood the Art of War, and that of their own Vassals had Followers enough to make up a Body of Men sufficient to encourage others to resort to it and form an Army: Now there is no such Thing, no warlike Leader, no great Man with such a following in all the Kingdom.[25]

The liberty of the people, therefore, was at risk, as they lacked any means to balance the extensive powers held by the Crown.

The debate between Morris and Carte provides a useful example of the ways in which credit, commerce and finance could provide the terrain for battles between Court Whigs and Tory/Jacobite polemicists. What is perhaps most interesting about their confrontation, however, is the shared assumptions they took into it. Both were concerned with the relationship between property and power and accepted Harrington's dictum that '*Dominion is founded only in Property*' – indeed, Morris quoted directly from Harrington to this effect.[26] Equally, however, they were in agreement that, for a monarch, it was not so much land that determined dominion, but rather income. As a consequence, prerogative without dominion was not, as Harrington suggested, a mere 'phantom'; rather, they agreed, a monarch could use prerogative to extract income from his or her people, thereby augmenting the Crown's property. Finally, and perhaps most importantly, there were some similarities between their historical narratives. Both accepted the suggestion that England's financial infrastructure had been transformed by the events of 1688 and that the roots of this shift lay in the reigns of the first two Stuarts. Their analyses, as such, constituted contrasting reactions to what they conceived of as an epoch-defining structural shift in government's economic foundations.

The analysis of credit which Carte advanced in his polemical works was to form an integral part of the *General History*. Indeed, by developing his previous account, he was able to provide a critique of two broad trends in historiography. On the one hand, he sought to reject the claims of both Tories such as Salmon and Court Whigs such as Morris regarding the poverty, political backwardness and barbarism of pre-modern societies. Rather, and in a similar manner to Rapin, he maintained that despite the beneficial institutional changes that had taken place over the course of England's history, a series of ancient political structures were key to the nation's political life and underpinned its happiness and prosperity. On the other hand, however, Carte unambiguously rejected Rapin's analysis of these structures. The Frenchman, and those opposition writers who drew on his work, had argued that England's constitution was based on the Saxon principle that popular consent was required to change laws or raise taxes. Carte, in contrast, sought to show that monarchs had a natural right both to determine laws and to raise revenue independently of any public assembly. Key to the *General History*'s treatment of these claims was an expanded version of the narrative of English financial history which Carte had outlined in his response to Morris. Thus he used his discussion of the nation's early history to trace the emergence and operation of the system of feudal military tenures, and his account of the sixteenth and seventeenth centuries to narrate the events surrounding its eventual demise. His discussion of the administration of Ireland in the seventeenth century, meanwhile, served to show that a modern version of the feudal system had the potential to bring real commercial and financial benefits. These elements of Carte's analysis will now be examined in turn.

2. Colonies and commerce in England's 'early' history

Carte's discussion of the emergence of political societies was based on the ideas of the seventeenth-century theorist of absolutism, Sir Robert Filmer. For Filmer, the origins of government lay in God's decree that Adam should rule over his wife and her desires be subject to his.[27] This power was then passed through Adam's body to his posterity, thereby maintaining a monarchical system through the flood to 'the confusion of Babel'.[28] 'When kingdoms were first erected, planted or scattered over the face of the world', Filmer continued,

> we find [Genesis X, II] it was done by colonies of whole families, over which the prime fathers had supreme power, and were kings, who were all the sons or grandchildren of Noah, from whom they derived a fatherly and regal power over their families.[29]

Such an account served to demonstrate both that patriarchal power was directly sanctioned by God and, as a result of the role played by Noah's descendants in settling European territories, that there was a direct historical link between sacred history and modern governments. Carte accepted this analysis and, in order to provide a narrative of the precise genealogical origins of England's monarchs, turned to the account of early Celtic history developed by the Breton abbé Paul-Yves Pezron. As Pezron had done, Carte opened his account with a discussion of Noah's eldest son, Japhet. In accordance with God's blessing and aided by an 'antediluvian vigour' that enabled extraordinarily lengthy lifespans, Japhet's progeny had increased rapidly in number.[30] As a result, two hundred years after the Deluge, men 'found themselves in a condition to send out colonies [...] into the different parts of the earth, to divide it among them, and as their families increased, to form many distinct nations'.[31] The first colonisers of Europe were Japhet's children, Jaones or Iones, and Tiras or Tirax.[32] The former occupied *Attica* and parts of Italy, while the latter, after settling in Phrygia, sent an 'amazing' number of colonies abroad, planting out territories in Poland, Russia, Germany, Gaul and later Spain. The dominance of these Phrygians was brought to an end by the Gomerians – also known as the Titans and Celtae – of Greater Asia, the descendants of Japhet's eldest son, Gomer. This group, led by their kings Saturn, Jupiter and Mercury, had defeated the Phrygians in battle and incorporated them into their numbers. Tempted by Britain's good air, fruitful soil and secure position, the Gomerians/Phrygians had travelled over from Gaul and populated and planted the empty territory.

The subsequent history of the island was characterised by violence and instability in the form of invasions from the Belgic-Celts, the Picts and later the Romans and Saxons. However, while each of these groups was socially and culturally distinctive, they had all, Carte argued, acted as colonisers of British lands, and with the exception of the Romans, had a common Gomerian/Phrygian heritage. This helped to ensure a shared approach to colonisation. On acquiring new territory, the head of a colony or clan – for Carte, the latter word was derived from the former – would divide up the land, taking what he wanted for himself and allotting to others distinct portions which they were to 'cultivate and improve'.[33] These lands became the property of their new proprietors 'with some dependence however, or subordination to the *chief* of the family'.[34] The core relationship was that between the 'vassal' and his clan leader, whereby the former received land from the latter in exchange for services and payments. Over time, the benefits and 'credit and glory' which attached itself to particular leaders as a result of territorial expansion led to the development of a hereditary royalty, whereby not just sovereignty of the clan but of the whole kingdom descended lineally.[35] Moreover, as the land acquired through conquest became too large to be managed by the king's personal followers, he was required to distribute territory to 'other adventurers'.[36] After a few generations, both these 'sorts of vassals' being blended together 'became equally obliged to pay to their common sovereign that obedience, which his own clan was always obliged to by the law of nature'.[37] What resulted, therefore, was a system of feudalism, and the effect of Carte's analysis, as Pocock has argued, was 'to telescope feudal kingship with patriarchal'.[38]

The most significant shift in this landholding system was that which followed the Norman invasion. Carte's analysis of William's reign, however, is by no means a straightforward one. On the one hand, the overthrow of England's rightful monarch by an invading foreign army made it difficult for a Jacobite like Carte to avoid parallels with England's more recent history. Indeed, when Carte describes the feudal law as having exposed the populace to 'various hardships, payments, and forfeitures unknown before', and reduced them 'to a state of more absolute dependence on the crown', he clearly has post-1688 events in mind as much as those that followed 1066.[39] On the other hand, however, Carte was anxious to stress that the feudal law itself was 'nothing but a collection of customs observed in the *German* and other nations with regard to the tenures of land'.[40] Indeed, under the Saxons, the populace still had to provide various military and monetary offerings to their lords and monarchs, and many of the customs associated with the Normans 'prevailed in *England* during the *Saxon* times'.[41] Consequently, the Norman invasion did not represent an absolute break in the system of landownership, and the ongoing survival of feudalism ensured that there was a broad political continuity both to English and European history.

In tracing this continuity, Carte sought to emphasise that the emergence of feudal government had coincided with the development of commerce. The key figure here was Mercury, the 'heathen' 'god of gain, of commerce and of merchandise, and [...] the patron of merchants and travellers'.[42] For Carte, Mercury was not a deity, but an ambitious and able Celtic ruler. The 'encouragement' of trade was one of his principal concerns, and he sought to link together his various kingdoms, which stretched from Asia to Spain, 'in society and friendship by a mutual intercourse in the way of merchandise'.[43] Such an approach brought considerable prestige, as commerce constituted 'the never-failing means of making a people rich, and a state powerful'.[44] Indeed, the period of Mercury's government, and that of his father Jupiter and his uncle Pluto, constituted one 'of industry, of plantations, and of commerce'.[45] Further discussion of commerce, meanwhile, is to be found across Carte's account of pre-Norman England. Thus while the Britons are presented as commercially backward, the Belgae who colonised England's southern maritime provinces are described as having knowledge of 'arts, wealth, and plenty of all things, the usual consequences of commerce, and a civilized manner of living'.[46] The skills of monarchs in economic statecraft are also noted. Athelstan, for example, is praised for having 'particularly encouraged' the commerce of his subjects, while Alfred is said to have built new trading vessels 'more commodious for commerce', thereby helping to ensure that wealth 'abounded in his realm; and gems, spices, with other oriental goods, were imported from the *East-Indies*'.[47]

A key effect of such analyses was to reduce the qualitative differences between ancient and modern history; indeed, monarchs such as Mercury and Alfred are shown to be ambitious, Stuart-style rulers committed to maintaining order and advancing the commercial interests of the nation and its people. Such an approach constituted a rejection of Whiggish claims about the deep historical roots of popular government, and served to demonstrate the historical priority both of feudal government and the political rights claimed by the Stuart kings and their Tory apologists. Equally significantly, through his discussion of commerce Carte supplemented these arguments by emphasising that feudal government was not a backward remnant of an oppressive age, but a system of political and social relations entirely compatible with the ambitions of a modern-style trading state. As a consequence, feudalism was vindicated by both its *de jure* historical status and the *de facto* benefits it was capable of generating.

3. Credit, commerce and modern history

In his discussion of the sixteenth and seventeenth centuries, Carte sought to trace the chain of events that had led to the breakdown of the monarchy in the 1640s. The most significant feature of his analysis in historiographical terms was its sophisticated account of the relationship between acts of statesmanship and social and economic change. Thus, on the one hand, Carte assumed that the shifts in property relations that took place in the period were products of specific actions on the part of monarchs. On the other, however, changes in the balance of property, and the gradual erosion of the relationship between property and power, were shown to restrict the capacity of individual monarchs to shape their own financial and, ultimately, political affairs. As such, England's economic foundations came to determine the character of its political superstructure.

Carte argued that the initial cause of these developments lay in a shift in the attributes of the landowning nobility. 'The old heroic race of nobility' had been characterised by their 'great qualities, noble sentiments, military glory, large estates, number of vassals, and unbounded hospitality'.[48] This group, however, had in a manner been 'extinguished by the civil wars between the houses of *York* and *Lancaster*'.[49] The few families who survived, meanwhile, had seen the material basis of their power undermined. Henry VII introduced legal reforms that weakened the lords' control over their vassals and permitted them to alienate their land. Later, they were attacked by Henry VIII, excluded from counsels by Elizabeth and debased by James, who, through ennobling a series of favourites and moneyed men, undermined the credibility of noble distinctions. As a result, a new type of nobility emerged distinguished by a very different spirit than their predecessors. As Carte observed:

> zeal for the publick good and the glory of their country, gave way to private interest: and the lust of power, the quest of profitable offices, and beneficial grants, the amassing of wealth by projects oppressive to the people, got the better of those generous sentiments, which a course of military service, and an emulation of the glory of great ancestors, seldom failed to inspire.[50]

It was, therefore, the demise of the old race of nobility, themselves the physical and spiritual successors of the feudal clan leaders, which had allowed the rise of a new class of individuals and a new and pernicious value system.

This shift was accompanied by a series of alterations in England's political infrastructure. While Carte conceived of the Commons as a recent addition to England's political infrastructure, he acknowledged its value and maintained that it needed to represent both landed and moneyed forms of property. However, in the current Parliament, whereas the landed interest was represented by 92 members 'and the trading or moneyed interest by about an hundred', there were '300 representatives of small, inconsiderable, and many of these beggarly, burroughs'.[51] The origins of this development could be traced back to the seventeenth century; while there had been no 'ill proportion' of representation in the reign of James, the Puritans had been able to wheedle their way into power at the 1640 election by corrupting the 'little freeholders of 40 shillings a year'.[52] The effect of this, meanwhile, was to render England an international laughing stock. As Carte noted,

> Foreigners, that know and reflect on this inequality in the representation, which cannot reconcile to common sense, stand amazed at hearing us brag of the excellency of our constitution, when it labours under so fundamental a defect: and are apt to doubt, whether the sense of parliament be really the sense of the nation.[53]

These developments, Carte argued, had had catastrophic consequences for the Stuart monarchy, the most significant of which was a debilitating credit crisis. Underpinning his analysis was the assumption that 'MONEY is necessary in all great undertakings' and, as a consequence, 'NOTHING hurts the affairs of a prince so much as indigence: it takes off from the influence of his authority, and is the ruin of his reputation'.[54] Such ideas meant that financial credit was of the utmost importance, and led Carte to provide a comparative history of the successes and failures of various monarchs in securing credit from their people. Key to this analysis was a paradigm shift in systems of credit which had taken place after Elizabeth's death. Under the Tudor monarchs, Carte showed, bad financial management had led to the demise of credit, just as good financial management had served to advance it. Mary I, for example, through confiscating estates and failing to pay the money she owed, lost the confidence of her people and, as a consequence, 'no body cared to trust her'.[55] This 'want of credit', Carte noted, 'proved the source of great inconveniences'.[56] Such conduct contrasted sharply with that of both her predecessor and her successor. Thus Edward was 'careful to pay his debts and maintain his credit'.[57] Similarly, it was, Carte argued, the City of London's perception of Elizabeth's 'œconomy' which 'kept up [her] credit'.[58]

The situation with regard to the Stuarts, however, was more complicated. Carte was by no means uncritical of James, and acknowledged that he lacked the frugality of his predecessor. Equally, however, as was conventional in Royalist/Tory accounts, the *General History* argued that James's approach to government was in line with Elizabethan precedents and that his financial problems had their origin in the debts he had inherited from Elizabeth and the necessary costs of funding the Court. James's inability to navigate his way out of this situation, meanwhile, was a product of the Puritan faction who 'wanted to keep the king necessitous, that they might the easier carry their point in depressing the royal prerogative'.[59] The result was a series of confrontations between the Stuarts and the Commons in which James and Charles always had right, conceived of in feudalistic terms, on their side. Thus taxation in the forms of 'fifteenth and tenths' was not a 'free gift' from the Commons, but rather

> a commutation for those services, and duties annexed to their tenures, in consideration whereof, their lands had been originally granted, and which being as much due to the king, as rent is from a lessee to a landlord, their estates would have been forfeited for want of payment and breach of covenants.[60]

As such, the Commons could not legitimately withhold taxation from their monarch. Similarly, forced loans to the monarchy were 'a seigniorial right, due to them in their necessities, from their tenants or vassals'.[61] These loans 'were due, by common right, to all lords of fiefs, according to the *feudal law*, which prevailed in all parts of *Europe*'.[62] Similarly, in his various discussions of taxes on commerce, Carte invoked the work of the legal scholars Sir Henry Finch and Sir John Davies to argue that it was the '*law merchant*' which gave the king the right both to levy impositions on his merchants and to decide the level of those impositions.[63] This area of law, he contended, formed part of the '*law of nations*' and was of 'equal force in all countries'.[64] As a result, the attempts by both supporters and critics of the Stuarts to justify or condemn commercial taxes by reference to specific precedents in statute and common law were fundamentally misguided; James's and Charles's right was grounded in a universal code, not a local one.

Such claims were the product of an absolute rejection of the ideas of English exceptionalism that had underpinned Rapin's analysis, and they allowed Carte to present resistance to the taxes of James and Charles from Parliament as a rebellion against both established practice and the natural order of things. However, while the Stuarts had right on their side, it was not *de jure*, but *de facto* material factors that determined events. Through their success in restricting the royal income, the Puritans, Carte argued, were able to impoverish the Crown. The consequences of this were catastrophic. James's 'want of money [...] was universally known; and [...] encouraged discontented persons at home [and] lessened his reputation and influence abroad'.[65] As a result, the King's 'royal dignity could not keep him from falling into a general contempt'.[66] By the time Charles succeeded to the throne, the monarchy was already doomed. The King,

Carte emphasised, had a range of enviable virtues, among them a 'love of order and oeconomy' and a 'constant application to business'.[67] Had he succeeded Elizabeth, he might, therefore, have preserved the prerogative.[68] However, 'this was now impracticable'.[69] Lacking the credit to raise money, 'his necessities laid him at the mercy of a parliament'.[70] This body, dominated as it was by a Puritan faction, secured ever more demeaning concessions from the King, among them the abandonment of the feudal duties that had previously been key to government finances.[71] As a result, the financial foundations on which the monarchy depended broke down, virtue and credit became entirely disassociated, and it became impossible for even a good monarch like Charles to hold on to power.

Such an argument enabled Carte, with rather more success than Salmon, to develop a Tory attack on Whiggism. This critique had two core elements. On the one hand, he provided a conventional, Tory-style defence of the Stuarts, which presented them not as the perpetrators but as the victims of unconstitutional practices. In doing so, he entirely rejected the Old Whig assumptions that underpinned the work of both Rapin and the Patriot opposition. On the other, his work contained a new version of his previous attack on the Court Whigs. Thus, whereas his response to Morris had been structured around a schematic comparison between pre- and post-1688 approaches to government revenue, the *General History* provided a narrative of the events that had led one set of practices to be replaced by the other. His account, however, retained a clear polemical focus. Carte's key point was that a system of property and power relations which was in line with both English and European historical practices and which brought real benefits to the nation had been unjustly and unwisely abolished. In its place had emerged an approach that severed the links between property and power, had no historical precedents, and served only to forward a self-interested Whiggish faction.

The *General History*'s defence of the old feudal system was further supported by its discussion of the growth of trade under the Tudors and Stuarts. Indeed, for Carte, while the first two Stuart kings had been unable to secure a workable level of income for themselves, their statecraft had, like that of their Tudor predecessors, played a central role both in advancing the nation's mercantile interests and bringing prosperity to its people. Showing how monarchs with very different characters and interests had, over an extended period of time, contributed to economic improvements was, however, no straightforward task. And, in forwarding such a thesis, Carte developed a complex and, at times, contradictory analysis of the commercial aspects of economic statecraft.

The tensions in his discussion can be seen particularly clearly in relation to Henry VII. Carte based his account of the King, which formed the closing section of the *General History*'s second volume, on the Tacitean principle that 'the vices of a man, and the necessity of his affairs, sometimes produce a conduct, which virtue would inspire into others'.[72] And while for Carte, Henry's 'insatiable' avarice ensured that 'never was prince so utterly devoid of all sentiments of honour, good-nature, generosity, and magnanimity', this vice had also been behind some of his key achievements in law and, perhaps most importantly, trade.[73] Thus Henry is said to have 'encouraged commerce, as it improved his customs, and brought money in to his subjects, which he could squeeze out at his pleasure'.[74] A rather different argument, however, emerges in the first pages of Volume 3 when Carte contrasts Henry VIII's approach to statecraft with that of his father. The use of 'divers heavy and illegal tolls and exactions' meant that the government of the first Tudor king had worked 'to the great discouragement of trade'.[75] It was only when his successor lifted these restrictions, Carte continued, that merchants began 'to resume with vigour the foreign commerce which they had been forced to interrupt'.[76]

The core contradiction here cannot be easily resolved; it is difficult to see how Henry VII could have simultaneously 'encouraged' and acted 'to the great discouragement' of commerce. Indeed, the consistency of Carte's analysis appears to have been weakened by, on the one hand, his respect for Bacon's *History*, from which he quotes frequently, and, on the other, his desire to emphasise that Henry VIII's government represented a complete departure from that of his father. As a result, a tension emerges between a Tacitean analysis concerning the potential benefits of vice and a Livian-style commentary on exemplary public-spirited achievement.

A similar combination of approaches is employed in relation to Elizabeth. Carte is more disparaging about the Queen than many of his contemporaries, and pays particular attention to her dissimulation. However, while this dissimulation is, on occasions, criticised, it is also seen as the root of many of Elizabeth's achievements. Indeed, Carte presents her much-celebrated 'prudence' as 'in many cases the effect of low cunning, and of the diffidence or jealousy of her nature'.[77] In relation to commerce, however, the analysis is rather more conventional. Thus he emphasised that the 'encouragement of commerce' and 'the reformation of the coin' were among the glories of her reign, and he paraphrased the *Annales*' accounts of, among other things, the Muscovy Company, the Turkey Company, coinage, the copper trade and the role played by Huguenot manufacturers.[78] In his commentary on the Queen's motivations, meanwhile, Carte attributed her interest in economic affairs to her desire to increase the trade of her subjects, and went on both to endorse and, on occasion, extend Camden's analysis. Thus he repeated the *Annales*' claim that the Queen's recall of debased money could not have been done without 'a very great loss to her'.[79] Carte, however, supplemented these remarks by adding that 'she gladly suffered that loss for the good of her subjects, and for retrieving the glory of the nation'.[80]

In relation to James, these ideas were given a polemical twist. 'Never prince took more pains for [the good of his people]', Carte noted, 'or was more truly desirous to promote their happiness, and advance their interests, particularly in the point of commerce.'[81] In demonstrating this, the *General History* made extensive use of the work of Howes, paraphrasing, for example, his accounts of James's role in establishing an English silk industry,[82] and drawing on his discussions of the East India trade[83] and England's Atlantic colonies.[84] The establishment of the latter, it was emphasised, constituted 'the almost onely advantageous trade, which exorbitant taxes and a general corruption have left us, that of our *American* colonies; all, except, *Jamaica*' had been 'planted by [James's] care', and throve as a result of his 'continual encouragement'.[85] What made such achievements in commercial statecraft particularly impressive were the difficult financial circumstances in which James operated. As Carte emphasised: 'The care, which the king was forced to take for his own subsistence, did not take off from his constant attention to the commerce of his subjects.'[86] This sort of analysis enabled Carte to develop a comparison between the approach of the King and that of his Puritan critics. Whereas James worked purely to protect the interests of his people, the Puritans, who were undermining his finances and authority, employed 'an arbitrary and tyrannical [approach]; as might naturally be expected from a sect, whose views were selfish, and whose chief aim was power'.[87] At the same time, Carte's account of commercial statecraft served to emphasise the unjustified nature of the rebellion against the Stuarts. By the time of Charles I's reign, 'the *English* were', he argued, 'in an happier state than any nation in *Europe*'.[88] Indeed, anyone who considered the state of the nation would have noted

> the plenty that reigned in every part of it, the impartial administration of justice, the lightness of the publick charge, [...] the flourishing condition of her trade, the credit of her merchants in all foreign exchanges, greater than that of any others in *Europe*, [and] the daily increase of her manufactures.[89]

The Puritans, therefore, had, for no good reason, dismantled a successful, natural and commercial mode of government.

4. Carte and Ireland

An examination of the ways in which this mode of government had collapsed forms the bulk of Carte's discussion of the seventeenth century and, as a result, the tone of his narrative is mournful and, on occasions, angry and despairing. A more positive form of analysis, however, emerges in relation to Ireland. Before James's reign, Carte argued, the territory was in a chaotic state. Its troubles had their origins in the actions of Henry II who, when England gained control of the island, granted vast tracts of Irish land to English 'adventurers'.[90] Free from direct monarchical control, these noblemen entered into a series of violent quarrels with one another, and treated the native population as slaves.[91] Moreover, despite a series of later land redistributions, the size of individual holdings remained far too large for individual undertakers, and this, in combination with the wars which ravaged the territory, reduced it to 'a desolate condition'.[92] The people of Ireland, meanwhile, were accustomed to simple food that cost them no labour and, as a result, had little motivation to work.[93]

To resolve these problems, James introduced a series of land reforms. Across the territory, he ensured that tenants were 'charged only with certain rents in lieu of all uncertain *Irish* exactions', thereby undermining the power and influence of the 'old chieftains' while giving the tenants increased independence.[94] More dramatic reforms took place in Ulster, where James embarked on an ambitious scheme of land improvement, dividing the northern counties into a series of plantations of 2,000, 1,500 and 1,000 acres.[95] To an extent, the aim of such a division was similar to Henry VII's attempts to prevent depopulation – as described by Bacon and Harrington – in the sense that it broke up large tracts of land into smaller, more easily cultivatable portions. However, whereas Harrington had seen such measures as leading to the demise of feudalism, Carte conceived of James's actions as a return to feudalistic first principles. Indeed, like the clan leaders who had first colonised Europe, James allotted 'distinct portions and dividends of land' to various individuals who were then charged with the task of cultivating and improving it, but who retained a 'subordination' to the chief.[96] This subordination was expressed in part through a series of services that were due to the monarch and that Carte described using the standard terms of feudal land tenure. Thus those with the largest territories held 'immediately of the crown *in capite* [, ...] those of 1500 by knights service' and the smaller grants 'in common soccage'.[97] The results of such reforms were dramatic. As a consequence of James's actions, Carte argued, Ulster was 'at present, perhaps, the best cultivated country in *Europe*'.[98] The rents he was able to obtain, meanwhile, ensured that it became a source of considerable government revenue and this, in turn, enabled him to instigate and, in part, to fund a series of reforms to support the clergy. These initiatives were accompanied by a scheme to introduce commerce through granting charters for markets and fairs in all 'the considerable towns'.[99] While such charters, Carte noted, were inconvenient for more advanced societies, they were necessary for a territory 'in infancy of trade' and were calculated to 'keep [the Irish] in subjection to the crown, and advance the interests of peace and commerce'.[100] Taken in sum, James's actions, Carte concluded in his character of the King, had reduced Ireland to 'a state of peace, order, civility, and industry' and laid 'the first foundation of that flourishing condition, to which it is now arrived'.[101]

This discussion of Ireland served as an important counterpoint to his analysis of England. The erosion of feudal values in England had created disorder and a system of public credit in which virtue was no longer able to determine credit. The restoration of a quasi-feudal system of land holdings in Ireland, meanwhile, was shown to have brought order to the territory and wealth to both its people and its monarch. At one level, therefore, Ireland represented a rejection of 'modern' approaches to finance and commerce. James's actions served to ground the funding of the Irish government not in large-scale borrowing and a system of public credit based on 'opinion', but rather in wealth derived directly from the land. As such, his statecraft had rather more in common with the actions of Mercury and England's Briton and Saxon chiefs than it did with the Robinocracy. For Carte, however, such an approach did not entail a retreat into a pre-commercial idyll; rather, its merit lay in its capacity to support a nation's trading and financial interests more effectively than any 'modern' alternative.

Conclusion

Thomas Salmon's *Modern History* and Thomas Carte's *General History* are rooted in the economic statecraft tradition. Their key sources on early modern finance and commerce were Bacon, Camden and Howes and, like these writers, Salmon and Carte provided narrative accounts of how England's monarchs had shaped the nation's economic successes and failures. Through doing so, they developed a series of examples of good and bad practice, which emphasised that successful government was a product of a monarch's capacity to ensure that his or her actions were shaped by the public's interests rather than any private desires for self-enrichment. In this sense, therefore, both writers offered moralistic and didactic analyses. Discussions of borrowing and credit could be slotted neatly into this framework. Indeed, both Salmon and Carte used their accounts of Tudor government to provide commentary on the ways in which public credit was boosted by virtuous statesmanship and destroyed by corruption and selfishness. Equally significantly, however, what distinguished their analyses from earlier accounts was a conception of modernity as an era in which conventional economic statecraft had broken down. For Salmon, the ongoing problems England had with debt were a symptom of this. Rather than being ruled by its own monarchs, the nation had become prey to a series of pernicious Genevan, Scottish and, most damagingly, Dutch influences. These groups had corrupted the people, led governments to act against the nation's interests, and through their influence encouraged a damaging programme of borrowing. In contrast, for Carte, it was debt that had caused the nation's problems. The difficult financial situation in which James found himself, and the failure of Parliament to provide the levies which were due to the King, served to undermine monarchical prerogatives. This ensured that, despite the commercial successes of James and Charles, by the start of the latter's reign the monarchy had lost the power to shape its own financial future. What unites Salmon's and Carte's work, therefore, is the idea that a significant shift had taken place both in the attitudes of the populace and the structure of England's economic institutions. For Salmon, there was some hope; a Tory government, free from Dutch influence, was shown to be capable of reviving, in part at least, England's fortunes. Carte, however, assumed that economic problems could no longer be solved simply through good statecraft; rather, a more far-reaching series of property reforms were required in order to return the constitution to first principles.

In developing such narratives, we see the beginnings of a new approach to historiography. The economic statecraft tradition assumed that a statesman's performance as a manager of the nation's financial and commercial interests would be determined by his or her character. Historians were, of course, aware that monarchs inherited kingdoms in varying degrees of affluence and poverty. However, even a debt-ridden kingdom such as that taken over by Elizabeth was shown to be revivable; as such, it provided further evidence of the power of skill and virtue to restore a nation's fortunes. In contrast to this, Salmon and Carte's discussions of Stuart England provided analyses of long-term economic changes, which had undermined the power of character to determine events. Indeed, Carte's account sought to show that in the modern era, the actions of monarchs were shaped by, rather than shaping, financial affairs. For the Tory historians with whom the last two chapters have been concerned, such a state of affairs was a highly troubling consequence of a loss of monarchical prerogative. Other writers, however, as we shall see, were to view these developments as evidence of the increasing success of England's commercial endeavours.

Part III

8

Economic statecraft and economic progress: William Guthrie's *General History*

The middle years of the eighteenth century saw the emergence of a new, enlightened approach to history. Underpinning this mode of writing was the assumption that the level of progress achieved in modern-day Europe distinguished it from any previous historical period.[1] To an extent, the novel qualities of the present were conceived of in political terms. With regard to England in particular, there was support for the Tory/Court Whig argument that the nation's much-celebrated liberty had its origins not in Saxon or pre-Saxon history, but rather in the constitutional and cultural shifts produced by the tumultuous events of the seventeenth century. Equally, there was a growing belief that a range of intellectual and cultural fields – among them technology, manufacture, the arts and sciences, and, perhaps most importantly, manners – had been transformed over the past hundred years and that, in some sense, these developments were interconnected.[2] Incorporating such diverse subject matter into a conventional narrative posed considerable challenges, and some writers, most famously the Scottish conjectural historians, dispensed with the chronological approach altogether.[3] Neoclassical conceptions, however, as Philip Hicks's account of the subject has shown, continued to shape the ways in which British writers and readers viewed history.[4] Consequently, there was a desire to provide an account that conformed to the conventional understanding of history as 'a continued Narration of things True, Great and Publick', but that was able to explain and narrate the recent shifts which had transformed Europe's nation states.[5] Such ideas served to alter the emphasis of English narrative history in two important ways. On the one hand, they expanded the genre's thematic range. And although politics remained the primary subject, England's political history was shown to have shaped and been shaped by a range of non-political developments. On the other hand, history's narrative focus tightened. The desire of post-Civil War party-political histories to show the benefits of government of a particular ideological hue led them to present the character and conduct of the monarch as the key force determining the character of a particular era. As a result, English history was conceived of as the site of a series of abrupt transformations in the nation's fortunes, as good and bad monarchs succeeded one another in rapid succession. While later writers did not necessarily ignore the character of individual statesmen, the impact of character was shown to be restricted by a wider set of institutional and ideological considerations. Attention, meanwhile, came to be focused around a single epoch-defining shift: the decay of a medieval, feudal society and the emergence of a modern, commercial one.

These ideas ensured that commerce acquired a unique degree of importance within historical narratives as both a significant agent in bringing about the demise of feudalism and the defining characteristic of the system that replaced it. An enlightened society, it was assumed, was necessarily a commercial one and it became a key task for historians to trace the causes and trajectory of England's economic progress. In giving commerce these roles, however, historians came to conceptualise it in new ways. It was not, in its modern form at least, simply an activity that could be promoted with varying degrees of effectiveness by a monarch. Rather it was a complex system of exchanging goods and services that had evolved over a substantial period of time and that, despite its dependence on government and the law, was partially independent from them. As such, commerce had its own history, and this history had a complex and frequently shifting relationship with political events.

The final part of this book examines the consequences of these developments for economic statecraft. Chapter 9 will show that David Hume's *History of England* used such an approach as the basis for an out-and-out attack on the record both of England's monarchs and previous historians as, respectively, managers and chroniclers of the nation's economic interests. This chapter, meanwhile, explores how the Scottish historian William Guthrie constructed a narrative of political and economic progress through drawing on and developing the ideas that underpinned the economic statecraft tradition.

1. Guthrie as a political journalist

The sophisticated account of the relationship between government, commerce and liberty that Guthrie developed in his *General History* (1744–51) had its origins in his career as a political journalist. Born in Forfarshire in around 1708, Guthrie moved to London in the early 1730s to become, as James Boswell described him, 'an Authour by Profession'.[6] From 1735 to 1740 he was employed by the *Gentleman's Magazine* as a parliamentary reporter, where he worked in close collaboration with his eventual successor, Samuel Johnson.[7] It was also in this period that he began his involvement in anti-ministerial polemic, serving as a writer for *Common Sense* (1737–44) and, from 1743 onwards, as co-editor with James Ralph of *Old England, or, the Constitutional Journal.*[8] The latter paper was superintended and, on occasions, written by the Patriot politician and propagandist Lord Chesterfield. Its primary aim was to undermine support for the Pelham government by showing how the administration's support for Hanover, particularly its controversial decision to take on 16,000 German troops, had been highly detrimental to British interests. While this line of argument failed to significantly dent Pelham's parliamentary majority, it did provoke excitement among Jacobites and considerable disquiet in government.[9] In March 1743 a clampdown was attempted. Following the simultaneous publication of anti-Hanoverian articles in *Old England* and *Common Sense,* Guthrie was arrested and his papers confiscated.[10] Such moves, however, did little to circumscribe *Old England*'s activities and, following a few days of incarceration, Guthrie took up his pen once more. Predictably, perhaps, the response from the opposition and its supporters contrasted sharply with that of the government. Whereas for William Pitt the paper was written with 'a truly British constitutional spirit', for the Marquis of Hartington it was 'direct treason' which, unless action was taken, would bring about 'an end of government'.[11]

Much of *Old England*'s invective was expressed through commentary on England's history, with particular reference to commercial and financial issues. The paper's main strategy was to explore the parallels between the most nefarious political figures from 'Old England' and leading figures in the Pelham administration. In the number for 5 March 1743, Guthrie, writing under the pseudonym Jeffrey Broadbottom, argued that while both the Stuart kings and Cromwell had made significant mistakes, these had been partially mitigated by their achievements.[12] James I's reign, for example, was dominated by the King's 'timorous cowardly Politics'.[13] However, the pernicious effects of such practices were counteracted 'by the Care then taken of the Commerce of *England* and the Establishment of several very useful Public Bodies'.[14] Similarly, 'the degenerate Court of the second Charles' was 'distinguished by several masterly Strokes in Politics, in Arms, and in Commerce'.[15] In contrast, Guthrie continued, 'for the present [government] what Merit can be pleaded; what Praise can even ingenious Adulation bestow upon it?'[16]

Similar ideas were expressed in an even more direct way in the paper's November 1744 account of Richard Empson. Empson, Guthrie observed, was one of the most unpopular ministers England had ever seen. By contemporary standards, however, his crimes were not of the utmost severity. The money he extorted was distributed 'amongst Men of Learning and Merit; and the Royal Coffers were always so full that the King was well served, both in his Household, Cabinet and Camps'.[17] Empson did not, however,

> sooth his Master's Passion for a *foreign* Interest, dangerous, incompatible with, and dishonourable to that of *England*. [...] He has not dar'd to contract with foreign Powers as a general Undertaker for burying, in Defence of a lowly Territory, the Commerce, Interest, Money, and Glory of *Old England*.[18]

Guthrie's polemical strategy here is, at one level, a straightforward one; the paper uses a comparative form of history to show the degenerate state of modern England and to highlight the failures of Hanoverian governments. What is noteworthy, however, is his Tacitean contention that, particularly with regard to economic affairs, statesmen with significant moral and political flaws had the capacity to advance the nation's interests. The comparison, therefore, was not between the virtue of the past and the vice of the present, but rather between the manageable and sometimes publicly advantageous vices and malpractices of 'Old England' and the modern age's catastrophic and publicly detrimental failings.

On other occasions, *Old England* developed a quasi-Harringtonian form of argument which owed much to the writing of Bolingbroke. In the number for 2 March 1745, for example, the paper launched an attack on the septennial Act, by providing a general outline of

England's history. Originally, Guthrie argued, the country had been an 'aristocratical' state in which the balance of the land was held by the king, nobility and Church.[19] The people joined sometimes with the king and sometimes with the nobility 'as they found either inclin'd to favour public Liberty'.[20] This balance survived until the reign of Henry VII, a 'designing Prince' who, using 'Methods foreign to the Design of this Paper', was able to terminally weaken the 'great Pin' which, on occasions at least, had linked the people's interests to those of the nobility.[21] Through the first part of the Tudor period the balance of property shifted from the nobility to the people, thereby ensuring that when Elizabeth came to the throne, 'the Government from Aristocratical came to be Popular'.[22] The Queen was aware of this and 'found her Government upon its natural Basis, the *Affections of her People*'.[23] The first two Stuart kings, in contrast, sought to restore aristocratic powers, first through imprisoning members of the Commons and later by extending the duration of Parliaments in order to render MPs 'independent of their Constituents'.[24] Guthrie's polemical point here was a conventional one: that modern governments, through extending the length of Parliaments to seven years, were behaving in an 'aristocratical' manner that resembled the Stuarts. Such an approach, however, was viewed as ill-advised not so much because it violated the ancient constitution, but rather because it unnaturally contravened the modern balance of property. The implication, therefore, was that the 'progress' achieved with regard to property relations rendered aristocratic government anachronistic.

2. The *General History*

The *General History* (1744–51) was published in weekly parts, the first of which went on sale on 25 February 1744.[25] At this time, Guthrie was still actively working as a political journalist, and advertisements for the *History* in *Old England* were frequently placed immediately alongside his articles for the paper. In 1746, however, using a time-honoured technique for eliminating troublesome polemicists, the government attempted to prise him away from the opposition with the offer of a pension.[26] The move appears to have been a successful one. Guthrie accepted the deal, retaining the £200 pension for the rest of his life and, as the historian and biographer Thomas Birch noted in a letter of July 1747, he went on to affect 'the character of a most zealous subject'.[27] To an extent, this change of circumstances, coupled with a seemingly genuine desire – even before financial inducements were offered – to produce a history devoid of a party-political agenda, served to ensure that his formal, historical writing was different in character to his journalism. The *General History* was principally concerned with providing a narrative of progress, an account of the interconnected development of liberty and commerce across England's history. Entirely absent from the work, meanwhile, were the direct commentaries on contemporary events, and the politically charged parallels between past and present, which had characterised his journalism.

Guthrie did not, however, reject his earlier ideas entirely. Two points are of particular significance here. First, underpinning his analysis of progress was a version of the Harringtonian thesis that he had employed in *Old England*. This aspect of his work was outlined in the *General History*'s preface where he noted his intention to conclude his account with a 'dissertation', which would aim

> above all things, to mark the progress of the English commerce through its several gradations; and to trace the true sources of the necessity of that great alteration of property which was then introduced, and which, in effect, completed the durable fabric of our constitution as it now exists.[28]

By the time he came to write the dissertation around seven years later, however, Guthrie was aware that he had been 'necessarily obliged, to take into the body of the [...] history' so much of this material that the dissertation itself was largely redundant.[29] Indeed, the *General History* is perhaps best understood as an attempt to transform the brief Harringtonian sketches that been mainstays of Patriot propaganda into a complete, classical-style narrative of English history.

Second, Tacitean ideas of statecraft were of central importance to Guthrie's historical work. And, as had been the case in *Old England*, he was particularly concerned with tracing the contribution that non-virtuous actions could make to economic affairs. Indeed, the *General History* sought to demonstrate that the self-interested and arbitrary practices of England's monarchs had been supported by and played a vital role in generating wise commercial and financial reforms. Such arguments, it will be shown, when combined with the Harringtonian elements of his analysis, helped to produce a complex and often paradoxical account of the ways in which monarchical achievements in economic statecraft could, potentially, both support and undermine liberty.

For Guthrie, as for other writers influenced by Harrington, the reign of Henry VII constituted a key turning point in England's history. Its chief glory was the King's programme 'to raise, to cherish, and to support [...] the industrious commoners', a group who 'not living in an abject, despicable dependance on the great, availed themselves of the rising arts, and flowing commerce, which began now to distinguish England'.[30] Henry was aware that the main threat to the commoners came from the nobility or barons, who had 'a strong tendency [...] to envy and oppress the wealthy merchant and the ingenious mechanic'.[31] Consequently, he sought to counteract this group's pernicious influence by undermining the system of feudal landownership on which their power was based. Guthrie's phrasing in this account is significant. The idea that Henry had supported the 'commoners' or 'middle people' in order to diminish the power of the nobility and advance his own authority was a standard theme in historical writing. As we have seen, this mode of analysis had its origins in the work of Bacon and had shaped the property-based analyses of Harrington and the neo-Harringtonian writers who followed in his wake, Bolingbroke among them. At the same time, discussion of Henry's successful management of England's commercial interests was a feature of much post-Baconian history. Guthrie's key move, however, was to fuse these elements together by arguing that Henry's support for the 'commoners' explicitly involved defending the interests of merchants and tradesmen. Indeed, Henry's aim, as was noted in the dissertation at the conclusion of the *General History*, was to 'put the industrious and trading part of the nation into a method of becoming proprietors in the soil'.[32]

To provide an account of the specific measures that Henry had employed, Guthrie turned to Rymer's *Foedera*, contemporary legal records and, most importantly, Bacon. Thus, he paraphrased Bacon's commentaries on the laws to counter depopulation and eliminate fines on the alienation and mortgaging of land, and repeated the former Lord Chancellor's account of Empson and Dudley.[33] All of these measures were presented as part of the King's grand plan to transfer property to the commons. At the same time, the Scotsman offered a full Baconian vindication of Henry's management of England's commercial interests. Guthrie accepted, therefore, Bacon's analysis of avarice, arguing that the King 'pursued many [...] measures for advancing the trade of his subjects, as being the most effectual manner of filling his own coffers'.[34] Finally, the *General History*'s principal verdict on Henry's economic statecraft was derived directly from Bacon: Henry's successes, it was noted, were a product of his ability to prioritise 'power' over 'plenty'.[35]

These Baconian borrowings were then used to support the standard Harringtonian conclusion on Henry's reign. During his lifetime, Guthrie noted, Henry had been an oppressive ruler who had brought a good deal of suffering to his people. However,

> the moment that [he] left the stage, and the curtain was dropped, the tricks of his cunning vanished, while the effects of his wisdom remained. His people, no longer oppressed by his craft, found themselves happy in his art; government then gave way to law, and justice succeeded to rigour.[36]

Underpinning this account, meanwhile, was a highly ambivalent view of the relationship between liberty and commerce. It was Henry's success in managing commerce and promoting the interests of the trading population, Guthrie argued, that had ensured that 'wealth and liberty' emerged during his reign from the 'pressure of corruption, oppression and prerogative'.[37] However, the wealth that commerce generated was also shown to have had a soporific effect on the populace. The fact that England, 'as an independent, trading state, was now in a higher pitch of happiness than perhaps it had ever known before' explained why the people were unwilling to resist the incursions Henry had made on popular liberties.[38] For Guthrie, therefore, as for Bolingbroke, 'drops of Manna' from trade had the capacity to soften any murmurs of complaint from the populace, and to ease the way for arbitrary forms of government.[39]

These arguments regarding property and commerce were developed further when Guthrie came to discuss the reign of Elizabeth. His key move – one that would have been rejected vociferously both by Whigs such as Rapin and Tories such as Salmon – was to present Elizabeth as continuing the approach to government developed by Henry. With regard to property, this link was made explicitly. Whereas the reigns of her predecessors had seen power slip back to the nobility, Elizabeth followed the plan of her 'wise grandfather' and took 'every opportunity to add to the growing property of the commons'.[40] In relation to economic issues the link was implicit, with Guthrie praising Elizabeth's measures in a similar manner to those of Henry. His key source here was Camden, and despite offering some criticism of the *Annales*, he used it frequently. Thus for Guthrie, as for Camden, the root cause of Elizabeth's success was her 'oeconomy', which ensured that she swiftly repaid any loans she took out, and administered her revenues frugally.[41] More generally, through summarising material from the *Annales*, he was able to present the Queen as a highly able manager of England's commercial interests. Indeed, Guthrie's discussions of the positive effect of Huguenot immigration on the textile trade,[42] his accounts of the establishment of the Turkey and East India Companies,[43] and his detailed commentary on Elizabeth's support for the Muscovy Company[44] all paraphrased Camden's work. What is noteworthy, however, is Guthrie's tendency to emphasise, even more directly than Camden had done, Elizabeth's personal responsibility for acts of economic statecraft. For example, while Camden had noted the role played by Elizabeth's negotiations with the Russian Tsar in ensuring that the Muscovy Company received trading privileges, he did not imply that she had directly managed Russian commerce.[45] For Guthrie, however, it was the Queen who personally 'improved' this line of trade.[46] Similarly, describing the commercial treaty with Portugal of 1571, Camden noted that Francis Gerard, the Portuguese ambassador, 'struck up a League with the Queen'.[47] Guthrie, however, maintained that Elizabeth was the active party, and had 'made a treaty of commerce with Portugal, by which she cut off a clandestine trade which the English had long carried on with the Portuguese settlements in Africa'.[48] The implication of such accounts – and this suggestion was to be developed in Guthrie's discussion of James I – was that the Queen's power and prerogative had supported the growth of English commerce.

Ideas about prerogative were also of importance to the *General History*'s discussion concerning the effects of Elizabethan commercial growth on English liberty. As had been the case in his account of Henry VII, Guthrie presented commerce's influence as working in two seemingly opposite directions. For example, the reforms that Elizabeth effected with regard to commerce and property were shown to have altered the people's relationship with government. In

1066, Guthrie noted, the Normans had only to defeat 'a few great Lords' to achieve a conquest; if they had landed in 1588, however, the Spanish would have faced a far more difficult task.[49] The shift in the balance of property meant that 'the spirit of national freedom would have disputed every foot of ground', as the commoners sought to defend all they 'had painfully earned by trade, by agriculture, by manufactures, or by the rising arts'.[50] Through spreading wealth among the populace, therefore, changing patterns of property ownership are shown to have protected liberty by giving a wider section of the population an interest in resisting arbitrary forms of power. However, while commerce and the arts may have helped to prevent dramatic affronts to liberty, the wealth they generated could also, as Guthrie had shown in his discussion of Henry VII, dull the senses of the populace to more minor incursions on their rights. Elizabeth, it was noted, had exercised 'high prerogative' in her management of domestic affairs.[51] But the fact that 'poverty [had] its protection, nobility its respect, religion its reverence, and commerce its encouragement' meant that 'the people thus happy, unattacked in property, and unloaded with taxes [...] almost lost sight of those constitutional rights, which alone distinguish a land of freedom'.[52] Ultimately, it was only the responsible way in which Elizabeth exercised her power that prevented popular liberties from being completely destroyed.

By the time Guthrie reached the Stuarts, the tensions in his accounts of property and commerce had become acute. On the one hand, he argued that the property held by the middling sort meant that the people's minds were now turned to 'foreign commerce and domestic freedom' and that they would not accept the oppressive precedents of former reigns.[53] It was this attitude and the arbitrary policies pursued by James and Charles that were responsible for the conflict between Parliament and the monarchy, and ultimately the Civil Wars of the 1640s. On the other hand, and far more provocatively, Guthrie sought to apply Bacon's and Bolingbroke's Tacitean arguments concerning Henry VII's management of commerce to the reign of James I, and to show that James's absolutist approach to government had benefited trade. Thus for Guthrie, the much-derided Italian and Spanish trading company that James established in 1605 was not a destructive monopoly, but a means to encourage commerce and a 'good effect' of the King's profligacy.[54] Similarly, James's need for finance, and his inability to obtain it from the landed classes in Parliament, made him dependent on the 'mercantile interest'.[55] This in turn led him to embark on a number of measures designed to support trade, including the promotion of commerce to the East and West Indies,[56] the enlargement of the East India Company's charter[57] and a series of contributions towards 'naval architecture'.[58] Such actions and the King's pacifistic foreign policy meant that it was James who had 'laid the foundation of those great schemes of commerce, that now both enrich and ennoble England'.[59] Moreover, while Guthrie saw the King's absolutist approach to government as politically reprehensible, he acknowledged that it had played a useful role in promoting economic efficiency. As is noted in the 'character' of James that concludes the *General History*'s discussion of his reign:

> The great increase of the commerce and manufactures of England under Elizabeth and James, could not have been effected but by force of prerogative, which was usefully and sometimes beneficially applied; especially by erecting companies, which, in the then, almost, infant state of commerce, was necessary for improving and extending it.[60]

The measures pursued by James also had important consequences for his successor. While the various customs and excises that Charles imposed were unpopular, the massive growth in trade that previous monarchs had helped to produce meant that such impositions were 'scarcely felt' by traders themselves.[61] The people, Guthrie notes, simply wanted to enjoy the sweets of commerce in peace and 'would willingly have indulged [Charles] in his arbitrary principles, which endangered both [liberty and property], if he had proved no more immoderate than theretofore'.[62]

At times Guthrie's position on commerce with regard to the Stuarts is paradoxical, if not outright contradictory, and he appears to argue that the wealth of the populace simultaneously both supported and undermined liberty. It is, however, possible to see how the two claims might work together, most notably in the *General History*'s discussions of the attempts by Charles to levy ship money.[63] The people, Guthrie argued, made a distinction between occasional arbitrary impositions on trade, which it was prudent for the affluent merchant class to pay, and attempts to turn – without parliamentary consent – such taxes into law, and use legal measures to enforce them. This, they were aware, would create a legal precedent, thereby ensuring that such impositions could be made in perpetuity. Charles, with disastrous consequences, failed to comprehend this position and assumed that the supine behaviour of the people in the face of his earlier impositions meant that they were losing their 'high sentiments of liberty'.[64] For Guthrie, therefore, the changes effected by Henry VII did not, as Bolingbroke had argued, ensure that a monarch would be forced to court the affections of his subjects; rather, while strengthening the monarch's prerogative and ability to raise revenue, they created a firm legal line over which a monarch could not cross without alienating his people.

However, what is perhaps most significant is that the consequences of crossing this line are presented as political rather than economic. Charles had rejected the constitution, shown contempt for the commercial classes, and had little interest or aptitude for the management of trade, thereby causing the merchant classes to enter into rebellion against him. However, the nation itself, it is emphasised, continued to prosper. As he noted:

> The increase of England's riches was such, that, with the Roman emperor, he might have said, "I received an empire of brick, but I leave it of marble." The use of plate became now common in the houses of artizans and peasants. Improvements were daily making in all the elegancies and luxuries of life; immense sums were expended in importing antique statues, fine paintings, and in erecting magnificent edifices in a much finer taste than had ever been known in England before, and in some respects, than she has ever known since.[65]

Guthrie's claim, therefore, was that the relentless promotion of commerce by Tudor and Stuart statesmen had ensured that, by the time of Charles I, a commercial spirit had entered into the English people, and, as a consequence, they no longer required direct 'encouragement' from the state.

Conclusion

Guthrie's position on issues of commerce and revenue marks a considerable departure from the other post-Civil War historians discussed in this study. Key to the historical writing of the period was the assumption that a public-spirited monarch was required in order to bring the nation economic success. It was this approach, moreover, which gave accounts of economic statecraft their polemical force. Through celebrating the virtues and commercial achievements of some monarchs and condemning the vices and failures of others, historians could provide a vindication of a particular political perspective, be it Republican or Royalist, Whig or Tory. There were, of course, a number of attempts to adapt this basic framework. Some Tory writers, most notably Carte, had argued that in certain retrograde circumstances even a virtuous monarch could fail. Bolingbroke, meanwhile, had acknowledged that Henry VII's self-interested management of commerce had brought some benefits to the public. Such achievements, however, were conceived of as an exception to the general pattern of English history. A ruler would, it was assumed, be far better off following the virtuous 'oeconomy' of Elizabeth than the manipulative avaricious politics of Henry. For Guthrie, however, such issues were rather less clear cut. His analysis presented Henry VII's reign – as described by Bacon – less as an exception to, and more as an exemplification of, good economic practices. As a consequence, he rejected the idea that a necessary relationship existed between virtue, good government and commercial and financial achievement. Moreover, he maintained that Henry VII, Elizabeth I and James I had succeeded in commercial terms, not in spite of their self-interest and absolutism, but because of them.

Two qualifications need to be provided for such an argument. First, Guthrie is not claiming that *every* selfish absolutist will be adept at promoting commerce. Rather, the point being made was that economic statecraft was a skill that required knowledge of the often complex workings of trade and finance. Self-interest might drive a statesman to seek this sort of expertise, but this would not always be the case. Second, and even more importantly, Guthrie was not calling for a commercially adept absolutist to take control of modern Britain. While he maintained that this sort of approach had helped commerce 'in its infant state', the implication of Guthrie's account is that it would be of no value in maturity. Such a conclusion is a product of his use of Harringtonian ideas. His key point was that the shifts in property that had taken place rendered the sort of statecraft that promoted commerce in the past undesirable and impossible in modern England. In this sense, the *General History*, despite its extensive use of ideas of economic statecraft, marked a move away from this tradition of historical analysis. For all the writers discussed thus far, a monarch is inevitably something of a merchant, and the prosperity of the nation is a direct consequence of his or her ability or inability to negotiate treaties with foreign powers and to provide a body of laws and regulations capable of advancing trade. Nevertheless, the implication of Guthrie's account is that the monarchical management of commerce represents a stage in the evolution of the English economy, not, as it had done for earlier writers, an inevitable feature of commercial life. England's continuing commercial success in the face of Charles's inept economic management demonstrated that, in the modern age, the desire of merchants and tradesmen to protect and advance their property was the key driver of national wealth. As a result, while the *General History* is a work of commercial statecraft, it is one that, in its latter pages, narrates the demise of the power relations on which that mode of writing had been based.

9

The end of economic statecraft: David Hume's *History of England*

The chronologies of David Hume's career as a political economist and his career as a historian are closely intertwined.[1] *Political Discourses*, the collection of essays containing his principal contribution to political economy, was published in January 1752.[2] The work went on to secure Hume a Europe-wide reputation as a writer on economic affairs and was, as he noted in his autobiography, his only book 'successful on the first publication'.[3] A second edition emerged later in 1752, and further versions – now forming the final section of his *Essays and Treatises on Several Subjects* – were issued in 1754, 1757, 1758, 1760, 1764, 1767, 1768, 1770, 1772 and 1777. Revisions, some minor, others more substantial, were included in each of these publications, and a new economic essay, 'Of the Jealousy of Trade', was attached to later versions of the 1758 text and all subsequent editions. At the same time, Hume continued to elaborate on and clarify the essays' arguments in his correspondence, entering into a series of exchanges with some of Europe's foremost economic thinkers, among them Josiah Tucker, Anne-Robert-Jacques Turgot, André Morellet and Adam Smith.[4]

The idea for a history, meanwhile, had first been mooted by Hume in the second half of the 1740s. Work began in the late summer of 1752 and the first volume, covering the reigns of James I and Charles I, was published as *The History of Great Britain* in the autumn of 1754.[5] Hume added a second volume in 1757, extending the narrative up to the Glorious Revolution, while 1759 saw the publication of the two-volume *History of England under the House of Tudor*.[6] The project was completed with two further volumes, published in 1761 and 1762, covering the period from the Roman invasion to the Battle of Bosworth Field.[7] The entire narrative was then republished as a single work later in 1762 under the title *The History of England from the Invasion of Julius Caesar to the Revolution in 1688*.[8] New editions, each containing significant revisions, followed in 1770, 1773 and 1778.[9]

Alongside the chronological coincidence between Hume's writings on history and political economy are, perhaps unsurprisingly, a series of intellectual links. This chapter explores these connections and provides an account of the relationship between the historical and economic facets of Hume's work.[10] My approach is, in a sense, analogous with that of a number of scholars, among them Duncan Forbes, Nicholas Phillipson and James A. Harris, who have discussed the relationship between Hume's historical and political writing.[11] For these commentators, the *History* formed part of Hume's career-long enterprise to, in the words of Forbes, develop a 'programme of political education'.[12] Only through such an endeavour, Hume assumed, could the disruptive influence of political factionalism be countered, and 'the established, Hanoverian regime' be provided with a 'a proper intellectual foundation'.[13] Running parallel with this project, and stretching across the *Political Discourses*, the *Essays* and the *History*, I argue, was an attempt to give England's commercial and financial interests – which were in Hume's estimation of vital importance to government – a similar grounding.[14] Such a programme contained a number of elements: an analysis of the conditions on which economic life in England depended; an account of the processes through which those conditions had been established; and commentary on the role that England's statesmen had played in its commercial and financial history. In discussing these matters, Hume developed a damning critique of the economic statecraft tradition; indeed, it was, in part, the misunderstandings of economic affairs committed by previous generations of historians that he sought to warn his readers against and correct.

The chapter is divided into six sections. Section one provides an account of Hume's views on history, commerce and finance as developed in his essays. Section two gives a general introduction to the *History of England*. Sections three, four and five look respectively at his discussion of Stuart, Tudor and pre-Tudor England. Section six investigates the changes Hume made to the *History* in its later editions.

1.1 Essays: 'Of the Rise and Progress of the Arts and Sciences'

Hume's approach to the histories of commerce and finance has its roots in the account of causality first advanced in *A Treatise of Human Nature* (1739–40) and subsequently adapted in the *Enquiry Concerning Human Understanding* (1748). His underlying claim in these works was that human perception of causality is rooted not in any necessary connection between objects, but rather in experience; it is the regular conjunction of events that leads individuals to the attribution of a causal relationship. In the opening section of the 1742 essay 'Of the Rise and Progress of the Arts and Sciences', Hume used this idea as the basis for an account of the epistemology of historical causation.[15] His aim here was to establish the types of events that are attributable to causes and, consequently, potential sites for the discovery of profound knowledge, and those that are a product of chance and thus not susceptible to further enquiry. The argument proceeded through two stages. In the first, Hume outlined his core thesis: events arising from a great number of people can be accounted for by '*determinate and known Causes*', as the presence of a large sample provides the observer with the regular conjunction of events required to attribute causation.[16] In contrast, events that depend on a few people do not provide a large enough sample for such a judgement, and may 'be ascrib'd to Chance, or secret and unknown Causes'.[17] Such arguments led Hume to conclude that some subjects were more suitable for 'general' analysis than others. 'The domestic and the gradual Revolutions of a State' – such as the 'Rise of the Commons in *England*' and the 'Increase of Trade and Industry' – depended on the passions of many and were, therefore, 'a […] proper Subject of Reasoning and Observation'.[18] In contrast, 'the foreign and the momentary' revolutions, 'which are commonly produc'd by single Persons, […] are more influenc'd by Whim, Folly, or Caprice, than by general Passions and Interests'.[19] 'For the same reason', Hume continued, 'tis more easy to account for the Rise and Progress of Commerce in any Kingdom, than for that of Learning.'[20] The former relied on 'Avarice, or the Desire of Gain', which was 'an universal Passion, that operates at all Times, in all Places, and upon all Persons'.[21] The latter was dependent on curiosity, or the love of knowledge, which has 'but a very limited Influence, and requires Youth, Leisure, Education, Genius, and Example, to make it govern any Person'.[22]

In the second stage of his argument, Hume considered the relationship between 'chance', particular occurrences, and 'caused' or 'general' ones. The historian of the arts and sciences, Hume warned, needed to proceed with caution; the small number of people who cultivate these subjects and the limited, delicate nature of their passion mean that chance must always play a significant part in their development. However, Hume continued, there was a sense in which general causes did influence scientific and artistic endeavour.

> Tho' the Persons, that cultivate the Sciences with such astonishing Success, as to attract the Admiration of Posterity, be always few, in all Nations, and all Ages; 'tis impossible but a Share of the same Spirit and Genius must be antecedently diffus'd thro' the People among whom they arise, in order to produce, form, and cultivate, from their earliest Infancy, the Taste and Judgement of those eminent Writers. The Mass cannot be altogether insipid. [...] The Question, therefore, concerning the Rise and Progress of the Arts and Sciences, is not altogether a Question concerning the Taste, Genius, and Spirit of a few, but concerning those of a whole People; and may, therefore, be accounted for, in some Measure, by general Causes and Principles.[23]

For Hume, therefore, 'chance' and 'causation' were not mutually exclusive categories. General causes, he acknowledged, do not have the capacity to explain specific individual events, such as the existence of Homer at a particular time or place.[24] Equally, though, as the 'Arts and Sciences' require certain conditions to prosper, an analysis of general causes has the potential to offer a partial explanation even for seemingly 'chance' occurrences. Given such an approach, a key task for the historian was to select an appropriate form of analysis for the phenomena being described. Certain events required a 'general' form of cultural history, which looked at changes in the behaviour of large groups and sought to identify clear patterns of causation. Other occurrences demanded the use of a 'particular' mode of analysis concerned with the actions of specific individuals. Moreover, the use of this latter approach obliged the analyst to distinguish between those historical phenomena that were a product of the general cultural context – and thus subject to causal analysis – and those that were not.

1.2 Essays: *Political Discourses*

Hume's comments on the development of commerce in 'Of the Rise and Progress of the Arts and Sciences', brief as they are, raise a number of important questions. His analysis presents avarice as the root of all commercial activity. However, while Hume assumed that avarice is a universal human phenomenon, one which 'operates at all Times, in all Places, and upon all Persons', commerce is not; rather, its emergence is a subject on which 'Reasoning and Observation' have the potential to shine some light.[25] Given such assumptions, what was it that enabled human beings' innate avarice to take a commercial turn?

An answer to this question was to be formulated in 'Of Commerce', the first essay in the *Political Discourses*. For Hume, there were significant differences between the behaviour of the populace in societies where manufactures and mechanic arts are not cultivated and those where they are. In the former, a habit of indolence prevails, as individuals have no motivation to produce more than they need. In the latter, proprietors of land and farmers have the opportunity to purchase a range of desirable commodities. Consequently, they 'study agriculture as a science [...], redouble their industry and attention', and, as a result, produce more from the land than they need for mere survival.[26] In most societies, Hume explained, the emergence of manufacturing was a consequence of the development of foreign trade and, more specifically, the introduction of luxury goods. The power of such products lay in their sudden entry on to the market; whereas domestic manufactures 'advance by slow degrees' and lack the capacity to 'affect us by their novelty', foreign commodities are experienced as something entirely new.[27] At the same time, the profit available through trading abroad is high, as goods that are unwanted and cheap in one country can be non-reproducible, highly desirable and consequently expensive in another locale. This ensured that it was overseas commerce that had provided the objects that could attract people's previously latent avarice. Through it 'men become acquainted with the *pleasures* of luxury and the *profits* of commerce; and their *delicacy* and *industry*, being once awaken'd, carry them to farther improvements, in every branch of domestic as well as foreign trade'.[28] What is particularly significant is that the historical narrative that Hume develops here is a 'general' history; as such, it depends not on the actions of particular elite individuals, but rather on a 'general' cause – the introduction of luxury goods – which exerts an influence on the passions of the multitude.

This 'general' approach to commercial history helped Hume to define his place within existing economic debates. Despite being the most important aspect of public affairs, he argued, commerce and finance were 'commonly treated in the loosest and most careless manner', with writers building their analyses on a series of 'groundless' assumptions.[29] In contrast to this, Hume emphasised, his own work would be concerned with a 'multitude of cases' and 'universal propositions, which comprehend under them an infinite number of individuals'.[30] These would then be used, albeit with extreme caution and an awareness of possible exceptions, to establish 'general principles'.[31] Such a 'refin'd' and 'subtile' method, Hume argued, was 'uncommon' and 'out of the common road'.[32] It served, however, to highlight the magnitude of the errors committed by previous economic commentators. Underpinning their conceptions of finance and commerce was an understanding of 'plenty of money' as the cause of national prosperity.[33] To an extent, this idea was simply misguided; as Hume forcefully demonstrated, the level of money in a country would naturally adjust itself to the level of industry, thereby ensuring that any sudden acquisition or loss of specie had no long-term consequences. Equally, however, attempts to retain money could be highly pernicious, as they led nations to adopt 'bars, obstructions, and imposts' on the movement of goods, which served to 'check industry, and rob ourselves and our neighbours of the common benefits of art and nature'.[34] The point being made here, it should be emphasised, was not that such regulations were wrong *per se*. Indeed, Hume endorsed a tax on German linen as it encouraged 'home manufactures, and thereby [multiplied] our people and industry', and supported the tax on brandy, noting that it increased the sale of rum and supported the southern colonies.[35] In 'Of Taxes', meanwhile, he showed that the general effect of a moderate increase in taxes on commodities was to increase the industry of the poor by obliging them to work harder to maintain their standard of living.[36] Hume's contention, therefore, was that the needs of commerce and industry, phenomena that could only be understood through a knowledge of people's natural passions and desires, provided the criteria for assessing economic policy.

2. Hume's *History of England*

The *History of England* was anchored in the broad historiographical framework that Hume had established in 'Of the Rise of the Arts and Sciences'. The result, as Pocock has argued, was a work written in 'the double key of political narrative and sociological generalisation'.[37] On the one hand, therefore, Hume conceived of his history in classical terms as a narrative of the deeds performed by particular individuals.[38] Indeed, as the letters he wrote in the period surrounding the publication of the *History* demonstrate, his aim was to overcome the failings in 'style, judgement, impartiality, [and] care' of previous historians of England by mimicking the practices of classical historiography.[39] Party polemics, transcribed documents, pedantic footnotes and the trivial and frivolous were all avoided and replaced by what Hume referred to as a conciseness 'after the manner of the Ancients'.[40] On the other hand, however, Hume provided a general 'cultural' history, an account of the various shifts in manners and opinions experienced by the general mass of England's population as they moved from a state of barbarism to one of civilisation.[41] And it was, for Hume, manners and opinions that determined the character of a particular age, shaping its approach to matters such as government, military affairs, learning and commerce. To an extent, and in the manner Hume had anticipated in the *Essays*, these different 'keys' of history are integrated. Indeed, Hume's main point is that the political upheavals of the seventeenth century cannot be understood without a knowledge of England's changing social and economic structure.

In structural terms, however, the 'general' cultural analysis is often separated from the main narrative. Sometimes this simply involves inserting a paragraph of contextual material into the discussion or an explanatory note. Elsewhere, the treatment of such issues is attached to the 'characters' of monarchs given after the narration of their deaths; as a consequence, these sections come to deal as much with the disposition of the age as they do with that of a particular king or queen. On four occasions, with regard to Norman, Saxon, Elizabethan and Jacobean England, Hume devotes a complete chapter to such issues. These sections are conceived of as, in a sense, separate from the 'main' historical project. In the first edition of the Stuarts' volume, Hume introduced his Jacobean chapter as a 'pause' in his account, which departed 'a little from the historical style'.[42]

This phrase was deleted in later versions of the text, but the labelling of the four 'cultural' chapters as 'appendices' in all editions from 1762 onwards served, perhaps more effectively, to emphasise their distinctiveness from the rest of the text. Equally, however, while such sections may not have quite been 'history', they were of vital importance to it. In relation to the Stuarts' volume, Hume noted that without 'cultural' information 'history can be very little instructive, and often will not be intelligible'.[43] A similar point was made in a more forceful manner before the non-narrative section concerning Charles I and the Interregnum, when Hume observed that 'The chief use of history is, that it affords materials for disquisitions of this nature; and it seems the duty of an historian to point out the proper inferences and conclusions.'[44]

Commerce and finance occupied a complex place within this schema. The narrative section of Hume's account is concerned with commercial and financial issues in so far as they directly shaped or provided a context for political events. Indeed, one of Hume's key aims was to show that the Civil War was, in part, a consequence of 'general' changes in England's social structure produced by the rise of commerce. His discussion of commerce in the non-narrative sections, meanwhile, accomplished three principal tasks. First, he outlined the organisation and extent of government revenue and commerce at particular moments in time. To provide a sense of perspective, particularly in relation to commerce, English approaches were then contrasted both with those of other European nations from the same period and contemporary practices. Second, he sought to account for changes in England's economic infrastructure. In doing so, Hume developed the analysis of luxury he had forwarded in 'Of Commerce', fusing it with the account of changes in property ownership advanced by, among others, Bacon, Harrington and Bolingbroke. The result was a cultural history of commerce that conceived of England's commercial development over the *longue durée* as a product of a shift in the way in which the passions of the multitude functioned. Third, and in spite of this, Hume continued to believe that commerce had a political history made up of the specific commercial and financial measures pursued by individual monarchs. As an account of 'the few' – individual monarchs and, on occasion, the small cabal of ministers who surrounded them – this history was shaped by chance or unknown causes. 'General' principles, however, were also important to such an endeavour. As Hume had demonstrated in his discussion of the arts and sciences, to be fully understood the actions of the few needed to be placed in the wider context of 'general' cultural history. Moreover, the 'general' principles concerning commerce that Hume had established in *Political Discourses* provided the criteria by which he judged the successes, and more commonly failures, of England's monarchs in the *History*.

The next three sections explore the way in which these ideas were developed in Hume's account. My treatment of the material here will be chronological by order of publication, and thus begins with discussion of the Stuarts, before moving on to the Tudor and then pre-Tudor volumes. To reflect the structure of Hume's analysis the accounts of the Tudors and Stuarts will be divided into two subsections. The first will look at the narrative part of Hume's analysis, where the economic material is primarily concerned with issues relating to finance. The second will be concerned with the non-narrative appendices and focus on their analyses of commerce. The less detailed discussion of pre-Tudor economic issues will be dealt with in a single section.

3.1 The Stuarts: narrative

The primary importance of Jacobean history, as Hume conceived of it, lay in its capacity to explain the origins of the conflict between 'Privilege & Prerogative' which had generated the modern party system, and which, as such, continued to shape English political life.[45] Hume was aware, as many previous historians had been, that disagreements regarding James's handling of revenue had played a key part in determining the period's emerging battle lines. His approach to the antagonists, however, as discussed in the narrative part of the first volume of his *History*, was at odds with that of both Whig and Tory accounts. Key to these analyses, as we have seen, had been an attempt to attribute blame. Thus for Whig writers, James's absolutist designs had led him to embark on a programme of revenue-raising that went against established constitutional precedents and threatened the liberties of the populace. For Tory historians, meanwhile, responsibility for the conflict lay with a group of power-hungry Presbyterians and Republicans who, in order to advance their own selfish agenda, had used Parliament to reject the monarch's legitimate requests for revenue. Hume had no sympathy with this sort of polemic. Indeed, rather than viewing the conflict as the product of an unwarranted power seizure from either king or commons, he sought to show how disagreements had emerged from a series of complex shifts in England's 'general' circumstances.

The key context for Hume was, in a sense, intellectual. In the first years of the seventeenth century, he argued:

> the minds of men, thro'out all Europe, but especially in England, seem to have undergone a general, but insensible revolution. Tho' letters had been revived in the preceding age, they had been little cultivated beyond the limits of the college; nor had they, till now, begun to spread themselves, in any degree, among men of the world. Arts, both mechanical and liberal, were every day receiving great improvements. Navigation had extended itself over the whole globe. Travelling was secure and agreeable. And the general system of politics, in Europe, was becoming more enlarged and comprehensive.[46]

However, just as the force of this revolution was different in England and mainland Europe, so were its effects. In the former, it was argued:

> the love of freedom, which, unless checked, flourishes extremely in all liberal natures, acquired new force, as well as more enlarged views, suitable to that cultivated understanding, which became, every day, more common, among men of birth and education.[47]

On the Continent, however, 'where the necessity of discipline had begot mercenary armies, the prince commonly established an unlimited authority, and overpowered [...] the liberties of the people'.[48] For Hume, the actions of the commons, specifically their increasing desire to defend their 'privileges', were a direct product of the English form of this 'general revolution'. The King's behaviour, meanwhile, was shaped by his contrasting understandings of English and European developments. 'Happily', Hume noted, he was entirely ignorant of the transformation taking placed in England, possessing 'neither sufficient capacity to perceive the alteration, nor sufficient art and vigour to check it in its early advances'.[49] Equally, however, he had full knowledge of the powers exercised by other European princes, even if he was unaware of how recently they had been acquired. It was this that led him to claim, even though he lacked the military backing of his fellow monarchs, the same kind of rights that they enjoyed and to assume, as they did, that his power was divine in origin.

The tensions between monarch and people created by such developments were further exacerbated by England's economic situation. The discovery and conquest of the West Indies in the 1490s, Hume argued, had produced a rise in the price of goods that served to reduce the relative wealth of the monarch. As a result, not only did the royal income fail to rise in proportion to that of his subjects, but the pressure for expenditure increased as improvements in 'art and industry' raised the expectations and financial demands of royal servants, courtiers and ministers.[50] At the same time, however, the very gold that had undermined the King's position also turned the populace against him. As Hume noted, 'riches', in association with the 'increasing knowledge of the age', produced in the people 'a spirit of freedom and independence, [disposing] them to pay little regard, either to the entreaties or menaces of their sovereign'.[51] Drawing on Harringtonian ideas about the relationship between property and power, Hume went on to attribute the origins of this 'spirit' to an alteration in landownership.[52] The 'increase of commerce' and regulations permitting the barons to alienate their lands had shifted the 'ballance of property' from the lords to the commons.[53] This development initially served to strengthen the influence of the monarchy, as free from the threat of the peers, sovereigns were able to expand their prerogative to the point where it threatened the survival of the constitution. Ultimately, however, the commons 'recovered from their lethargy' and, no longer tied to the monarch by a shared fear of the disruptive barons, sought 'to secure liberty by firmer barriers, than their ancestors had hitherto provided for it'.[54]

For Hume, it was the simultaneous presence of a necessitous monarch, with only a limited understanding of the contemporary economic situation, and an increasingly wealthy, knowledgeable and rebellious commons that had generated the period's disputes about revenue. The King, Hume emphasised, desirous of raising his 'pomp and splendor' to the levels enjoyed by previous English monarchs and contemporary European ones, sought to enlarge his revenue.[55] The newly acquired 'spirit and judgement' of the House of Commons, however, led it to protect what it considered its privileges, and attempt a series of economic reforms.[56] Constitutional precedent, meanwhile, provided only limited help in adjudicating between conflicting claims. On occasions, the problem here was a lack of clarity. Describing James's attempts to increase his income through raising customs and levying new impositions on goods, Hume noted that 'the precedents for so dangerous an exercise of power were neither very recent nor very numerous'.[57] However, the fact that there were precedents in the reigns of Mary and Elizabeth served 'to throw a kind of doubt and ambiguity on this question, which was of so great moment to the constitution'.[58] Elsewhere, measures advanced by the King and opposed by the Commons – for example monopolies – were supported by 'many and recent precedents'.[59] They remained, nonetheless, both 'diametrically opposite to all the principles of a free government' and highly damaging to the nation's growing commercial interests.[60]

Hume's account, therefore, was premised on the notion that the origins of the struggle between privilege and prerogative could not be understood without an account of the ways in which general, contextual factors shaped action. This is not to claim, it should be emphasised, that his account was rooted in a form of economic determinism. As he made clear though a series of counterfactual speculations, war was not inevitable. If the King had possessed 'a very rigid frugality' or if the Commons had acted 'with more generosity and kindness', events would have unfolded in a very different way.[61] Moreover, as the *History* consistently emphasised, the conflict would not have taken the direction it did without the pernicious influence of religious enthusiasm. Nevertheless, it was through giving 'general' factors a much more significant role than other writers that Hume was able to reduce the culpability of both the Commons and the King. Thus, despite accepting the argument of Salmon and Carte that the Commons were an innovating force, by presenting the lower house's actions as part of a wider, intellectual and economic shift, Hume was able to account for and justify their actions. Similarly, while Hume's discussion of changes in the balance of property has something in common with Bolingbroke's equally Harringtonian account, there is an alteration of emphasis. Bolingbroke had used James's failure to act in a manner appropriate for a 'popular' polity as evidence of his fundamental demerit, emphasising both that the conduct of his predecessor and the 'constitution' provided clear markers of the sort of conduct required.[62] Hume, in contrast, maintained that the King's only crime – if it could be so labelled – was his failure to fully comprehend a series of complex and highly novel circumstances. What James lacked, therefore, was not virtue, but knowledge and understanding of economic and intellectual change.

3.2 The Stuarts: non-narrative

Ideas regarding knowledge and understanding were also key to Hume's account of commerce in the non-narrative sections of the Stuarts' volume. James's reign, Hume sought to demonstrate in the first of the Stuart 'appendix' chapters, was a time of rapid economic development. Indeed, 'during no period of English history, was there a more sensible increase [...] of all the advantages, which distinguish a flourishing people'.[63] When judged in relation to other European countries of the time and modern standards, however, the nation's commerce appeared rather less successful. The Dutch, it was noted, possessed three times more shipping, and 'all the more elaborate and curious arts were only cultivated abroad, particularly in Italy'.[64] Similarly, 'a catalogue of manufactures, for which the English were then eminent, would appear very contemptible, in comparison of those, which flourish among them at present'.[65] Fine linen manufacture was 'totally unknown', silk manufacture 'had no footing' and, because of a lack of expertise, wool, which accounted for nine-tenths of the commerce of the kingdom, had to be exported to be dyed and dressed.[66]

This general picture of English economic development was then placed alongside an account of James's performance as a manager of the nation's financial and commercial interests. While a range of material is drawn upon, including Rymer's *Foedera* and the *Journal of the House of Commons*, Hume's greatest debt was to Howes, who Hume, under the misapprehension that a single author had written the whole of the *Annales*, referred to as 'Stowe'.[67] Thus Hume utilised the *Annales* as a source, quoted at length from the 'honest' historian's work in a footnote, and endorsed his arguments about the increase in commerce that had taken place under James, arguing that:

> Not only the peace, which he procured, was favorable to industry and commerce: His turn of mind inclined him to promote the peaceful arts: And trade being as yet in its infancy, all additions to it would be the more evident to every eye, which was not blinded by melancholy prejudices.[68]

What distinguished Hume's account from Howes's, however, was its analysis of James's role in these changes. Indeed, whereas the English chronicler provided numerous examples of the King's economic successes, the Scottish historian struggled to find any. A proclamation that James issued against exporting undressed cloth, Hume noted, was deeply unpopular and quickly retracted. His attempt to introduce silk manufacture was defeated by the English climate and he failed to protect English interests in the Spice Islands.[69] Moreover, when James did recommend wise measures, such as 'greater freedom of trade and an exemption from the restraint of exclusive companies', the opposition he faced from 'men [...] imprisoned by their own prejudices' made him, understandably in Hume's estimation, reluctant to force the issue.[70]

Similar differences are also apparent in Hume's and Howes's treatment of the North American colonies. Howes would surely have endorsed Hume's pronouncement that it was the commencement of the American colonies which 'chiefly renders the reign of James memorable'.[71] For Hume, however, this achievement was only indirectly attributable to the reigning monarch. The colonies had been 'peopled', he argued, by a group of 'necessitous and indigent' individuals, who were discontented with the established Church and monarchy and who had done little to increase the wealth or the population at home.[72] Possessed of 'the spirit of independency, which was reviving in England', in America it was these individuals, not the monarch, who 'promoted the navigation, encouraged the industry, and even multiplied the inhabitants of their mother-country'.[73] His views, meanwhile, are made even clearer in his concluding comments. Outlining the relative progress of commerce and learning in the Jacobean era, Hume noted: 'the endeavours of James, *or more properly speaking*, *those of the nation*, for the promotion of trade, were attended with greater success than those for the encouragement of learning'.[74]

Hume's conception of the relationship between 'general' and 'particular' history here is a complex one. To an extent, while he moves rapidly between the two modes, they remain causally unconnected; James may well have been an ineffective manager of the nation's commercial interests, but commerce, agriculture and manufacture continued to improve at an expeditious rate. Equally, however, there was a sense in which 'general' factors shaped 'particular' actions. Underlying Hume's analysis is a conception of economic affairs as a discrete area of knowledge. In James's reign, however, a series of 'general' factors had prevented this knowledge from making any headway. Self-interested tradesmen, seeking to protect their own monopolies, had resisted reforms successfully, and, as a result, the King's wiser actions had been defeated by the prejudice of the times. Consequently, knowledge had exerted little influence on policy.

These ideas shaped the rest of the Stuarts' volume. The whole period, Hume maintained, was one of rapid and accelerating economic growth. During the 'peaceable' part of Charles's reign, 'commerce and industry [...] encreased extremely' and, although trade met with some 'convulsions' as a result of the Civil War, 'it soon recovered after the establishment of the Commonwealth'.[75] Commerce, meanwhile, 'did never, during any period, encrease so fast as from the restoration to the revolution'.[76] Such developments are explained as products of three principal triggers. First, the ongoing persecution of religious minorities both in England and abroad is shown to have produced a series of beneficial economic consequences. The severities exercised by Laud ensured that by the start of the Civil War, 25,000 people were resident in New England, while the oppression of the Catholics following the Civil War helped to populate Maryland.[77] Later, the restraints imposed on Dissenters served to further expand the colonies and helped to ensure that England's shipping doubled between the Restoration and the Glorious Revolution.[78] At the same time, knowledge of dyeing woollen cloth, an innovation that saved England 'great sums of money', was brought to England by a Dutchman, who fled the Low Countries fearing a French invasion.[79]

Second, English commerce had benefited from a series of fortuitous military conflicts. Hume's position here was by no means a straightforward one. He believed, in general, that peace was necessary for commerce.[80] At the same time, he was unconvinced that war against a trading rival would necessarily, as was widely assumed, bring commercial benefits. As he argued in relation to the Anglo-Dutch conflicts:

> even were the naval force of Holland totally annihilated, the acquisition of the Dutch commerce to England could not be relied on as a certain consequence; nor is trade a constant attendant of power, but depends on many other, and some of them very delicate, circumstances.[81]

Despite such observations, however, Hume maintained that, in England's case, war *had* proven to be advantageous. The conflicts with the Dutch during the Interregnum, 'by distressing the commerce of so formidable a rival, served to encourage trade in England'.[82]

Similarly, the two Dutch wars waged under Charles II, 'by disturbing the trade of that republic, promoted the navigation of this island; and after Charles had made a separate peace with the States, his subjects enjoyed unmolested the trade of Europe'.[83]

Finally, Hume argued that the ascendancy of 'democratical principles' following the regicide produced an important cultural shift in English views on trade, as country gentlemen became willing to apprentice their sons to merchants, and commerce became 'more honourable in England than in any other Europæan kingdom'.[84] England's commercial ascendancy, therefore, is presented as an unforeseen and unintended consequence of three of Hume's principal bugbears: religious intolerance, war and republicanism. In no sense was it the product of a deliberate strategy pursued by the nation's monarchs. Indeed, it is not until the reign of James II that Hume was able to find examples of a Stuart encouraging trade in a 'judicious' manner.[85]

4.1 The Tudors: narrative

Writing to the physician John Clephane in September 1757, Hume announced his plans to extend his history to cover the reigns of the Tudor kings. 'I wish, indeed', he observed,

> I had begun [with the reign of Henry VII]: For by that means, I should have been able, without making any digression, by the plain course of the narration, to have shown how absolute the authority was, which the English Kings then possessed, and that the Stuarts did little or nothing more than continue matters in the former tract, which the people were determined no longer to admit.[86]

In the narrative sections of his account, Hume developed this thesis by emphasising that arbitrary measures were a consistent feature of the financial practices of the Tudor monarchs. With regard to Henry VII, Hume paraphrased Bacon's discussion of the various perversions of the law through which the King, aided by his 'instruments of oppression' Empson and Dudley, raised his income.[87] Attention is also drawn to Henry VIII's attempt to arbitrarily impose taxes on his people in 1525, and his more successful schemes for seizing goods and land from the monasteries, and demanding loans and benevolences from his subjects.[88] In relation to Elizabeth, meanwhile, Hume used material from the transcripts assembled by the antiquarian Simonds

D'Ewes to provide some detailed discussion of parliamentary debates that had taken place concerning the Queen's various monopolies.[89] The arbitrary programme of the Tudors, he argued, had serious economic consequences for England's populace. Henry VII is presented as 'enriching himself with the spoils of his oppressed people', while Elizabeth's monopolies are said to have put 'invincible restraints upon all commerce, industry, and emulation'.[90] As a consequence, these latter measures constituted grievances that were 'the most intolerable for the present, and the most pernicious in their consequences, that ever were known in any age or under any government'.[91]

Hume's primary interest, however, was less in the economic consequences of such incidents than their significance for Tudor politics. Arbitrary monarchical impositions, he maintained, were an unintended consequence of the populace's ancient privileges. These privileges ensured, as was noted with regard to Henry VII, that the English were secured 'from all taxations and impositions, except such as were levied by their own consent'.[92] 'Had the King', Hume continued, 'been empowered to lay on general taxes at his pleasure, he would naturally have abstained from these oppressive expedients, which destroyed all security in private property, and begot an universal diffidence thro' the nation.'[93] Similarly, Elizabeth's limited income ensured that she lacked the financial means to reward those persons who had distinguished themselves in military and civil employments, and, consequently, had turned to monopolies to raise revenue.[94]

However, while such measures may have had their origins in financial weakness, that monarchs were consistently able to employ them demonstrated both the strength of the Crown and the supine nature of Parliament. Henry VII, for example, had such power over his parliamentarians that they were willing to make Dudley, 'the very man who was the chief instrument of [the King's] oppressions', their speaker.[95] Henry VIII, meanwhile, through his use of prerogative, imprisonment and extorted loans, became 'in a manner, absolute master of the person and property of every individual'.[96] Hume's most detailed discussion of parliamentary weakness, however, came in his account of monopolies, which he presented as a corrective for those who 'are prepossessed with an idea of the antient privileges of the people, and of the liberty enjoyed under the administration of Elizabeth'.[97] In the 1601 debate about monopolies, the Commons asserted that:

> The Queen possessed both an enlarging and a restraining power: by her prerogative she might set at liberty what was restrained by statute or otherwise, and by her prerogative she might restrain what was otherwise at liberty: That the royal prerogative was not to be canvassed nor disputed nor examined; and did not even admit of any limitation: That absolute princes, such as the sovereigns of England, were a species of divinity: That it was in vain to attempt tying the Queen's hands by laws or statutes; since, by means of her dispensing power, she could loosen herself at her pleasure [...].[98]

Hume went on to summarise the Commons' reaction to Elizabeth's decision to cancel the most grievous of the patents, drawing on material from D'Ewes:

> A member said, with tears in his eyes, that, if a sentence of everlasting happiness had been pronounced in his favour, he could not have felt more joy than that with which he was at present overwhelmed. [...] And it was farther remarked, that in the same manner as the Deity would not give his glory to another, so the Queen herself was the only agent in their present prosperity and happiness.[99]

What is perhaps most noticeable about Hume's account here is the information he does not include. Specifically, no mention is made of the sections of the debate, covered at length in his source material, where speakers, among them Sir Francis Bacon and Sir Walter Raleigh, defended the social and economic efficacy of some types of monopoly. Indeed, Hume's account assumed that there was an agreement concerning the pernicious nature of patents. As a result, Hume was able to use the monopolies debate to emphasise the shared sentiments that underlay the comments made by the various speakers, and to show that these sentiments were 'more worthy of a Turkish divan than of an English house of commons, according to our present idea of this assembly'.[100] Such a methodology served two purposes. On the one hand, it supported the claim that Hume had made in his letter to Clephane. As he presented them, the Stuart kings were not the unconstitutional innovators of Whiggish accounts, but were acting in accordance with well-established and widely supported ideas about English government. On the other hand, however, it served to emphasise the historical distance that lay between the mid-eighteenth and early seventeenth centuries. For Hume, the Elizabethan world he was describing, with its sycophantic and lachrymose parliamentarians, was one that was alien to the present to the point of absurdity. To comprehend the politics of the period, however, it was necessary to acquire some sort of understanding of the opinions and 'general' values on which government had been based.

4.2 The Tudors: non-narrative

Such an approach ensured that, while the tone of Hume's discussion of Tudor financial practices was sometimes supercilious, he also exhibited a good deal of sympathy for the actions both of monarchs and Parliament. Both, after all, were acting in conformity with established practices. When he came to deal in more detail with the government's management of commerce in the non-narrative sections of his discussion, however, he was a good deal more critical.

In his discussion of Henry VII, Hume provided both an account of the origins of English and European commercial development during the King's reign, and an analysis of Henry's skills in the management of commerce. With regard to the former issue, the *History* built directly on the argument advanced in 'Of Commerce', maintaining that an influx of luxury goods had transformed commerce and manufacture in England, and later, as a consequence, its social structures and political institutions. However, whereas in his essay Hume had offered a historical generalisation – 'in most nations foreign trade has preceded any refinement in home manufactures' – in the *History* he outlined the specific events that had caused these developments to take place in fifteenth-century Europe:

> It was during this reign, on the second of August 1492, a little before sun set, that Christopher Columbus, a Florentine, set out from Cadiz on his memorable voyage for the discovery of the western world; and a few years after, Vasquez de Gama, a Portuguese, passed the cape of Good Hope, and opened a new passage to the East Indies. These great events were attended with the most important consequences to all the nations of Europe, even to such as were not immediately concerned in those naval enterprizes.[101]

The most significant of these consequences, as Hume argued, was a change in the spending habits of the nobility; rather than using their income to fund an army of retainers, they spent their money, and sometimes exhausted it entirely, on luxury goods.[102] Such actions ensured that the common people were no longer 'maintained in a vicious idleness' and 'were obliged to learn some calling or industry'.[103] At the same time, merchants and tradesmen directly benefited from the spending habits of their social superiors, and 'both acquired a share in the landed property, and created to themselves a considerable property of a new kind, in stock, commodities, art, credit, and correspondence'.[104]

These developments meant that, for Hume, as for other historians operating in the Baconian/Harringtonian tradition, Henry VII's reign constituted a key axis in English history. However, while Hume acknowledged the role played by Henry in fomenting beneficial political change, his contributions to commercial policy are presented as a good deal less successful. The reasons for this distinction lay in the nature of the subjects:

> The more simple ideas of order and equity are sufficient to guide a legislator in every thing that regards the internal administration of justice: But the principles of commerce are much more complicated, and require long experience and deep reflection to be well understood in any state.[105]

To an extent, Hume's comments here echo his earlier statements concerning the difficulties inherent in commercial affairs. Their function, however, was rather different. In 'Of Commerce', Hume had sought to prepare his readers for an approach to commerce and finance that was 'refin'd', 'subtile' and 'out of the common road'.[106] Here, however, Hume's concern is with the pre-history of this understanding of commerce. As he observed, these matters were 'often misunderstood' during Henry's reign, and 'even in the age of Lord Bacon, very imperfect and erroneous ideas were formed on that subject'.[107]

It is this conception of Tudor and Stuart ignorance concerning commerce that shaped Hume's engagement with the work of Bacon and Camden. In relation to Henry VII, Hume repeated and endorsed Bacon's account of the King's character. It was, therefore, avarice that shaped Henry's conduct and led him, ever anxious to increase his customs revenue, 'to encourage commerce'.[108] However, whereas Bacon had seen this encouragement as producing a series of beneficial regulations, for Hume 'trade and industry were rather hurt than promoted by the care and attention which were given to them'.[109] In demonstrating this, Hume did not use Bacon as a source, but rather followed his methodological lead by turning to the statute book and basing his analysis on the King's record as a lawmaker. To give a sense of the general approach Hume took, a series of examples have been transcribed below:

> Severe laws were made against taking interest for money, which was then denominated usury. Even the profits of exchange were prohibited, as savouring of usury, which the superstition of that age zealously proscribed. All evasive contracts, by which profits could be made from the loan of money, were also carefully guarded against. It is needless to observe how unreasonable and iniquitous these laws, how impossible to be executed, and how hurtful to trade, if they could take place.[110]

> Laws were made against the exportation of money, plate, or bullion: A precaution, which serves no other purpose than to make more be exported.[111]

> Horses were forbid to be exported; as if that exportation did not encourage the breed, and render them more plentiful. To promote archery, no bows were to be sold at a higher price that [*sic*] six shillings and four pence, reducing money to the denomination of our time. The only effect of this regulation must be either that the people would be supplied with bad bows or none at all. Prices were also affixed to woollen cloath, to caps and hats. And labourers wages were regulated by law. It is evident, that these circumstances ought always to be left free, and must be trusted to the common course of business and commerce.[112]

> There is a law of this reign, containing a preamble, from which it appears, that the company of merchant adventures in London, had, by their own proper authority, debarred all the other merchants of the kingdom, from trading to the great marts in the low countries, unless each trader previously payed them the sum of near seventy pounds. It is surprising that such a by-law (if it deserves that name) could ever be carried into execution, and that the authority of Parliament should be requisite to abrogate it.[113]

Hume's concern in these examples, as Bacon's had been, was not with the specific empirical consequences of Henry's legislation, and neither writer provided evidence to explore the ways in which legal changes had affected England's fortunes. Rather, the laws themselves are the sole source material referred to, and an assessment of the King's success is made by measuring his actions against a normative conception of good economic practice. Where the two writers differed, however, was in their conception of these norms. Bacon conceived of commerce as a powerful, unruly force that required careful regulation if it was to advance national interests. Prices, wages, interest rates, navigation and the organisation of individual trades and markets could, he argued, all benefit from legal control. Hume, in contrast, maintained that people's natural avaricious desires were the key shaping factor in producing the world's economy, something that he conceived of as a large, complex, but highly propitious economic system. Legislators, for Hume, still had a significant role to play in maintaining the order and justice that commercial exchange required, and in establishing a series of mechanisms for equitably collecting government revenue. At the same time, government could encourage industry, as Henry VII had done, by providing loans for his people.[114] However, matters such as prices, wages, interest rates and the organisation of individual trades and markets should emerge naturally as products of interactions between sellers and consumers. For Bacon, therefore, a history of economic development was necessarily an elite history, a narrative of how politicians had regulated commerce. Hume, however, as he had argued in 'The Rise and Progress of the Arts and Sciences', and demonstrated in 'Of Commerce', saw 'the Increase of Trade and Industry' and the 'Rise and Progress of Commerce' as developments requiring general analysis.[115] Nevertheless, within Hume's schema an elite account had a role to play either in showing how legislators had supported such 'general' developments or, as was the case with Henry VII, by examining how their actions had impeded them.

Bacon and Hume also conceived of the function of their analyses in contrasting ways. The former was careful to establish the basic economic principles contained within Henry's actions. For example, the law preventing wines being imported in anything but English ships was said to have arisen from the King subordinating plenty to power, while his regulation of the price of cloth was based on the notion not of 'prescribing prices, but stinting them not to exceed a rate'.[116] The implication here, in line with standard humanist ideas about history, was that these principles were still relevant, and that the reader might learn from the wise acts performed by historical figures. Hume also traced the ideas underlying Henry's actions, but, in rejecting them, did not seek to justify his own economic principles. No attempt was made, therefore, to explain why restricting exports of specie caused more to be exported, or why wages and prices 'must be trusted to the common course of business and commerce'.[117] Similarly, it was 'needless to observe' the negative consequences that resulted from prohibitions on usury.[118] The interested reader could, of course, find ample support for these principles both in Hume's essays and in a range of other works of political economy. However, the key feature of Hume's polemical strategy was, in a sense, his failure to develop his argument further. The ostensible assumption of the passages is that, while these principles may have been entirely alien to those such as Henry and Bacon living in Tudor and Stuart England, for his polite eighteenth-century readership they were obvious to the point of being self-evident.

Similar ideas underlay Hume's account of Elizabeth's management of commerce. The Queen's awareness that England was dependent on its naval power made her, Hume argued, 'desirous to encourage commerce and navigation'.[119] Some success was achieved in this area, and Hume provided details of the Queen's role in expanding the number of ships and protecting the interests of English merchants in the face of aggression from the Hans Towns.[120] Nevertheless, 'the general train of her conduct was very ill calculated to serve the purpose at which she aimed'.[121] The key problem was the Queen's monopolies, which worked to 'extinguish all domestic industry' and acted as 'an immediate check on foreign trade'.[122] Hume went on to argue that 'the spirit of the age was strongly bent on naval enterprizes', and proceeded to examine the profitable trade links that England forged over the course of Elizabeth's reign.[123] However, his point here is that these developments were achieved in spite of, not because of, monarchical support. With regard to the East Indies and Turkey, Hume simply noted the Queen's role in granting patents and, as a consequence, confining trade.[124] In relation to Russia, however, a more extended analysis was provided which, paraphrasing Camden's *Annales*, discussed the founding of the Muscovy Company and its acquirement of an exclusive patent for Russian trade; the successful attempt by the Tsar John Basilides ('a most furious tyrant') to obtain an alliance with Elizabeth; his unsuccessful attempt to secure an English wife; the trading of the Muscovy Company in Russia; and the attitude of Basilides' successor Theodore to trade.[125] Within these discussions, Hume acknowledged that the exclusive patent granted by John Basilides had encouraged the English trade. Ultimately, however, his conclusion drew attention to Elizabeth's failings:

> After the death of John Basilides, his son Theodore revoked the patent, which the English enjoyed for a monopoly of the Russian trade; and when the Queen remonstrated against this innovation, he told her ministers, that princes must carry an indifferent hand, as well between their subjects as between foreigners; and not convert trade, which by the laws of nations ought to be common to all, into a monopoly for the private gain of a few. So much juster notions of commerce were entertained by this barbarian, than were practised by the renowned Queen Elizabeth![126]

A comparison between Hume's account of this incident and that of other historians is instructive. Camden passed over this incident without comment. Rapin and Salmon, seemingly unwilling to acknowledge that a tyrant might lecture Elizabeth on trade, ignored it. Guthrie, focusing on the resolution of the crisis, saw it as further evidence of Elizabeth's skills as a statesman.[127] Carte, meanwhile, drew attention to the fact that, in defending liberty of trade, the Tsar argued the case 'very reasonably'.[128] Hume would clearly have endorsed such a verdict. However, it is noteworthy that, uniquely among the sources discussed, he used the incident to develop a direct criticism of the Queen's commercial policy. Indeed, as his jaunty exclamation mark implies, Hume revels in demonstrating that Elizabeth's reign was not a glorious age of monarchical commercial endeavour, but rather, in economic terms, a period of sub-barbarian ignorance.

5. The early history of England

The concluding part of Hume's discussion of economic affairs in the pre-Tudor volumes of the *History* performed two principal tasks. First, he developed an explanation of the reasons why commerce had been unable to prosper in England until the latter part of the period. Second, he provided an analysis of the changes that had ultimately enabled a successful trading culture to emerge. The result was both a direct challenge to the approaches of Rapin and Carte and the development of a pre-history to the analysis he had advanced in 'Of Commerce'.

For Hume, the avaricious desires of the populace functioned as the key motor driving economic development. While, as had been the case in the *Essays*, he treated these desires as innate, certain conditions were shown to be required to direct individuals towards economically useful forms of industry. In England's early history these conditions were entirely absent. Economic activity, Hume maintained, required a stable and equitable legal system with the capacity to protect private property; without this, individuals could not have confidence that they would receive any benefits from their work. The precariousness of property within both Saxon government and the feudal system that emerged under the Normans served, as a consequence, to reduce the potential for profit from trade and manufacture, and fundamentally inhibited these activities.[129] At the same time, the period's primitive bellicosity was incompatible with labour and commerce. The habitual plundering of the Danes, for example, rendered them 'incapable of industry'.[130] Under feudalism 'every profession was held in contempt but that of arms' and any merchant or manufacturer who acquired a degree of opulence 'found himself but the more exposed to injuries, from the envy and avidity of the military nobles'.[131] A few exceptional individuals, foremost among them Alfred the Great, had been able to transcend the values of their time and successfully promote England's commercial interests.[132] Ultimately, however, the long-term effects of such actions were negligible. Deprived of the peace and order it required to prosper, England's commerce remained in a consistently 'low' and 'languishing' state.[133]

To explain how this commercial backwardness was overcome, Hume provided both a general and a more specific argument. The general argument was built on the assumption that the upshot of encounters between relative refinement and relative barbarity would be the civilising of the latter by the former. A key example of this process came in Hume's discussion of the spread of Christianity from the conquered ancient Britons to the conquering pagan Saxons. The hostilities between the two peoples 'naturally' indisposed the Saxons against the faith of the Britons.[134] Nonetheless, he continued,

> however limited in their views [the Saxons were], they could not but have perceived a degree of cultivation in the southern counties [of Britain] beyond what they themselves possessed; and it was natural for them to yield to that superior knowledge, as well as zeal, by which the inhabitants of the Christian kingdoms were even at this time distinguished.[135]

Similarly, when the English Court became filled with Normans during the reign of Edward the Confessor, the fact that the new arrivals were 'distinguished, both by the favour of Edward, and by a degree of cultivation somewhat superior to that of the English in those ages, soon rendered their language, customs and laws fashionable in the kingdom'.[136]

These developments were aided by a specific alteration in English government. The demise of the feudal system in the thirteenth century, Hume argued, had caused a diminution both of the power and revenue of English monarchs. In order to restore their position, therefore, monarchs sought inspiration abroad:

> During the course of two centuries, the kings of England, in imitation of other European princes, had embraced the salutary policy of encouraging and protecting the lower and more industrious orders of the state; whom they found well disposed to obey the laws and civil magistrate, and whose ingenuity and labour furnished commodities, requisite for the ornament of peace and support of war.[137]

Initially, this encouragement took the form of a series of measures that enabled citizens to 'enjoy unmolested the fruits of their industry', including 'liberty of trade' and permission to farm their own tolls and customs.[138] Later, to facilitate the raising of revenue, Edward I had initiated a system where local boroughs sent two deputies to Parliament, with the power to consent, on behalf of those they represented, to measures forwarded by the King and his council. These reforms laid the foundation for a 'free and equitable government' and resulted, in time, in the emergence of the third estate.[139] 'And by this means', Hume concluded, a section of the population, 'formerly so abject in England, as well as in all other European nations, rose by slow degrees to their present importance; and in their progress made arts and commerce, the necessary attendants of liberty and equality, flourish in the kingdom.'[140]

To an extent, the effect of Hume's analysis was to emphasise the fundamental remoteness of medieval history. For Hume, as for writers such as Brady, Salmon and the Court Whig authors, this was a period in which the economic features that defined modern society existed only, at best, in primitive form and were little understood by contemporary observers. As a consequence, the *History* was not exemplary in the manner of earlier accounts. There was little that a modern politician could learn about commerce by observing the workings of a society that was entirely different to his own, and in which economic knowledge was grossly inferior to the present. Despite this, however, there remained an important didactic component to Hume's analysis. By tracing the transition from a non-commercial society to a primitive commercial one in the medieval volumes, he provided an account of the preconditions necessary for economic activity. Like government, it was emphasised, commerce was dependent on opinion. A tradesman needed to have confidence that property would be respected, and he needed to feel valued within the society of which he formed a part. Hume was, of course, aware that commerce had evolved a good deal since these foundations were established. Equally, however, as foundational values, these patterns of opinion played a fundamental role in holding up the commercial edifice on which English prosperity was based. As a consequence, his account provided both a powerful demonstration of the need to preserve England's commercial foundations, and a warning regarding the consequences – essentially a return to the barbarism of the early medieval period – of not heeding history's lessons.

6. Revisions to the *History of England*

While Hume was initially disappointed both by the critical reception and sales of his history, particularly with regard to its first two volumes, the work was to be a considerable success, spawning a successful French translation and multiple further editions in his lifetime. In preparing these new editions, Hume made a number of changes to the text, correcting errors, revising the phrasing and, on occasion, adding whole new paragraphs and sections.[141] The most significant of these alterations were to the sections of the *History* concerning the Stuarts where, as previous commentators have noted, Hume adapted his analysis in the wake of his concerns about popular unrest both in England and the North American colonies.[142] Equally importantly, however, these later editions saw Hume rework and expand his commentary on England's financial history.

The key changes he made concerned James's approach to taxation. In the first edition of the Stuarts' volume, as we have seen, Hume had argued that the attempts James made to levy impositions on merchandise had been based on precedents 'neither very recent nor very numerous'.[143] The research he completed on the Tudors, however, led him to substantially revise this verdict. In the 1762 edition of the text, the comment on the lack of precedents was deleted, and instead, after noting the existence of the impositions, Hume observed: 'This exercise of power will naturally, to us, appear arbitrary and illegal; yet, according to the principles and practices of that time, it might admit of some apology.'[144] Hume went on to provide just such an apology, explaining that the fact that Parliament had gifted the duties of tonnage and poundage to Henry V and all succeeding monarchs 'for life' led monarchs to consider these sources of income as their 'own proper right and inheritance'.[145] Equally, it was natural for the King to question the rates of poundage, given that these rates had been determined before the discovery of the West Indies. He also revised his comments on previous approaches to taxation, noting that 'The King was supported [...] by two direct precedents, one in the reign of Mary, another in the beginning of Elizabeth.'[146] These comments were then further strengthened in the 1773 edition, when Hume once again rephrased his account, this time arguing that the King had been supported by 'direct precedents, some in the reign of Mary, some in the beginning of Elizabeth'.[147] An extended footnote was provided to justify this assertion. The overall effect of such changes, and similar alterations made to the non-narrative sections of the text, was to reduce still further James's personal culpability for the arbitrary practices followed during his reign.[148] Indeed, given the specific situation in which the King found himself and the extent to which his actions were supported by precedent, it is difficult to see, Hume shows, how he could have acted otherwise.

These revisions concerning James's financial management, it should be emphasised, were not accompanied by any changes to Hume's essential argument regarding the King's handling of commerce. As a result, the gap between his often sympathetic attitude to the monarchical administration of revenue and his critical approach to the commercial aspects of statecraft becomes even more marked in the later editions of the text. In part this was a methodological issue. Hume tended to view matters of revenue as products of a particular context. Commercial schemes, in contrast, were assessed using the sort of 'general' and seemingly universal principles that Hume had laid out in *Political Discourses*. The reasons for such a distinction are hinted at in the final set of revisions that Hume made to the *History* shortly before his death. As part of his remarks on the civil government in England in the Jacobean appendix, Hume had argued that on the accession of the Stuarts, kings of England possessed 'an authority, in the judgement of all, not exactly limited; in the judgement of some, not limitable'.[149] However, he continued, this authority had its roots not in 'money' or 'force of arms', but rather 'merely on the opinion of the people, influenced by antient precedent and example'.[150] It was this that explained the extreme jealousy of monarchs towards their prerogative. In the 1778 edition, Hume added the following sentence to his analysis:

> And it seems a necessary, though perhaps a melancholy truth, that, in every government, the magistrate must either possess a large revenue and a military force, or enjoy some discretionary powers, in order to execute the laws, and support his own authority.[151]

Such comments provide a useful gloss on Hume's contrasting approaches to finance and commerce. For Hume, the power of monarchs to alter impositions on goods formed a part of their prerogative. The ways in which they used this prerogative in the past had, by contemporary standards, been arbitrary and crude. However, they had been rooted in precedent – the key force in maintaining the authority of government – and they had helped government to fulfil its basic function: the maintenance of order. As such, while Tudor and Stuart monarchs clearly had no conception of the sort of advanced ideas about finance that Hume had discussed in 'Of Taxes', when evaluated using political criteria their actions were justifiable. In relation to commerce, however, an area which for Hume required more complex types of knowledge, the fundamental ignorance of the Tudors and Stuarts meant they had achieved little of real value. Hume's analytical approaches reflected, therefore, the nature of the subjects he discussed. The administration of finance, at its most basic, only required a knowledge of precedent. To manage commerce successfully, however, statesmen needed a sophisticated understanding of a broad range of 'general' material.

Conclusion

Taken in sum, Hume's *History of England* constitutes a rejection of the economic statecraft tradition as outlined over the course of this book. Three points are of particular significance here. First, in so far as previous generations of historians had dealt with economic history, they had conceived of it as the study of economic policy. 'Exemplary', Livian accounts maintained that, just as virtuous monarchs produced good policies and commercial success, so self-interested rulers promoted unsuccessful measures and damaged a nation's commercial interests. For more Tacitean historians it was not a monarch's virtue that made him or her successful, but skill and cunning. Nevertheless, the assumption was still that the individual qualities of a statesman were the decisive factor in determining the advancement (or not) of trade and national prosperity. Hume disagreed. Despite the incompetence and ineffectiveness of England's monarchs with regard to economic affairs, in the Tudor and Stuart periods trade and commerce had flourished. There was, therefore, no necessary connection between economic statecraft and economic development.

Second, historians of economic statecraft emphasised the close connection between the management of economic policy and other aspects of a statesman's role. The sort of virtue or skill that enabled a monarch to produce success in commerce, it was assumed, would naturally bring about political and military achievements, and ensure that he or she was a competent protector of the Church. For Hume, however, the differences between politics and commerce as fields of knowledge meant that it was very possible – as the reign of Henry VII demonstrated – for a ruler to have success in the former area and be an abject failure in the latter. Commerce remained dependent on a government's capacity to provide justice and order; nevertheless, the lower order political skills required to maintain the basic conditions for commercial life were not the same as the more subtle and refined approaches necessary for its successful management.

Third, and largely as a consequence of this, Hume rejected previous ideas regarding the function of historical writing. Authors working in the economic statecraft tradition had assumed that the past had provided examples of both successful and unsuccessful economic management. As a consequence, through studying English history, one could learn about both the approaches to commerce and finance which could be fruitfully imitated, and those which needed to be avoided. For Hume, however, history fulfilled a rather different didactic function. His historical narrative of commercial ineptitude demonstrated the need for modern statesmen to, in a sense, turn away from the past, and engage with the sort of modern programme of commercial analysis that he had developed in *Political Discourses*. At the same time, however, an account of the steps through which England had become a commercial power served to illustrate the patterns of opinion on which successful economic activity relied. Maintaining these conditions, Hume sought to demonstrate, would be a considerable challenge, but one of vital importance to the nation's future prosperity.

Conclusion

The *Monthly Review* for September 1790 contained a lengthy discussion of the final volume of John Sinclair's *The History of the Public Revenue of the British Empire* (1785–90). While appreciative of Sinclair's work, the anonymous reviewer opened his discussion with some general, and rather less positive, comments on the treatment of financial issues by previous English historians:

> History, till of late, was chiefly employed in the recital of warlike transactions. [...] The *people* were not known; the circumstances that affected *their* domestic prosperity and happiness were entirely overlooked; and the records of many ages might have been perused without obtaining the least information concerning any fact that led to a knowledge of the internal economy of the state, or the private situation of individuals. Thanks, however, to the more enlightened spirit of modern times, things are much altered in this respect. Readers now expect to find, not only the *warlike* exploits, but the *civil* transactions, of princes, recorded in the historic volume.[1]

Such ideas are in many ways an eighteenth-century commonplace. The historian Robert Henry, for example, noted that English historians had given us 'only a detail of our civil, military, and ecclesiastical affairs'; not one of them had 'pretended or designed to give, any thing like a history of learning, arts, commerce, and manners'.[2] Thomas Carte, meanwhile, complained that much previous historical writing contained little other than the 'relations of battles, sieges, and other warlike exploits'.[3] What the nation required, however, was a faithful history of its 'Constitution, Laws, Affairs, Commerce, and Situation in all Ages'.[4] Similar ideas underpinned Hugh Blair's discussion of history in his 1783 work *Lectures on Rhetoric and Belles Lettres.* 'I cannot', Blair observed,

> conclude the subject of History, without taking notice of a very great improvement which has, of late years, begun to be introduced into Historical Composition; I mean, a more particular attention than was formerly given to laws, customs, commerce, religion, literature, and every other thing that tends to show the spirit and genius of nations. It is now understood to be the business of an able Historian to exhibit manners, as well as facts and events; and assuredly, whatever displays the state and life of mankind, in different periods, and illustrates the progress of the human mind, is more useful and interesting than the detail of sieges and battles.[5]

For many commentators, therefore, commerce and 'the internal economy of the state' were, in historiographical terms, new subjects.

This book constitutes a rebuttal of such arguments. As has been shown, from the first years of the seventeenth century onwards writers engaged with economic issues: they examined monarchical approaches to the regulation of trade; they discussed the emergence of international trading companies and debated their value to the nation; they reflected on the relationship between commerce and war; and they offered detailed analysis of the ways in which kings and queens had managed their revenues. Moreover, these analyses were not in any sense peripheral to the period's historiography. The extent of England's trade, the management of its finances and the prosperity of its people, at particular points in time, were important flashpoints in historical debates, and the subject of extensive commentary.

It would, however, be wrong to conclude that writers such as Blair were simply ill-informed. Rather, his comments should be seen as the product of a particular conception of economic issues that was to achieve increasing popularity over the course of the eighteenth century. When discussing commerce and finance, earlier generations of historians were primarily concerned with economic policy and, as such, the specific actions performed by monarchs. This ensured that they treated trade and finance as part of their discussion of what Blair referred to as 'facts and events'. Blair himself, however, considered commerce to be something entirely different: an aspect of 'manners' and a product of the 'progress of the human mind'. As a consequence, whereas Bacon's and Camden's views of economic activity were political – they conceived of it as an aspect of statecraft – Blair's was not. Indeed, he conceptualised commerce as an emanation of a particular age's 'spirit and genius' and, as such, an activity that existed far beyond the Court and Westminster. Given such assumptions, Blair's verdict on previous historical writing seems fair; with the notable exception of Howes, the accounts of commerce and finance discussed in this book tell us almost nothing about the specific lived experience of individuals outside the higher echelons of power.

The sort of ideas that underpin Blair's comments did much to shape approaches to historical writing in the second part of the eighteenth century. Indeed, what we see in this period is a new desire to capture the nature and extent of the nation's economic activity. A useful bellwether for such shifts can be found in the various additions that Hume made to his accounts of commerce in the seventeenth-century volumes of his *History*. While these changes did little, if anything, to alter his argument, they provided a mass of extra information. Much of this material sought to quantify commercial activity. In his Jacobean appendix, Hume included precise figures concerning England's imports and exports and the volume of its coinage, while the Caroline and Commonwealth non-narrative chapter was supplemented with details about customs, the postal service and more discussion of coinage.[6] On occasion, readers were invited to compare these figures with more modern experiences. Elsewhere, Hume augmented his analysis with information about changes in the fabric of everyday life:

> The planting of hops encreased much in England during this reign.[7]

> The first mention of tea, coffee, and chocolate, is about 1660. Asparagus, artichoaks, colliflower, and a variety of sallads, were about the same time introduced into England.[8]

Such accounts are hardly the material of a grand political narrative. They provided, however, a series of intimations for Hume's readers of the tiny, incremental steps through which the 'ancient' world had receded, and the modern world – replete as it was with exotic vegetables, decorative tableware and beverages – had emerged.

Running alongside such developments was a shift in attitudes regarding the relationship between political and economic activity. Earlier writers, particularly those influenced by Livian conceptions of exemplary virtue, had assumed that just as a good monarch could be expected to produce an expansion of trade, a bad one would initiate a period of commercial decline. Such approaches both enabled economic statecraft to function within a conventional humanist framework and allowed it to fulfil a polemical, political function. By mid-century, however, other ideas were coming to the fore. Indeed, even a self-consciously political historian such as Catharine Macaulay argued that while the actions of a monarch such as James I had done much to undermine the constitution, English trade had 'increased much in [his] reign'.[9] As such, in Macaulay's work, the histories of political statecraft and economic activity were not directly connected. This partial separation of the commercial and the political also shaped the organisation of historical narratives. Bacon and Camden had both been able to integrate discussion of finance and trade into their chronological narratives of statesmanship. Later writers came to organise their work differently. Hume, as we have seen, placed much of his discussion of commerce and finance in a series of appendices. Macaulay pursued the same approach. Even more innovatively, Robert Henry's *History of Great Britain* (1771–93) was divided into seven parallel narratives, each of which engaged with a different theme. The effect of such a move was to ensure that 'civil and military history' (theme 1) was separated from the 'history of commerce, of shipping, of money or coin, and of the prices of commodities' (theme 6).[10]

This period also saw the publication of a series of historical accounts concerned exclusively with economic concerns. Sinclair's *History of the Public Revenue* was an important example of this sort of writing.[11] Another key text was Adam Anderson's hugely ambitious *An Historical and Chronological Deduction of the Origin of Commerce* (1764), a two-volume account that traced the development of trade from the earliest time to the present, 'comprehending therein the Discoveries, Inventions, and Improvements, in Navigation, Colonization, Manufactures, [and] Agriculture'.[12] Such subjects were, Anderson stressed, of the utmost importance, as it was 'to the instrumentality of Commerce *alone*, the Britannic Empire is most peculiarly indebted; for its Opulence and Grandeur; – its Improvements in Arts and Knowledge; – and in general, for the great Bulk of its solid Comforts and Conveniencies'.[13] As a result, Anderson concluded, commerce clearly deserved its own history.

In the face of such developments, what happened to ideas about economic statecraft? In the short term, discussion of the cultural aspects of commerce did not bring about an end to reflection on government's commercial and financial roles. Historians continued to provide accounts of the economic 'events' of the Tudors and Stuarts and to assess their successes and failures as managers of England's commercial interests. Equally, in dealing with these issues, they remained reliant on the works of writers such as Camden, Bacon and Rymer. Indeed, it notable that Anderson not only used Bacon's *History of the Reign of Henry VII* as one of his principal sources, but also endorsed, in a way that Hume did not, aspects of its positive verdict on the King's commercial achievements.[14] In this sense, therefore, what we see is not so much an elimination of interest in the political aspects of commerce and finance, but rather the addition into historical narratives of a semi-autonomous economic sphere. As a consequence, the task for historians was no longer simply to trace the ways in which monarchs shaped commerce and finance. Rather they needed to examine a series of complex and multifaceted interactions between commercial and political spheres, each of which could affect the other, but neither of which was necessarily dominant.

Over the longer term, however, a different approach to economic affairs, albeit one shaped by Hume's analysis, was to emerge. For Hume, as we have seen, attempts to promote commerce by England's monarchs had been largely unproductive. Once stable property relations had been established, it was the desires of the populace that shaped trade's expansion, not the 'encouragement' offered by government. The effect of such a move was undoubtedly to downgrade the importance of the history of economic policy. Indeed, whereas a writer such as Guthrie maintained that the statecraft of England's monarchs had been the driving force behind the creation of modern commercial societies, Hume saw their actions as, at best, an irrelevance. In attacking the record of England's monarchs, it should be emphasised, Hume's point was an empirical, historical one; his claim was not that governments were unable to promote commerce, but rather that, in the main, they *had not* done so. And, from a Humean perspective, it was to be hoped that future statesmen might, particularly if armed with copies of *Political Discourses* and the *History of England*, do rather better than their predecessors in administering the nation's trading interests.

Ultimately, however, the critique of early modern policies that Hume helped to inaugurate played a vital role in clearing the way for the development of new approaches to commerce and finance. And although other writers, foremost among them Adam Smith, were to construct the most influential of the intellectual edifices that emerged, they did so on Humean foundations. Indeed, Smith's account of the 'progress of opulence' draws on Hume's 'general' approach to history, just as his attack on the 'commercial, or mercantile system' continued and developed the *History of England*'s critique of Tudor and Stuart practices.[15] Smith's many heirs on both the left and right of the political spectrum, meanwhile, would turn still further away from economic statecraft. Indeed, one thing that Chicago and Marxist economic theorists agree on is that the answers to the world's problems do not, in any sense, lie in the study of the history of economic policy, particularly that of a mercantilist bent. Hume, it is true, might well have been appalled at the actions of his intellectual heirs. Equally, as a historian preoccupied with the unintended consequences of actions, he might, perhaps, have appreciated the ironies of his historical thought's afterlife.

Notes

Introduction

1 Francis Bacon, *The History of the Reign of King Henry VII* (1622), ed. Brian Vickers (Cambridge: Cambridge University Press, 1998); William Camden, *The History of the Most Renowned and Victorious Princess Elizabeth Late Queen of England* (1615, 1625), 4th edn (London, 1688); Thomas Carte, *A General History of England*, 4 vols (London, 1747–55); William Guthrie, *A General History of England*, 4 vols (London, 1744–51); David Hume, *The History of England from the Invasion of Julius Cæsar to the Revolution in 1688* (1754–62), 6 vols (London, 1762); Paul de Rapin de Thoyras, *Histoire d'Angleterre depuis l'invasion de Jules César*, 13 vols (La Haye, 1724–27); Thomas Salmon, *Modern History, or the Present State of all Nations*, 31 vols (London, 1724–38). With regard to James I, the principal accounts to be consulted are John Stow and Edmund Howes, *Annales, or a General Chronicle of England* (London, 1631); Richard Baker, *A Chronicle of the Kings of England* (London, 1643); Anthony Weldon, *The Court and Character of King James, written and taken by sir A.W.* (London, 1650); William Sanderson, *Aulicus Coquinariæ, or a Vindication in Answer to a Pamphlet, entitled the Court and Character of King James* (London, 1650); Arthur Wilson, *The History of Great Britain* (London, 1653); William Sanderson, *A Compleat History of the Lives and Reigns of Mary Queen of Scotland, And of Her Son and Successor James the Sixth, King of Scotland; And (After Queen Elizabeth) King of Great Britain, France, and Ireland* (London, 1656); Roger Coke, *Detection of the Court and State of England* (1694), 2 vols, 3rd edn (London, 1697).

2 Mark Salber Phillips, *Society and Sentiment: Genres of Historical Writing in Britain, 1740–1820* (Princeton, NJ: Princeton University Press, 2000); Noelle Gallagher, *Historical Literatures: Writing About the Past in England, 1660–1740* (Manchester: Manchester University Press,

2012). See also Ben Dew and Fiona Price (eds), *Historical Writing in Britain, 1688–1830: Visions of History* (Basingstoke: Palgrave, 2014).

3 Gallagher, *Historical Literatures*, pp. 63–110.

4 Gallagher, *Historical Literatures*, pp. 111–56.

5 Gallagher, *Historical Literatures*, pp. 13–62; Phillips, *Society and Sentiment*, pp. 295–321; Devoney Looser, *British Women Writers and the Writing of History, 1670–1820* (Baltimore, MD: Johns Hopkins University Press, 2000), pp. 28–60.

6 Phillips, *Society and Sentiment*, pp. 131–46; Karen O'Brien and Susan Manning, 'Historiography, Biography and Identity', in Susan Manning (ed.), *The Edinburgh History of Scottish Literature, Volume 2: Enlightenment, Britain and Empire* (Edinburgh: Edinburgh University Press, 2007), pp. 142–52. Older, although still useful, is Judith H. Anderson, *Biographical Truth: The Representation of Historical Persons in Tudor-Stuart Writing* (New Haven, CT: Yale University Press, 1984).

7 Philip Hicks, 'Women Worthies and Feminist Argument in Eighteenth-Century Britain', *Women's History Review*, 24:2 (2014), 174–90; Philip Hicks, 'Female Worthies and the Genres of Women's History', in Ben Dew and Fiona Price (eds), *Historical Writing in Britain, 1688–1830: Visions of History* (Basingstoke: Palgrave, 2014), pp. 18–31; Barbara Taylor, 'Enlightenment and the Uses of Woman', *History Workshop Journal*, 74:1 (2012), 79–87; Karen O'Brien, *Women and Enlightenment in Eighteenth-Century Britain* (Cambridge: Cambridge University Press, 2009).

8 For some useful comments on the status of history writing in this period, see Karen O'Brien, 'The History Market in Eighteenth-Century England', in Isabel Rivers (ed.), *Books and their Readers in Eighteenth-Century England: New Essays* (London: Continuum, 2003), pp. 105–34. See also Philip Hicks, *Neoclassical History and English Culture: From Clarendon to Hume* (Basingstoke: Macmillan, 1996); Anthony Grafton, *The Art of History in Early Modern Europe* (Cambridge: Cambridge University Press, 2007). The extensive literature on Hume will be discussed in the chapter concerning his work.

9 Everett Zimmerman, *The Boundaries of Fiction: History and the Eighteenth-Century British Novel* (Ithaca, NY: Cornell University Press, 1997); William Ray, *Story and History: Narrative Authority and Social Identity in the Eighteenth-Century French and English Novel* (Oxford: Basil Blackwell, 1990). A similar point has been made by Karen O'Brien, who notes that 'although many have argued that the boundary between history and fiction was porous, they have, in fact, tended to treat history as an unchanging kind of writing against which

the evolution of the novel can be measured and mapped'. See Karen O'Brien, 'History and the Novel in Eighteenth-Century Britain', in *The Uses of History in Early-Modern England* (San Marino, CA: Huntingdon Library, University of California Press, 2006), pp. 389–405 (p. 390).

10 Laird Okie, *Augustan Historical Writing: Histories of England in the English Enlightenment* (Lanham, MD: University Press of America, 1991); Duncan Forbes, *Hume's Philosophical Politics*, rev. edn (Cambridge: Cambridge University Press, 1978), pp. 233–323. In relation to Rapin, see also Karen O'Brien, *Narratives of Enlightenment: Cosmopolitan History from Voltaire to Gibbon* (Cambridge: Cambridge University Press, 1997), pp. 17–19. A notable exception to this trend is Noelle Gallagher, 'Early-Enlightenment Historiography in Britain', in Sophie Bourgault and Robert Sparling (eds), *A Companion to Enlightenment Historiography* (Leiden: Brill, 2013), pp. 343–71.

11 See: J. H. Clapham, *An Economic History of Modern Britain*, 3 vols (Cambridge: Cambridge University Press, 1926–38); Phyllis Deane and W. A. Cole, *British Economic Growth, 1688–1959: Trends and Structure* (Cambridge: Cambridge University Press, 1962).

12 Donald Coleman, 'What is Economic History?', *History Today*, 35:2 (1985), 35–6 (p. 35). See also Douglass C. North, *Structure and Change in Economic History* (London: W.W. Norton, 1981).

13 Coleman, 'What is Economic History?', 35.

14 The literature on contextualist approaches to intellectual history is large, but see in particular Quentin Skinner, 'Meaning and Understanding in the History of Ideas', in *Visions of Politics, Volume 1: Regarding Method* (Cambridge: Cambridge University Press, 2002), pp. 57–89; J. G. A. Pocock, 'Introduction: The State of the Art', in *Virtue, Commerce and History* (Cambridge: Cambridge University Press, 1985), pp. 1–36.

15 Roland Barthes, 'The Death of the Author', in *Image Music Text* (London: Fontana, 1977), pp. 142–48 (p. 146).

16 Hicks, *Neoclassical History*, p. 10.

17 Political economy was closely tied to political polemic for much of the period under discussion. For a useful discussion of political economy's emergence as a genre, see Julian Hoppitt, 'The Context and Contours of British Economic Literature', *The Historical Journal*, 49:1 (2006), 79–110.

18 Such an approach has something in common with that outlined by Hayden White in the introduction to *Metahistory*. White argues that 'the historical work represents an attempt to mediate among [...] the *historical field*, the unprocessed *historical record*, *other historical accounts*,

and an audience'. And for White, the manner in which historians completed these acts of mediation was a product of a series of interconnected ideological and narratalogical concerns. Despite forwarding such a model, however, 'what one [...] misses in White', as Dominick Lacapra has argued, is 'an analysis of the way in which the formalized schemata and patterns he elicits actually function in texts'. It is just this sort of detailed textual analysis that I aim to provide. See Hayden White, *Metahistory: The Historical Imagination in Nineteenth-Century Europe* (Baltimore, MD: Johns Hopkins University Press, 1973), pp. 1–42 (p. 5); Dominick Lacapra, *Rethinking Intellectual History: Texts, Contexts, Language* (New York: Cornell University Press, 1983). p. 81. See also Herman Paul, *Hayden White: The Historical Imagination* (Cambridge: Polity, 2012), pp. 73–4.

19 Translated as Hannah Arendt, *The Human Condition* (Chicago: University of Chicago Press, 1958).

20 Arendt, *Human Condition*, p. 28.

21 Arendt, *Human Condition*, p. 30.

22 Arendt, *Human Condition*, p. 29.

23 Arendt, *Human Condition*, p. 28.

24 J. G. A. Pocock, *The Machiavellian Moment: Florentine Political Thought and the Atlantic Republican Tradition*, 2nd edn (Princeton, NJ: Princeton University Press, 2003 [1975]); for Pocock's comments on Arendt, see p. 550. He also makes reference to Arendt in *Political Thought and History: Essays on Theory and Method* (Cambridge: Cambridge University Press, 2008), p. 135. For other accounts of Pocock's debt to Arendt, see Ellen M. Rigsby, 'The Failure of Success: Arendt and Pocock on the Fall of American Republicanism', *Theory & Event*, 6:1 (2002); Mira L. Siegelberg, 'Things Fall Apart: J.G.A. Pocock, Hannah Arendt, and the Politics of Time', *Modern Intellectual History*, 10:1 (2013), 109–34.

25 Pocock, *Machiavellian Moment*, p. 445.

26 See Pocock, *Machiavellian Moment*, pp. 423–505; Istvan Hont and Michael Ignatieff (eds), *Wealth and Virtue: the Shaping of Political Economy in the Scottish Enlightenment* (Cambridge: Cambridge University Press, 1983). Politeness and manners constitute a major thread in accounts of the relationship between wealth and virtue. On this issue, see Nicholas Phillipson, 'Politics and Politeness: Anne and the Early Hanoverians', in J. G. A. Pocock, Gordon J. Scochet and Lois G. Schwoerer (eds), *The Varieties of British Political Thought* (Cambridge: Cambridge University Press, 1993), pp. 211–45; Lawrence E. Klein, 'Liberty, Manners, and Politeness in Early Eighteenth-Century England', *The Historical Journal*, 32:3 (1989),

583–605; J. G. A. Pocock, 'Virtues, Rights and Manners: A Model for Historians of Political Thought', in *Virtue, Commerce and History: Essays on Political Thought and History, Chiefly in the Eighteenth Century* (Cambridge: Cambridge University Press, 1985), pp. 37–50; Nicholas Phillipson, 'The Scottish Enlightenment', in Roy Porter and Mikuláš Teich (eds), *The Enlightenment in National Context* (Cambridge: Cambridge University Press, 1983), pp. 19–40.

27 Hicks, *Neoclassical History*, p. 8.

28 Hicks, *Neoclassical History*, p. 8.

29 Hicks, *Neoclassical History*, p. 30.

30 Hicks, *Neoclassical History*, p. 33.

31 See Hicks, *Neoclassical History*, pp. 182–8.

32 Phillips, *Society and Sentiment*, p. 16.

33 Phillips, *Society and Sentiment*, pp. xii, 16.

34 Phillips, *Society and Sentiment*, p. 16.

35 Philips sees commerce as a 'principal agent' shaping these changes, but also demonstrates that for Hume and his followers, the 'possibilities of political action were shaped in a hundred ways by the often invisible movements of economy, custom, or opinion'. Phillips, *Society and Sentiment*, p. 17.

36 Mark Salber Phillips, *On Historical Distance* (New Haven, CT: Yale University Press, 2013), p. 65.

37 Phillips, *Society and Sentiment*, p. xii.

38 The public, political aspect of financial affairs is also discussed by Aristotle. In his account of 'the art of acquisition' in the *Politics*, he noted that 'cities, like households, but to an even greater extent, are often in want of financial resources and in need of more ways of gaining them. This is the reason why some of those who adopt a political career confine their activity to matters of finance'; Aristotle, *Politics*, tr. Ernest Baker, rev. tr. R. F. Stalley (Oxford: Oxford University Press, 1995), I, 11, 1259a. In such passages, as Ricardo F. Crespo has argued, 'elements of both house and *polis* realms are mixed up' and the economy is viewed as 'dealing not only with the house, life and needs, but also with the *polis*, with what is useful and free and, thus, moral, as well as with the good life or happiness (*eudaimonia*)'; Ricardo F. Crespo, *A Reassessment of Aristotle's Economic Thought* (London: Routledge, 2013), p. 25.

39 Adam Smith, *An Inquiry into the Origins and Causes of the Wealth of Nations* (1776), ed. R. H. Campbell, A. S. Skinner and W. B. Todd, 2 vols (Indianapolis, IN: Liberty Press, 1981), IV.i–viii. For Smith's view on mercantilism, see Lars Magnusson, *Mercantilism: The Shaping of an Economic Language* (London: Routledge, 1994), pp. 25–8.

40 Smith, *Wealth of Nations*, IV.i.35.
41 Smith, *Wealth of Nations*, IV.i.34.
42 Joseph A. Schumpeter, *History of Economic Analysis* (London: George Allen & Unwin, 1954), p. 473. Schumpeter's discussion of Ricardo draws on the work of the English economist Herbert Foxwell. On this connection, see Erik S. Reinert, 'Schumpeter in the Context of Two Canons of Economic Thought', *Industry and Innovation*, 9:1–2 (2002), 22–39 (p. 32). Schumpeter, it should be emphasised, saw Keynes's work as rooted in the 'Ricardian vice'. See Schumpeter, *History*, p. 473, n. 3.
43 John Maynard Keynes, *The Collected Writings of John Maynard Keynes: Volume 7, The General Theory of Employment, Interest and Money* (London: Macmillan for the Royal Economics Society, 1973), p. 33.
44 Robert Skidelsky, 'Economists vs the Economy', *Project Syndicate*, 23 December 2016, www.project-syndicate.org/commentary/mathematical-economics-training-too-narrow-by-robert-skidelsky-2016-12 (accessed 9 December 2017).
45 See Schumpeter, *History*, pp. 159–60. See also Magnusson, *Mercantilism*, p. 41.
46 Keynes, *General Theory*, p. 333.
47 Erik S. Reinert, *How Rich Countries Got Rich... and Why Poor Countries Stay Poor* (London: Constable, 2007). See also Sophus A. Reinert, *Translating Empire: Emulation and the Origins of Political Economy* (Cambridge, MA: Harvard University Press, 2011).
48 Reinert, *How Rich Countries Got Rich*, p. 308.
49 Reinert, *How Rich Countries Got Rich*, pp. 23–4.
50 Contributors to this project include Ha-Joon Chang, Jürgen Backhaus and Patrick O'Brien.
51 www.othercanon.org/documenting
52 See Steve Pincus, 'Rethinking Mercantilism: Political Economy, the British Empire, and the Atlantic World in the Seventeenth and Eighteenth Centuries', *William and Mary Quarterly*, 69:1 (2012), 3–34. This article provides an expansion of Pincus's earlier discussion in Steve Pincus, *1688: The First Modern Revolution* (New Haven, CT: Yale University Press, 2009) pp. 366–99; Carl Wennerlind, *Casualties of Credit, The English Financial Revolution, 1620–1720* (Cambridge, MA: Harvard University Press, 2011).
53 The first reference in the *OED* to this conception of 'finance' is from 1770 (see n. 7). It quickly became popular and begins to feature frequently in the titles of pamphlets from 1776 onwards. See, for example, John Shebbeare, *An Answer to the printed speech of Edmund Burke [...] In which his Knowledge in Polity, Legislature, Humankind,*

History, Commerce and Finance, is candidly examined (London, 1776). Hume, writing in the 1750s, opts for the plural form, 'finances', in the marginal notes to his *History* to refer to the same concept. As this account demonstrates, the cluster of ideas associated with the term 'finance' had a long-standing connection before the term was coined.

54 When discussing historical material, I do not use the term 'the economy' as this might be seen to imply the existence of a separate economic sphere, independent from political control. As such, it is not in line with the understandings of commerce and finance which inform accounts of economic statecraft.

55 My focus on political histories of finance or commerce should not be taken to imply that that these were the only form of writing to discuss the economic aspects of England's past. Coexistent with the economic statecraft tradition were a series of discussions of what Francis Bacon labelled the 'history of trades', which included notable contributions from William Petty, John Evelyn and Thomas Boyle. Equally significantly, there were a number of attempts from writers interested in commercial affairs to provide historical or partially historical accounts. English works of this sort included John Evelyn's *Navigation and Commerce: their Original and Progress* (1674), the anonymous *A Brief History of Trade* (1702) and Daniel Defoe's *A General History of Trade* (1713). However, while these accounts addressed some similar issues to those I deal with, they were rarely engaged with by narrative historians, and thus do not form a part of the story outlined here. For the history of trades, see W. E. Houghton, Jr, 'The History of Trades: Its Relation to Seventeenth-century Thought', *Journal of the History of Ideas*, 2:1 (1941), 33–60; K. H. Ochs, 'The Royal Society of London's History of Trades Programme: An Early Episode in Applied Science', *Notes and Records of the Royal Society of London*, 39:2 (1985), 129–58. For histories of commerce, see N. S. B. Gras, 'The Rise and Development of Economic History', *Economic History Review*, 1:1 (1927), 12–34.

Chapter 1

1 Markku Peltonen, 'Bacon, Francis, Viscount St Alban (1561–1626)', *Oxford Dictionary of National Biography*, Oxford University Press, 2004; online edn, October 2007. This paragraph draws on material from Jonathan Marwil, *The Trials of Counsel, Francis Bacon in 1621* (Detroit, MI: Wayne State University Press, 1976); Brian Vickers, 'Introduction' to Francis Bacon, *The History of King Henry VII*, ed. Brian Vickers (Cambridge: Cambridge University Press, 1998);

Michael Kiernan, 'Introduction' to Francis Bacon, *The Historie of the Raigne of King Henry the seventh*, ed. Michael Kiernan (Oxford: Oxford University Press, 2012).

2 Peltonen, 'Bacon'.

3 Kiernan, 'Introduction', p. xxvi; Francis Bacon to James I, 21 April 1621, in *The Works of Francis Bacon*, ed. James Spedding, 14 vols (London: Longman, 1857–74), 14: 242.

4 Polydori Vergilii, *Anglicæ Historiæ* (Basel, 1532). I have used the following translations. For the 1513 draft of the text: Polydore Vergil, *The Anglica Historia of Polydore Vergil*, ed. and tr. Denys Hay (London: Office of the Royal Historical Society, 1950). For later versions of the text: Polydore Vergil, *Anglica Historia* [1555 edn], tr. Dana F. Sutton, www.philological.bham.ac.uk/polverg/1e.html. Edward Hall, *The Union of the Famous and Illustre Families of Lancastre and York* (London, 1548); John Speed, *History of Great Britaine* (London, 1611). The pioneering study of sources in the *History* was Wilhelm Busch's *England Under the Tudors. Vol. 1 – King Henry VII*, tr. Alice M. Todd (London: A.D. Innes, 1895). Busch's finding have been supplemented by the work of Marwil and Kiernan.

5 Peter's pence was an annual tax paid to the papal see at Rome.

6 Thomas More, *The History of King Richard III and Selections from the English and Latin Poems*, ed. R. S. Sylvester (New Haven, CT: Yale University Press, 1976).

7 Antonia Gransden, *Historical Writing in England ii, c. 1307 to the Early Sixteenth Century* (London: Routledge Kegan Paul, 1982), p. 425. See also F. J. Levy, *Tudor Historical Thought* (San Marino, CA: Huntingdon Library, 1967), pp. 33–78; Paul Dean, 'Tudor Humanism and the Roman Past: A Background to Shakespeare', *Renaissance Quarterly*, 41:1 (1988), 84–111.

8 *Anglica Historia* (1555), 1: 1.

9 *Anglica Historia* (1555), 1: 1. For a discussion of Vergil's specific stylistic debts to Roman historians (principally Sallust), see Thomas S. Freeman, 'From Catiline to Richard III: The Influence of Classical Historians on Polydore Vergil's *Anglica Historia*', in Mario A. Di Cesare (ed.), *Reconsidering the Renaissance* (Binghampton, NY: Medieval and Renaissance Texts and Studies, 1992), pp. 191–214.

10 Scott Lucas, 'Holinshed and Hall', in Paulina Kewes, Ian W. Archer and Felicity Heal (eds), *The Oxford Handbook of Holinshed's Chronicles* (Oxford: Oxford University Press, 2013), pp. 203–16 (p. 203).

11 Gaius Suetonius Tranquillus, *The Twelve Caesars*, tr. Robert Graves, rev. J. B. Rives (London: Penguin, 2007); Bartolomeo Platina, *Lives*

of the Popes (1479), ed. and tr. Anthony F. D'Elia (Cambridge, MA: Harvard University Press, 2008).

12 Hay, 'Introduction', p. xxx.

13 Vergil, *Anglica Historia* (1555), 1: 1.

14 Vergil, *Anglica Historia* (1555), 1: 1.

15 Livy, *The Rise of Rome, Books 1–5*, tr. R. J. Luce (Oxford: Oxford University Press, 1998), p. 4. For a discussion of the significance of this passage and Livy's approach to *exempla*, see Jane D. Chaplin, *Livy's Exemplary History* (Oxford: Oxford University Press, 2000).

16 Hay, 'Introduction', p. xxxiii.

17 Alexander Barclay, 'Dedication' to *Here begynneth the famous cronycle of the warre by Sallust*, tr. Alexander Barclay (London, 1525). A 'monycion' or 'monition' is an 'instruction, direction [or] prompting' (*OED*).

18 Thomas Blundeville, *The True Order and Methode of Wryting and Reading Hystories* (London, 1574), dedication. Blundeville's work was an abridgement and translation of Ancesco Patrizi's *Della Historia Diece Dialoghi* (Venice, 1560) and Iacob Acontius' unpublished manuscript *Della osservationi et avvertimenti che haver si debbono nel leger delle historie.*

19 For example, Tacitus, *The Annals of Imperial Rome*, tr. Michael Grant (London: Penguin, 1996), pp. 76, 308; Livy, *The Rise of Rome*, pp. 80, 172, 280, 303–4, 309.

20 For example, Tacitus, *Annals*, p. 206; Livy, *Rise of Rome*, pp. 106, 126, 230, 243.

21 For example, Tacitus, *Annals*, pp. 207–8; Livy, *Rise of Rome,* p. 97. Tacitus also provides discussion of regulations used to control luxury, e.g., *Annals,* pp. 92, 143.

22 Polybius, *The Histories*, tr. Robin Waterfield (Oxford: Oxford University Press, 2010), p. 124.

23 Blundeville, *True Order*, n.p.

24 Blundeville, *True Order*, n.p.

25 Vergil, *Anglica Historia* (1513), p. 145.

26 Vergil, *Anglica Historia* (1513), p. 147.

27 Vergil, *Anglica Historia* (1513), p. 147.

28 Vergil, *Anglica Historia* (1513), p. 127.

29 Vergil, *Anglica Historia* (1513), p. 127.

30 Vergil, *Anglica Historia* (1513), p. 127.

31 Vergil, *Anglica Historia* (1513), p. 129.

32 Vergil, *Anglica Historia* (1513), p. 129.

33 Vergil, *Anglica Historia* (1513), p. 129.

34 Vergil, *Anglica Historia* (1513), p. 131.

35 Vergil, *Anglica Historia* (1513), p. 147.

36 Vergil, *Anglica Historia* (1555), 26: 51. For Empson (or Hemson as he is referred to) and Dudley, see 26: 46.
37 Vergil, *Anglica Historia* (1555), 26: 50.
38 Vergil, *Anglica Historia* (1555), 26: 50.
39 Hall, *Union*, Kyng Henry the vii, Fol. iiii, lxi.
40 Speed, *History*, p. 728. Speed is quoting from a manuscript by John Davies of Hertfordshire.
41 Speed, *History*, p. 728. Stow is Speed's source here.
42 Hall, *Union*, p. lvii.
43 Speed, *History*, p. 750.
44 Speed, *History*, p. 728.
45 Speed, *History*, p. 729.
46 Peter Burke, 'A Survey of the Popularity of the Ancient Historians', *History and Theory*, 5:2 (1966), 135–52 (p. 149). Burke estimates that at least 110 commentaries on Tacitus were published between 1450 and 1700 and has identified 87 such works from the seventeenth century. The literature on the influence of Tacitus in the early modern period is large. The classic account is Richard Tuck, *Philosophy and Government, 1572–1651* (Cambridge: Cambridge University Press, 1993), pp. 31–119. I have also drawn on the following: Alan T. Bradford, 'Absolutism and the "Utility" of Tacitus', *Huntingdon Library Quarterly*, 46:2 (1983), 127–55; J. H. M. Salmon, 'Stoicism and Roman Example: Seneca and Tacitus in Jacobean England', *Journal of the History of Ideas*, 50:2 (1989), 199–225; David Womersley, 'Sir Henry Savile's Translation of Tacitus and the Political Interpretation of Elizabethan Texts', *The Review of English Studies*, 42:167 (1991), 313–42; Alexandra Gajda, 'Tacitus and Political Thought in Early Modern Europe, c. 1530-c. 1640', in A. J. Woodman (ed.), *The Cambridge Companion to Tacitus* (Cambridge: Cambridge University Press, 2008), pp. 253–68.
47 Levy, *Tudor Historical Thought*, p. 251.
48 See F. J. Levy, 'The Making of Camden's *Britannia*', *Bibliothèque d'Humanisme et Renaissance*, 26 (1964), 70–97 (pp. 84–5). See also Levy, *Tudor Historical Thought*, p. 251.
49 Levy, *Tudor Historical Thought*, p. 251, n. 27.
50 Robert Johnson, 'Of Histories', *Essaies, or Rather Imperfect Offers* (London, 1601), pp. 17–23 (the page numbers used in the copy I consulted are handwritten).
51 Johnson, 'Of Histories', p. 17.
52 Johnson, 'Of Histories', p. 17.
53 Johnson, 'Of Histories', p. 17.
54 Johnson, 'Of Histories', p. 18.

55 Johnson, 'Of Histories', pp. 18–19. 'Sithens' is an archaic form of 'since'.
56 The term is particularly associated with the work of Émile Durkheim. See his *Rules of Sociological Method* (1895), 2nd edn, ed. Steven Lukes (Basingstoke: Palgrave, 2013).
57 Johnson, 'Of Histories', p. 18.
58 Francis Bacon, 'Letter of Advice to Fulke Greville', in *The Oxford Francis Bacon Early Writings 1584–1596*, ed. Alan Stewart (Oxford: Oxford University Press, 2012), pp. 207–11 (p. 210).
59 Francis Bacon, *The Advancement of Learning*, ed. Michael Kiernan (Oxford: Oxford University Press, 2000), p. 14.
60 Francis Bacon, *De Augmentis Scientiarum*, in *The Philosophical Works of Francis Bacon*, ed. John M. Robertson (Freeport, NY; Books for Libraries Press, 1970), pp. 413–638 (p. 573). *De Augmentis* is an expanded Latin translation of *The Advancement of Learning*.
61 *The Advancement* used a quadripartite division of history into natural, civil, ecclesiastical and literary forms.
62 Bacon, *De Augmentis*, p. 427.
63 Bacon, *De Augmentis*, p. 431.
64 Bacon, *De Audgmentis*, pp. 432, 431.
65 Bacon, *De Augmentis*, p. 431.
66 Bacon, *De Augmentis*, p. 432.
67 Bacon, *De Augmentis*, p. 433.
68 Francis Bacon, *The History of King Henry VII*, ed. Brian Vickers (Cambridge: Cambridge University Press, 1998), pp. 203–4.
69 I have not been able to establish which version of the *Anglica Historia* Bacon consulted. His analysis bears most resemblance to the 1513 draft, but it seems highly unlikely he would have had access to this.
70 Bacon, *History*, p. 18.
71 Bacon, *History*, p. 174.
72 Bacon, *History*, p. 178.
73 Vergil, *Anglica Historia* (1555), 27: 19. For the equivalent passage in the 1513 edition, see p. 51.
74 Vergil, *Anglica Historia* (1555), 27: 21. See also (1513), p. 57.
75 Bacon, *History*, p. 84.
76 Bacon, *History*, p. 94.
77 Bacon, *History*, p. 84.
78 Bacon, *History*, pp. 84–5.
79 Bacon, *History*, p. 133.
80 The King's avarice is also shown to have made him more merciful than other monarchs, although Bacon's attitude to his leniency is distinctly ambivalent. In relation to the battles at Exeter and Blackheath, it was

noted that 'there were never so great rebellions expiated with so little blood drawn'. However, this leniency was attributed not to Henry's merciful nature but rather to his avarice. As Bacon wryly observed: 'the less blood Henry drew the more he took of treasure'. See Bacon, *History*, p. 198.

81 Bacon, *History*, p. 64.

82 Bacon, *History*, p. 65.

83 Bacon, *History*, p. 195.

84 Bacon, *History*, p. 31.

85 Bacon, *History*, p. 40. In addition, see p. 93. Vergil also emphasised Maximilian's poor finances: *Anglica Historia* (1555), 27: 20. The 1515 version presents Maximilian as 'unprepared' rather than suffering from a dearth of funds (p. 53).

86 Bacon, *History*, p. 199.

87 Hall, *Union*, Kyng Henry the vii, Fol. iiii. Bacon does not provide an account of the law-making process under Henry VII. However, although the origins of specific laws are described in a variety of ways, the majority of legislation is attributed to the King. The laws of the Parliament of 1487 are presented as reflections of Henry's personal 'cares' at that point in time (pp. 56–60), while the description of the Parliament of 1489 begins the majority of its paragraphs with 'the King made a law that [...]', 'he ordained [...]' or a similar construction (pp. 63–9). In the King's 'character', meanwhile, it is noted that 'he did much maintain and countenance *his laws*' (my italics), and throughout the text law-making is conceived of as one of the King's principal virtues. Such a presentation does not appear to be based on any documentary evidence. Bacon did not have access to records of debates, draft legislation or parliamentary diaries.

88 Seldon to Bacon, 20 August 1621. Reprinted in Daniel Woolf, 'John Seldon, John Borough, and Francis Bacon's History of Henry VII, 1621', *Huntingdon Library Quarterly*, 47 (1984), 47–53.

89 For Hayward's comments, see John Hayward, *The Life and Reign of King Edward the Sixt* (London, 1630), p. 47.

90 Bacon, *History*, p. 68.

91 Bacon, *History*, p. 121.

92 Bacon, *History*, p. 64.

93 'An act that no foreigner or denizen shall carry any woollen out of this realm [...]', 3 Henry VII, c. 30; 'An act against bringing wine into this realm in foreign vessels', 4 Henry VII, c. 39; 'For silkwomen', 19 Henry VII, c. 31. Please note, I have used the chapter numbers from the Rolls of Parliament not *Statutes of the Realm*. The Rolls of Parliament can be accessed at www.sd-editions.com.

94 'An act that denizens shall pay custom and subsidy', 1 Henry VII, c. 69 [74]; 'An act that all foreigners and denizens shall pay customs', 11 Henry VII, c. 54.

95 'An act against the excessive price of longbows', 3 Henry VII, c. 31; 'Woollen cloth', 4 Henry VII, c. 25.

96 'An act for weights and measures', 7 Henry VII, c. 19; 'An act for weights and measures', 11 Henry VII, c. 44; 'An act for weights and measures', 12 Henry VII, c. 9.

97 'Merchant Adventurers', 7 Henry VII, c. 10.

98 'An act against usury and unlawful bargains', 3 Henry VII, c. 29; 2 [29]; 'An act against usury', 11 Henry VII, c. 48.

99 'An act against exchange and rechange without the king's licence', 3 Henry VII, c. 28.

100 'An act against counterfeiting foreign coin', 4 Henry VII, c. 47; '[…] For the reform of the coinage', 19 Henry VII, c. 12.

101 'An act for fifteenths and tenths', 12 Henry VII, c. 12; 'An act for a subsidy to be granted to the king […]', 12 Henry VII, c. 13.

102 On this issue, see Lisa Jardine, *Francis Bacon: Discovery and the Art of Discourse* (Cambridge: Cambridge University Press, 1974), pp. 150–68.

103 For a useful discussion of these issues in relation to Bacon, see Markku Peltonen, 'Bacon's Political Philosophy', in Markku Peltonen (ed.), *The Cambridge Companion to Bacon* (Cambridge: Cambridge University Press, 1996), pp. 283–310 (see pp. 300–6). See also Markku Peltonen, *Classical Humanism and Republicanism in English Political Thought, 1570–1640* (Cambridge: Cambridge University Press, 1995), pp. 190–228. Peltonen presents Bacon's account of greatness as straightforwardly Machiavellian. The discussion that follows aims to show that while Bacon employs elements of Machiavelli's account, he also substantially modifies the Florentine's analyses of wealth and trade.

104 Niccolò Machiavelli, *Discourses on Livy* (1531), tr. Julia Conway Bondanella and Peter Bondanella (Oxford: Oxford University Press, 2008), p. 36.

105 Machiavelli, *Discourses*, p. 177.

106 Machiavelli, *Discourses*, p. 178.

107 Machiavelli, *Discourses*, p. 114.

108 Machiavelli, *Discourses*, p. 100.

109 Machiavelli, *Discourses*, pp. 317–18.

110 Machiavelli, *Discourses*, p. 318. Machiavelli's analysis of the relationship between wealth and virtue was not entirely consistent. On occasions, he acknowledged that private wealth could contribute to a nation's

greatness, and elsewhere he advocated that Princes should allow their subjects to pursue both agriculture and commerce in tranquility. See *Discourses*, p. 160; Niccolò Machiavelli, *The Prince* (distributed from c. 1513), tr. and ed. Peter Bondanella (Oxford: Oxford University Press, 2005), p. 79. See also Mark Jurdjevic, 'Virtue, Commerce, and the Enduring Florentine Republican Moment: Reintegrating Italy into the Atlantic Republican Debate', *Journal of the History of Ideas*, 62:4 (2001), 721–43 (p. 739).

111 See Tuck, *Philosophy and Government*, pp. 31–119.

112 Justus Lipsius, *Sixe Bookes of Politickes or Civil Doctrine*, tr. William Jones (London, 1594), p. 136.

113 See Giovanni Botero, *A Treatise, Concerning the Causes of the Magnificencie and greatnes of cities*, tr. Robert Peterson (London, 1606).

114 See, for example, Botero, *Treatise*, p. 53.

115 Cunning in the sense of 'knowledge [of] how to do a thing; ability, skill, expertness, dexterity, cleverness' (*OED*).

116 Botero, *Treatise*, p. 52.

117 Botero, *Treatise*, p. 52.

118 Botero, *Treatise*, p. 52.

119 Botero, *Treatise*, pp. 52–3.

120 For an account of the relationship between Machiavelli and Bacon, see Michelle Tolman Clarke, 'Uprooting Nebuchadnezzar's Tree', *Political Research Quarterly*, 61:3 (2008), 367–78. See also Howard B. White, 'The English Solomon: Francis Bacon on Henry VII', *Social Research*, 24:4 (1957), 457–81.

121 Francis Bacon, 'Of the True Greatness of the Kingdom of Britain', in *The Works of Francis Bacon*, vol. 7, ed. James Spedding (London: Longmans, 1872). The dating of this work has been the subject of a good deal of dispute. For a summary, see Markku Peltonen, 'Politics and Science: Francis Bacon and the True Greatness of States', *Historical Journal*, 35:2 (1992), 279–305 (p. 282, n. 9).

122 Bacon, 'True Greatness', p. 48.

123 Bacon, 'True Greatness', p. 55.

124 Bacon, 'True Greatness', pp. 56–7.

125 Bacon, 'True Greatness', p. 58.

126 Bacon, 'True Greatness', pp. 60–1.

127 Bacon, *History*, pp. 53–4. This speech is presented as having been authored by Henry, but delivered to Parliament by his Chancellor, the Archbishop of Canterbury, John Morton. Like the other speeches in the *History*, it is not based on historical record, but was invented by Bacon.

128 Bacon, *History*, p. 68.

129 Bacon, *History*, p. 181.
130 Bacon, *History*, p. 54.
131 Bacon, *History*, p. 60. 'An act against usury and unlawful bargains', 3 Henry VII, c. 29; 'An act against exchange and rechange without the king's licence', 3 Henry VII, c. 28. Similar language is used to discuss usury in Henry's speech to Parliament; Bacon, *History*, p. 54. However, in his 1625 essay on usury, Bacon argued that since 'there must be borrowing and lending, and men are so hard of heart, as they will not lend freely, usury must be permitted'. What was required, however, was government regulation which would control money lending and reduce interest rates. See Bacon, 'Of Usury', in *The Essays or Counsels* (London: J. Booth, 1818), pp. 157–62.
132 Bacon, *History*, p. 68; 'Woollen Cloth', 4 Henry VII, c. 25. The preamble to the law notes that 'Drapers, tailors and others in the city of London and other places in this realm who sell woollen cloth retail by the yard, sell a yard of cloth at an excessive price and make unreasonable profits, to the great harm and impoverishment of the king's liege people who buy the same cloth, against equity and good conscience.'
133 Bacon, *History*, p. 133; 'Merchant Adventurers', 12 Henry VII, c. 10; Bacon, *History*, p. 181; 'Against the making of private and unlawful statutes', 20 Henry VII, c. 17. The latter law notes that 'wardens and members of guilds, fraternities, and other corporate companies dwelling in various parts of the realm [...] had often made among themselves many unlawful and unreasonable ordinances both for the prices of goods and for other things, for their own private profit, and to the common harm and damage of the people'.
134 Bacon, *History*, p. 18. 'An act that denizens shall pay custom and subsidy', 1 Henry VII, c. 69[74].
135 Bacon, *History*, p. 67.
136 'An act against bringing wine into this realm in foreign vessels', 4 Henry VII, c. 39.
137 4 Henry VII, c. 39.
138 Bacon, *History*, p. 67.
139 Bacon, *History*, p. 67.
140 Bacon, *History*, p. 67.
141 'An act against pulling down towns', 4 Henry VII, c. 48.
142 Bacon, *History*, pp. 65–6.
143 Bacon, *History*, p. 65.
144 Bacon, *History*, p. 66.
145 Bacon, *History*, p. 66.
146 Bacon, *History*, p. 66.
147 Bacon, *History*, p. 66.

148 Bacon, *History*, p. 66.
149 Bacon, *History*, p. 67.
150 Bacon, *History*, p. 67.

Chapter 2

1 William Camden, *The History of the Most Renowned and Victorious Princess Elizabeth Late Queen of England* (1615, 1625), 4th edn (London, 1688), 'The Author to the Reader'. Subsequent references to this work use its standard Latin title, *Annales*. For a discussion of the importance of the Latin edition, see Patrick Collinson, 'William Camden and the Anti-myth of Elizabeth: Setting the Mould?', in *This England: Essays on the English Nation and Commonwealth in the Sixteenth Century* (Manchester: Manchester University Press, 2011), pp. 270–86.
2 Camden, *Annales*, 'The Author to the Reader'.
3 For an account of 'politic history', which stresses the links between Bacon and Camden, see F. J. Levy, *Tudor Historical Thought* (San Marino, CA: Huntingdon Library, 1967), pp. 237–85. See also F. J. Levy, 'Hayward, Daniel, and the Beginnings of Politic History in England', *Huntington Library Quarterly*, 50:1 (1987), 1–34.
4 Camden, *Annales*, 'The Author to the Reader'. Similar comments are to be found elsewhere in the text: Camden, *Annales*, pp. 110, 233.
5 Wyman H. Herendeen, *William Camden: A Life in Context* (Woodbridge: Boydell Press, 2007), p. 48. This paragraph draws on Herendeen's account.
6 Wyman H. Herendeen, 'Camden, William (1551–1623)', *Oxford Dictionary of National Biography*, Oxford University Press, 2004; Herendeen, *William Camden*, p. 102
7 William Camden, *Britannia* (London, 1586).
8 Camden, *Annales*, 'The Author to the Reader'.
9 Camden, *Annales*, 'The Author to the Reader'.
10 Hugh Trevor-Roper, *Elizabeth's First Historian: William Camden and the Beginnings of English 'Civil History'* (London: Jonathan Cape, 1971); Daniel Woolf, *The Idea of History in Early-Stuart England: Erudition, Ideology and the Light of Truth* (Toronto: University of Toronto Press, 1990), pp. 115–25.
11 See George Buchanan, *Rerum Scoticarum Historia* (Edinburgh, 1582).
12 For the former opinion, see Daniel Woolf, 'Two Elizabeths? James I and the Late Queen's Famous Memory', *Canadian Journal/Annales Canadiennes d'Histoire*, 20:2 (1985), 167–91. For the latter, see Kevin

Sharpe, 'The Foundation of the Chairs of History at Oxford and Cambridge: An Episode in Jacobean Politics', in *Politics and Ideas in Early Stuart England* (London: Pinter, 1989), pp. 207–29.

13 Camden, *Annales*, 'The Author to the Reader'.

14 See Trevor-Roper, *Elizabeth's First Historian*, p. 24; Sharpe, *Politics and Ideas*, p. 214; Herendeen, *William Camden*, p. 398.

15 The discussion of Cecil is based on material derived from Frederick C. Dietz, *English Public Finance, 1558–1641* (London: Frank Cass, 1964 [1932]), pp. 30–85; Norman Jones, *Governing by Virtue: Lord Burghley and the Management of Elizabethan England* (Oxford: Oxford University Press, 2015), pp. 137–69.

16 Dietz, *English Public Finance*, p. 33.

17 Anonymous, *The Life of the Great Statesman, William Cecil, Lord Burghley*, ed. Arthur Collins (London, 1732), pp. 68–71.

18 Jones, *Governing by Virtue*, p. 141.

19 Anonymous, *Life of Burghley*, p. 71.

20 Anonymous, *Life of Burghley*, p. 70.

21 Anonymous, *Life of Burghley*, p. 70.

22 Anonymous, *Life of Burghley*, p. 70.

23 Anonymous, *Life of Burghley*, p. 69.

24 Anonymous, *Life of Burghley*, p. 69.

25 Anonymous, *Life of Burghley*, p. 71.

26 The manuscript is to be found at SP12/255 f. 142–161. The comments on it are from Dietz, *English Public Finance*, p. 85.

27 SP 12/255 f. 157.

28 SP 12/255 f. 157.

29 SP 12/255 f. 157–8.

30 SP 12/255 f. 158.

31 SP 12/255 f. 158.

32 SP 12/255 f. 158.

33 SP 12/255 f. 158.

34 SP 12/255 f. 158.

35 Camden, *Annales*, pp. 439–40. For a discussion of the sources of the figures Camden uses here, see Howell A. Lloyd, 'Camden, Carmarden and Customs', *The English Historical Review*, 85:337 (1970), 776–87 (p. 778). Lloyd concluded that cross-referencing the *Annales* with extant state papers demonstrates 'Camden's remarkable reliability in factual matters' (p. 786).

36 Camden, *Annales*, p. 440.

37 Camden, *Annales*, p. 440.

38 Camden, *Annales*, p. 440.

39 Camden, *Annales*, p. 440.

40 Camden, *Annales*, p. 441.
41 These comments are placed between his discussion of Elizabeth's reforms to customs, and his discussion of taxation.
42 Camden, *Annales*, p. 440. Caermarden is Richard Carmarden (sometimes rendered as 'Carmarthen'), surveyor of the custom-house at London.
43 Camden, *Annales*, p. 440.
44 Camden, *Annales*, p. 440.
45 Mervyn James, 'English Politics and the Concept of Honour, 1485–1642', in *Society, Politics and Culture* (Cambridge: Cambridge University Press, 1986), pp. 308–415.
46 James, 'Concept of Honour', pp. 340–1.
47 James's conception of an abrupt transformation of honour has, in recent years, been developed by a number of accounts which, in the words of Richard Cust, seek to show the 'simultaneous existence of a variety of concepts, or discourses of honour in early modern England'. However, while honour was undoubtedly multifaceted in the period, and a variety of ways of discussing it were available, Camden's account is rooted in the humanist-inflected version of the concept identified by James. Richard Cust, 'Honour and Politics in Early Stuart England: The Case of Beaumont v. Hastings', *Past and Present*, 149 (1995), 57–94. See also Linda A. Pollock, 'Honour, Gender, and Reconciliation in Elite Culture, 1570–1700', *The Journal of British Studies*, 46:1 (2007), 3–29; William Palmer, 'Scenes from Provincial Life: History, Honour, and Meaning in the Tudor North', *Renaissance Quarterly*, 53:2 (2000), 425–48.
48 James, 'Concept of Honour', p. 375.
49 James, 'Concept of Honour', p. 375.
50 Markku Peltonen, *Classical Humanism and Republicanism in English Political Thought, 1570–1640* (Cambridge: Cambridge University Press, 1995), pp. 18–53. Machiavelli also maintained that 'glory' could be achieved through both political and military means. For a useful discussion, see Hillay Zmora, 'A World Without a Saving Grace: Glory and Immortality in Machiavelli', *History of Political Thought*, 28:3 (2007), 449–68.
51 Peltonen, *Classical Humanism*, p. 39.
52 Peltonen, *Classical Humanism*, p. 43.
53 Camden, *Annales*, p. 558.
54 Camden, *Annales*, p. 191.
55 Camden, *Annales*, p. 191.
56 Camden, *Annales*, p. 596.
57 Camden, *Annales*, p. 596.

58 Camden, *Annales*, p. 125.
59 Camden, *Annales*, p. 125.
60 D. M. Palliser, *The Age of Elizabeth: England Under the Tudors, 1547–1603*, 2nd edn (Harlow: Longman, 1992), p. 157.
61 See 'Summary of certain reasons which have moved the Queen to proceed in the reformation of her base and coarse moneys', TNA SP 12/13 fols 109–119. A draft version of this document with annotations by Burghley can be found at TNA SP 12/13 fols 103–107. For a discussion of these documents, see Jones, *Governing by Virtue*, p. 143. Burghley's role in the re-coinage was discussed by Robert Cotton and his contemporary biographer. See Palliser, *The Age of Elizabeth*, p. 162; Anonymous, *The Life of Burghley*, p. 15.
62 John Stow, *A Summarie of the Chronicles of Englande* (London, 1570), f. 395, v.
63 Raphael Holinshed, *The First Volume of the Chronicles of England* (London, 1577) p. 1814; John Stow, *A Summarie of the Chronicles of England* (London, 1575), p. 506; John Stow, *The Annales of England* (London, 1592), pp. 1099, 1101; John Stow and Edmund Howes, *The Annales or a Generall Chronicle of England* (London, 1615), pp. 646–7.
64 Camden, *Annales*, p. 48.
65 Camden, *Annales*, p. 48.
66 Camden, *Annales*, p. 48. 'A Summary of Certain Reason' notes that 'by continuing of base monies, divers persons both in foreign partes, and within the Realm, have counterfayted from tyme to tyme no smal quantitie [of coin]' (TNA SP 12/13 fol 113). The pamphlet also discusses the advantages of the re-coinage for 'all meane gentlemen that lived upon pensions and stipendes, all souldiours and servyng men' (TNA SP 12/13 fol 114).
67 Camden, *Annales*, pp. 49, 48.
68 'Brass' was used as a term for 'copper' in this period. Camden had made a similar comment about the copper mines at Keswick in his *Britannia* where he had noted that 'the mines not onely serve England over, but also afford great plenty beside, that is carried yeerely forth of the Realme'. See William Camden, *Britannia*, ed. Dana F. Sutton (2004), http://www.philological.bham.ac.uk/cambrit/cumbeng.html#cumb1, para 7.
69 Camden, *Annales*, p. 119.
70 Camden, *Annales*, p. 119.
71 Camden, *Annales*, p. 205.
72 Camden, *Annales*, p. 205.
73 Camden, *Annales*, p. 206.
74 Camden, *Annales*, p. 206.

75 Camden, *Annales*, p. 214.
76 Camden, *Annales*, pp. 215, 466.
77 Camden, *Annales*, p. 538.
78 Camden, *Annales*, p. 538.
79 Camden, *Annales*, p. 169.
80 Camden, *Annales*, p. 206.
81 Camden, *Annales*, p. 466.
82 David Harris Sacks, 'The Countervailing of Benefits: Monopoly, Liberty, and Benevolence in Elizabethan England', in Dale Hoak (ed.), *Tudor Political Culture* (Cambridge: Cambridge University Press, 1995), pp. 272–91.
83 For the Parliament of 1601, see J. E. Neale, *Elizabeth I and Her Parliaments, 1584–1601* (London: Jonathan Cape, 1957).
84 Camden, *Annales*, p. 635.
85 Camden, *Annales*, p. 635.
86 Camden, *Annales*, p. 636.
87 Camden, *Annales*, p. 636.
88 Camden, *Annales*, p. 636.
89 See John Cramsie, 'Commercial Projects and the Fiscal Policy of James VI and I', *The Historical Journal*, 43:2 (2000), 345–64 (p. 347); Simon Adams, 'The Patronage of the Crown', in John Guy (ed.), *The Reign of Elizabeth: Court and Culture in the Last Decade* (Cambridge: Cambridge University Press, 1995), pp. 20–45.
90 In 1603 James launched a review of monopolies made under Elizabeth, insisting that the Privy Council review all grants. Monopolies continued to multiply, however, leading to complaints from Parliament in 1606 and 1610. A monopolies Act followed in 1621, which was passed by the Commons, but rejected by the Lords. A revised version of this bill was passed in May 1624. See Chris R. Kyle, '"But a New Button to an Old Coat": The Enactment of the Statute of Monopolies 21 James I cap. 3', *The Journal of Legal History*, 19:3 (1998), 203–23. See also John Cramsie, *Kingship and Crown Finance under James VI and I* (Woodbridge: Boydell Press, 2002).
91 One other partial exception here is the Queen's legislation of clothing. While, for Camden, her measures were well-intentioned, they did not succeed in restricting extravagant practices. See *Annales*, p. 206.
92 Hunter, cited in Philip Lawson, *The East India Company: A History* (London: Routledge, 2003), p. 23. Hunter is referring specifically to the East India Company, but the same point can equally well be made in relation to other trading bodies.
93 The key account of this issue is Astrid Friis, *Alderman Cockayne's Project and the Cloth Trade: The Commercial Policy of England in its*

Main Aspects, 1603–1625 (London: Oxford University Press, 1927), pp. 149–56. See also Theodore K. Rabb, 'Sir Edwyn Sandys and the Parliament of 1604', *American Historical Review*, 69 (1963/4), 646–70; Robert Ashton, 'The Parliamentary Agitation for Free Trade in the Opening Years of James I', *Past and Present*, 38 (1967), 40–55; Theodore K. Rabb, 'Free Trade and the Gentry in the Parliament of 1604', *Past and Present*, 40 (1968), 165–73; Robert Ashton, 'Jacobean Free Trade Again', *Past and Present*, 43 (1969), 151–7; Pauline Croft, 'Free Trade and the House of Commons', *Economic History Review*, 28:1 (1975), 17–27.

94 The bills were tendered on 18 and 19 April and were 'for all the merchants to have free Liberty of Trade into all Countries and is used by other Nations' and 'for the Enlargement of Trade for his Majesty's Subjects in foreign Countries'.

95 *The Journals of the House of Commons*, 117 vols (London, 1803–63), 1: 218–19.

96 See Croft, 'Free Trade'.

97 *Journals*, 1: 220. Sandys labelled the Muscovy Company 'a strong and a shameful Monopoly' (1: 220).

98 On this issue, see K. N. Chaudhuri, 'The East India Company and the Export of Treasure in the Early Seventeenth Century', *The Economic History Review*, 16:1 (1963), 23–38. See also Lawson, *East India Company*, p. 36.

99 See Lynn Muchmore, 'A Note on Thomas Mun's "England's Treasure by Forraign Trade"', *The Economic History Review*, 23:3 (1970), 498–503. See also Thomas Mun, *England's Treasure by Forraign Trade* (London, 1664). This work was written at some point in the 1620s.

100 Camden, *Annales*, p. 596.

101 Camden, *Annales*, pp. 285–6.

102 SP 91/1 f. 59. A translation of the original letter can be found in George Tolstoy (ed.), *The First Forty Years of Intercourse between England and Russia, 1553–1593* (St Petersburg: A. Travshelya, 1875), pp. 350–3.

103 Camden, *Annales*, p. 14.

104 J. G. A. Pocock, *The Machiavellian Moment: Florentine Political Thought and the Atlantic Republican Tradition* (Princeton, NJ: Princeton University Press, 1975), p. 431.

Chapter 3

1 The scholarly literature on historians of James I is less extensive than on Bacon and Camden. The best account is to be found in Daniel

Woolf, *The Idea of History in Early Stuart England: Erudition, Ideology, and 'The Light of Truth' from the Accession of James I to the Civil War* (Toronto: University of Toronto Press), pp. 243–65. Other useful discussions can be found in Marc L. Schwarz, 'James I and the Historians: Toward a Reconsideration', *Journal of British Studies*, 13:2 (1974), 114–34; Royce Macgillivray, *Restoration Historians and the English Civil War* (The Hague: Martinus Nijhoff, 1974).

2 Christina DeCoursey, 'Howes, Edmund (*fl.* 1602–1631)', *Oxford Dictionary of National Biography*, Oxford University Press, 2004. See also David B. Quinn, 'Advice for Investors in Virginia, Bermuda, and New Foundland, 1611', *The William and Mary Quarterly*, 23:1 (1966), 136–45 (pp. 140–3); Gabriel Heaton and James Knowles, '"Entertainment Perfect", Ben Jonson and Corporate Hospitality', *The Review of English Studies*, NS, 54:217 (2003), 587–600 (pp. 588–9).

3 John Stow and Edmund Howes, *The Abridgement or Summarie of the English Chronicle* (London, 1607); *The Abridgement of the English Chronicle* (London, 1611); *The Abridgement of the English Chronicle* (London, 1618); *Annales, or, a generall chronicle of England* (London, 1615); *Annales, or, a generall chronicle of England* (London, 1632). Unless otherwise stated, all subsequent references are to the 1632 edition.

4 A short account of Charles I was also included in the 1632 edition.

5 Howes, *Annales* (1615), 'To the right high and mightie Prince Charles…'; *Annales*, p. 1087.

6 Howes, *Annales*, p. 1087

7 Barrett L. Beer, *Tudor England Observed: The World of John Stow* (Stroud: Sutton Publishing, 1998), p. 12.

8 Heaton and Knowles, 'Entertainment Perfect', p. 588.

9 Susan Myra Kingsbury (ed.), *Records of the Virginia Company of London*, 4 vols (Washington DC: Government Printing Office, 1906), 2: 16.

10 *Calendar of State Papers Colonial, East Indies, China and Persia, 1625–1629*, ed. W. Noel Sainsbury (London: Her Majesty's Stationery Office, 1884), p. 668.

11 *Calendar of State Papers Colonial, East Indies, China and Persia, 1630–1634*, ed. W. Noel Sainsbury (London: Her Majesty's Stationery Office, 1892), p. 342.

12 Beer, *Tudor England*, p. 13.

13 It is also noteworthy that Richard Hakluyt was both an investor in, and propagandist for, the Virginia Company.

14 Howes, *Annales*, 'To the Honest and Understanding Reader' and 'An Historicall Preface to this Booke'.

15 Howes, *Annales*, 'To the Honest and Understanding Reader'.

16 Howes, *Annales*, p. 866.

17 Howes, *Annales*, p. 1021.
18 Howes, *Annales*, p. 868.
19 Howes, *Annales*, p. 866.
20 Howes, *Annales*, p. 868.
21 Howes, *Annales*, pp. 866–70, 898, 1040.
22 Howes, *Annales*, p. 867.
23 Howes, *Annales*, p. 870.
24 Howes, *Annales*, pp. 895, 897 (these are consecutive pages), 869.
25 Howes, *Annales*, p. 869.
26 Howes, *Annales*, p. 869.
27 Howes. *Annales*, p. 869.
28 Howes, *Annales*, p. 869.
29 Howes, *Annales*, p. 869.
30 On this issue, see, for example, Andrew Hadfield, *Literature, Travel and Colonial Writing in the English Renaissance* (Oxford: Oxford University Press, 2007 [1998]), pp. 69–133. See also David Armitage, *The Ideological Origins of the British Empire* (Cambridge: Cambridge University Press, 2000).
31 Howes, *Annales*, pp. 993–5, 1022.
32 Howes, *Annales*, pp. 1017–21.
33 Howes, *Annales*, p. 1017.
34 The focus here is predominantly on very recent history – the 1615 edition of the text continued its narrative right up until 1614 – a move which enabled Howes to cover events not discussed by Hakluyt in the final, 1598 edition of the *Travels*.
35 Howes, *Annales*, p. 1020.
36 Howes, *Annales*, p. 1021.
37 Richard Hakluyt, *The Principal Navigations, Voiages and Discoveries of the English Nation, made by Sea or Over Land* (London, 1589), 'To the Right Honourable Sir Francis Walsingham'.
38 Howes, *Annales*, p. 994.
39 Howes, *Annales*, p. 1018.
40 Howes, *Annales*, pp. 1018, 1019.
41 Howes, *Annales*, p. 1019.
42 Howes, *Annales*, p. 1018.
43 Howes, *Annales*, p. 992.
44 Howes, *Annales*, p. 992.
45 Howes, *Annales*, p. 992.
46 Howes, *Annales*, p. 992.
47 Howes, *Annales*, p. 894.
48 Howes, *Annales*, p. 894.
49 Howes, *Annales*, p. 894.

50 Howes, *Annales*, p. 898.
51 Howes, *Annales*, p. 898.
52 Howes, *Annales*, p. 898.
53 Howes, *Annales*, p. 845.
54 Howes, *Annales*, p. 994.
55 Howes, *Annales*, p. 994. A similar account is provided in relation to the charter granted to the Muscovy Company. Here the excessive expenses incurred by the company are said to have resulted in it being given 'certaine priviledges, confirmed by act of Parliament, granting to them solely, the use both of the said trade, and of what places and lands soever should afterwards bee found and discovered by them' (*Annales*, p. 1017).
56 Howes, *Annales*, p. 890.
57 Howes, *Annales*, p. 891.
58 Howes, *Annales*, p. 994.
59 Richard Baker, *A Chronicle of the Kings of England from the Time of the Romans' Government unto the Death of King James* (London, 1643). On Baker, see Martine Watson Brownley, 'Sir Richard Baker's "Chronicle" and Later Seventeenth-Century English Historiography', *Huntingdon Library Quarterly*, 52:4 (1989), 481–500. Baker's account is divided into four parts, each of which begins its page numbering from '1'.
60 Baker, *Chronicle*, 'An Epistle to the Reader'.
61 Baker, *Chronicle*, 'An Epistle to the Reader'.
62 Baker, *Chronicle*, 'An Epistle to the Reader'.
63 Howes, *Annales*, p. 898; Baker, *Chronicle*, part 4, p. 135.
64 Howes, *Annales*, p. 994; Baker, *Chronicle*, part 4, p. 136.
65 Howes, *Annales*, p. 994; Baker, *Chronicle*, part 4, p. 136.
66 Howes, *Annales*, pp. 890–1; Baker, *Chronicle*, part 4, p. 134.
67 Baker, *Chronicle*, part 4, p. 146.
68 Baker, *Chronicle*, part 4, p. 146.
69 John Smith, *The Generall Historie of Virginia, new-England, and the Summer Islands* (London, 1624). Both the specific details that Baker uses, and the order in which he uses them, follow Smith's work.
70 John Smith, *A Map of Virginia* (London, 1612); Silvester Jourdain, *A Plaine Description of the Barmudas* (London, 1613).
71 Baker, *Chronicle*, part 4, p. 157.
72 Baker, *Chronicle*, part 4, p. 157.
73 Baker, *Chronicle*, part 4, p. 159.
74 See Lars Magnusson, *Mercantilism: The Shaping of an Economic Language* (London: Routledge, 2002), pp. 62–4. The discussion below draws on Magnusson's account.

75 See Gerrard Malynes, *The Maintenance of Free Trade* (London, 1622). This work developed claims made in Malynes' earlier work, *Saint George for England* (London, 1601) and *A Treatise of the Canker of Englands Commonwealth* (London, 1601). Misselden advanced an argument that was broadly similar to Malynes in his early work. See Edward Misselden, *Free Trade. Or, The Means to Make Trade Flourish* (London, 1622).
76 Thomas Mun, *England's Treasure by Forraign Trade* (London, 1664); Edward Misselden, *The Circle of Commerce. Or the Ballance of Trade* (London, 1623).
77 Misselden, *The Circle of Commerce*, p. 117.
78 Magnusson, *Mercantilism*, p. 79.
79 Mun, *England's Treasure*, p. 169.
80 Malynes, *Free Trade*, Dedication.
81 Mun, *England's Treasure*, p. 204.

Chapter 4

1 For the effects of the English Revolution on historical writing, see Daniel Woolf, *The Idea of History in Early Stuart England: Erudition, Ideology and 'The Light of Truth' from the Accession of James I to the Civil War* (Toronto: Toronto University Press, 1990), pp. 247–65.
2 Hamon L'Estrange, *The Reign of King Charles: An History* (London, 1655), The Epistle Dedicatory.
3 Peter Heylyn, *Observations on the Historie of the Reign of King Charles* (London, 1656).
4 Thomas Fuller, *The Appeal of Iniured Innocence* (London, 1659), dedication. Heylyn had alleged that Fuller was 'BY ASSED'. Fuller responded by confidently declaring that he had used 'as UPRIGHT BOWLES as ever any that enter the *Alley* of History, since our *Civil Dissensions*' (p. 10).
5 Thomas May, *The History of the Parliament of England* (London, 1647), preface.
6 May, *History of the Parliament*, preface.
7 Fuller, *Appeal*, p. 1. L'Estrange also echoed these sentiments, arguing that while writing about 'recent times' made good history, it usually brought 'the *Relater* under a cloud'. L'Estrange, 'The Preface'.
8 J. G. A. Pocock, *The Ancient Constitution and the Feudal Law: A Study of English Historical Thought in the Seventeenth Century*, 2nd edn (Cambridge: Cambridge University Press, 1987 [1957]), p. 46.
9 David Norbrook, 'The English Revolution and English Historiography', in N. H. Keble (ed.), *The Cambridge Companion to the*

Writing of the English Revolution (Cambridge: Cambridge University Press, 2001), pp. 233–50 (p. 234).

10 Michael Sparke, *The Narrative History of King James for the first fourteen years* (London, 1651). Detailed discussion is also to be found in Thomas Frankland's *Annals of King James* (London, 1680), pp. 9–12.

11 In its examination of the economic debate between supporters of the Stuarts and their critics, my account has some resemblance to Steve Pincus's recent work on mercantilism. For Pincus, the economic thought of the seventeenth and early eighteenth centuries was not structured, as has been widely assumed, around a universally supported mercantilist consensus. Rather the period saw the emergence of a series of politically charged debates, which eventually generated competing Whig and Tory conceptions of commerce. Tories, he argues, conceived of property as 'finite and tied to the land and its products' and trade as a zero sum game between competing nations. In contrast, for 'Whig polemicists, traders, and politicians [...] property was potentially infinite and depended on the product of human labour'. Pincus's account provides a useful corrective to more schematic approaches to mercantilism, and the Whiggish position he discusses clearly informs some of Coke's arguments. Generally, however, the battle-lines in the historical accounts discussed here were not drawn around land, but rather Livian/exemplary ideas of virtue and vice. See Steve Pincus, 'Rethinking Mercantilism: Political Economy, the British Empire, and the Atlantic World in the Seventeenth and Eighteenth Centuries', *William and Mary Quarterly*, 69:1 (2012), 3–34.

12 References are to the 1651 edition: Anthony Weldon, *The Court and Character of King James* (London, 1651). For Weldon, see Joseph Marshall and Sean Kelsey, 'Weldon, Sir Anthony (*bap.* 1583, *d.* 1648)', *Oxford Dictionary of National Biography*, Oxford University Press, 2004; online edn, January 2008.

13 Weldon, *Court and Character*, p. 173. For an account of the considerable impact this image of James has exerted, see Jenny Wormald, 'James VI and I: Two Kings or One', *History*, 68 (1983), 187–209.

14 Aristotle, *Nicomachean Ethics*, tr. David Ross (Oxford: Oxford University Press, 1980), p. 82.

15 Weldon, *Court and Character*, p. 53.

16 Weldon, *Court and Character*, p. 170.

17 Weldon, *Court and Character*, p. 51. The Latin section can be translated as 'By lawful or unlawful means'.

18 Weldon, *Court and Character*, p. 60.

19 Weldon, *Court and Character*, p. 80. The kennel is 'the surface drain of a street; the gutter' (*OED*).
20 Weldon, *Court and Character*, pp. 154–5.
21 Weldon, *Court and Character*, p. 11.
22 Weldon, *Court and Character*, pp. 11–12.
23 Weldon, *Court and Character*, p. 171.
24 Weldon, *Court and Character*, p. 171.
25 Weldon, *Court and Character*, p. 53.
26 Arthur Wilson, *The History of Great Britain* (London, 1653).
27 This section is derived from information in Graham Parry, 'Wilson, Arthur (*bap.* 1595, *d.* 1652)', *Oxford Dictionary of National Biography*, Oxford University Press, 2004; Arthur Wilson, 'Observations of God's Providence', in F. Peck (ed.), *Desiderata curiosa*, new edn, 2 vols in 1 (1779), pp. 460–83.
28 Wilson, *Observations*, p. 475.
29 Wilson, *History*, 'Proeme'.
30 Wilson, *History*, 'Proeme'.
31 Wilson, *History*, 'Proeme'.
32 Wilson, *History*, 'Proeme'. Wilson's comments are rooted in a Galenic understanding of medicine, and the idea that particular illnesses were the product of a build-up of humours in specific parts of the body. For a clear explanation, see Thomas Wright, *Circulation: William Harvey's Revolutionary Idea* (London: Vintage, 2013), pp. 30–4, 150–1.
33 Wilson, *History*, 'Proeme'.
34 Wilson, *History*, 'Proeme'. By 'personating' Wilson means 'describing' or 'depicting'.
35 Wilson, *History*, 'Proeme'.
36 Wilson, *History*, p. 146.
37 Wilson, *History*, 'Proeme'.
38 Wilson, *History*, 'Proeme'.
39 Wilson, *History*, 'Proeme'.
40 Wilson, *History*, 'Proeme'.
41 Wilson, *History*, 'Proeme'.
42 Wilson, *History*, pp. 185, 177.
43 Wilson, *History*, p. 185.
44 Wilson, *History*, p. 185.
45 Wilson, *History*, pp. 148–9.
46 Wilson, *History*, p. 91.
47 Wilson, *History*, p. 91.
48 Wilson, *History*, p. 190. This idea was then supported with a quotation from Livy: *Instum id bellum quibus necessarium*.
49 Wilson, *History*, p. 91.

50 Wilson, *History*, p. 91. For similar comments, see Wilson, *History*, p. 190.
51 Wilson, *History*, p. 91.
52 Wilson, *History*, pp. 289–90.
53 Wilson, *History*, p. 289.
54 Wilson, *History*, p. 171.
55 Wilson, *History*, p. 91.
56 This paragraph draws on Daniel Woolf, 'Sanderson, Sir William (1586–1676)', *Oxford Dictionary of National Biography*, Oxford University Press, 2004; Anita McConnell, 'Sanderson, William (1547/8–1638)', *Oxford Dictionary of National Biography*, Oxford University Press, 2004.
57 William Sanderson, *A Compleat History of the lives and reigns of, Mary Queen of Scotland, and of her son and successor, James the Sixth, King of Scotland, and (after Queen Elizabeth) King of Great Britain, France and Ireland* (London, 1656), 'Proeme to the Second Part'. These comments are given further credence by the fact that Sanderson's wife, Margaret (née Snedale) was to become a maid of honour to Catherine of Braganza and Mary of Modena, rising to the position of Mother to the Maids of Honour.
58 The monument is located in the west aisle of the north transept.
59 Carew Raleigh responded to some of the criticisms Sanderson made of his father, Sir Walter Raleigh, in *Observations upon some particular persons and passages* (London, 1656). Sanderson countered with *An Answer to a Scurrilous Pamphlet* (1656). Sanderson also produced an account of Charles I shortly after his accounts of Mary and James (*A Compleat History of the Life and Raigne of King Charles* (London, 1658)) and a work on drawing (*Graphice: Or, the Use of the Pen and Pencil* (London, 1658)).
60 The phrase appears repeatedly through his account. See, for example, Sanderson, *History of Mary and James*, pp. 333, 360, 431, 494.
61 See W. Sanderson, *Aulicus Coquinariæ, or a Vindication in Answer to a Pamphlet, entitled the Court and Character of King James* (London, 1650), pp. 58–8, 204; Sanderson, *History of Mary and James*, p. 360.
62 Sanderson, *History of Mary and James*, p. 410.
63 Sanderson, *History of Mary and James*, p. 366.
64 Sanderson, *History of Mary and James*, p. 366.
65 Sanderson, *History of Mary and James*, p. 366.
66 Sanderson, *History of Mary and James*, p. 366.
67 Sanderson, *History of Mary and James*, p. 367.
68 Sanderson, *History of Mary and James*, 'Proeme to the Second Part'.

69 Sanderson, *Aulicus Coquinariae*, pp. 160–1. See also *History of Mary and James*, pp. 495, 572.
70 Sanderson, *Aulicus Coquinariae*, p. 161; *History of Mary and James*, p. 572.
71 Sanderson, *Aulicus Coquinariae*, p. 161; *History of Mary and James*, p. 572.
72 Sanderson, *Aulicus Coquinariae*, p. 162; *History of Mary and James*, p. 572.
73 Sanderson, *Aulicus Coquinariae*, pp. 184–5. See also *History of Mary and James*, p. 384.
74 Sanderson, *History of Mary and James*, pp. 413, 409.
75 Sanderson, *History of Mary and James*, p. 573.
76 Roger Coke, *Detection of the Court and State of England* (1694), 2 vols, 3rd edn (London, 1697). For Coke, see John Callow, 'Coke, Roger (c.1628–1704)', *Oxford Dictionary of National Biography*, Oxford University Press, 2004. See also Henry Snyder, 'David Jones, Augustan Historian and Pioneer English Annalist', *Huntington Library Quarterly*, 44:1 (1980), 11–26.
77 Coke, *Detection*, 1: 6–7.
78 Coke, *Detection*, 1: 7.
79 Coke, *Detection*, 1: 3.
80 Coke, *Detection*, 1: 5.
81 Coke, *Detection*, 1: 4.
82 Coke, *Detection*, 1: 5.
83 Coke, *Detection*, 1: 5
84 Coke, *Detection*, 1: 5.
85 Coke, *Detection*, 1: 59.
86 Roger Coke, *A Discourse of Trade* (London, 1670); *England's Improvements* (London, 1675). His other publications on commercial themes included *Reflections upon the East-Indy and Royal African Countries* (London, 1695) and *A Treatise Concerning the Regulation of English Coin* (1696).
87 For England's advantages, see *Discourse on Trade*, p. 40. For Coke's comments on the importance of greater numbers of people, see *England's Improvements*, p. 3.
88 Coke, *Detection*, 1: 55.
89 Coke, *Detection*, 1: 55.
90 Coke, *Detection*, 1: 56.
91 Coke, *Detection*, 1: 56.
92 Coke, *Detection*, 1: 84.
93 Coke, *Detection*, 1: 56.
94 Coke, *Detection*, 1: 56–7.

95 Coke, *Detection*, 2: 681.
96 Coke, *Detection*, 2: 681.

Chapter 5

1 Philip Hicks, *Neoclassical History and English Culture: From Clarendon to Hume* (Basingstoke: Macmillan, 1996), pp. 82–109.
2 John Milton, *The History of Britain* (London, 1670). Milton got as far as the Norman invasion. Temple's plans for a history were discussed in his *An Introduction to the History of England* (London, 1695). Swift's history was never published. For discussion of his historical endeavours, see Hicks, *Neoclassical History*, pp. 101–2. See also James Tyrrell, *General History of England, both ecclesiastical and civil*, 3 vols (London, 1696–1704); Robert Brady, *A Complete History of England*, 2 vols (London, 1685–1700).
3 John Hughes (ed.), *A Complete History of England, Volumes 1 and 2* (London, 1706); White Kennet, *A Complete History of England, Volume 3* (London, 1706). For Kennet, see Hicks, *Neoclassical History*, pp. 112–14; Laird Okie, *Augustan Historical Writing: Histories of England in the English Enlightenment* (Lanham, MD: University Press of America, 1991), pp. 27–32.
4 Laurence Echard, *The History of England*, 3 vols (London, vol. 1, 1707, vols 2 and 3, 1718). For Echard, see Hicks, *Neoclassical History*, pp. 102–9; Okie, *Augustan Historical Writing*, pp. 32–9; Deborah Stephan, 'Laurence Echard – Whig Historian', *Historical Journal*, 32:4 (1989), 843–66.
5 Paul de Rapin de Thoyras, *Histoire d'Angleterre depuis l'invasion de Jules César*, 13 vols (La Haye, 1724–27).
6 The translations were Paul de Rapin de Thoyras, *The History of England*, tr. and ed. Nicholas Tindal, 15 vols (London, 1725–31); *The History of England*, tr. and ed. John Kelly and Joseph Morgan, 3 vols (London, 1732–7); *The History of England*, tr. and ed. J. Templeman, 2 vols (London, 1734). A final translation followed in the nineteenth century: Paul de Rapin de Thoyras and Henry Robertson, *The History of England from the earliest periods*, tr. and ed. Henry Robertson, 2 vols (London, 1820). Unless otherwise stated, references to Rapin's *History* are to the first edition of the Tindal translation. In addition, page references have been provided for the first French edition – these have been labelled *Histoire*.
7 For Rapin's sales figures, see Hicks, *Neoclassical History*, p. 147.
8 See, for example, John Lockman, *A New History of England, in English and French by question and answer. Extracted from the most*

celebrated English historians particularly M. de Rapin Thoyras (London, 1729). Lockman's text proved to be enduringly popular, running to twenty-five editions, the last of which was published in 1811. Tindal and Robertson also extended Rapin's narrative beyond its original end point, the former taking it to the accession of George II and the latter to 1820. See Robertson above and Paul de Rapin de Thoyras and Nicholas Tindal, *The History of England*, tr. Nicholas Tindal, 2 vols (London, 1744–47).

9 Hugh Trevor-Roper, 'Our First Whig Historian', in *From Counter-Reformation to Glorious Revolution* (London: Secker and Warburg, 1992), pp. 249–65 (p. 262).

10 Trevor-Roper, 'Whig Historian', p. 263.

11 See D. W. L. Earl, 'Procrustean Feudalism: An Interpretive Dilemma in English Historical Narration, 1700–1725', *The Historical Journal*, 19:1 (1976), 33–51; Duncan Forbes, *Hume's Philosophical Politics*, rev. edn (Cambridge: Cambridge University Press, 1978 [1975]), pp. 238–40; Okie, *Augustan Historical Writing*, p. 60; Steven Stryer, 'The Style of Discontinuity: Prose Patterning and Historical Change in Paul de Rapin de Thoyras and Thomas Salmon', *Clio: A Journal of Literature Philosophy and the Philosophy of History*, 42:2 (2013), 137–60.

12 Okie, *Augustan Historical Writing*, p. 61.

13 Okie, *Augustan Historical Writing*, p. 61.

14 This biographical information is drawn from M. G. Sullivan, 'Rapin de Thoyras, Paul de (1661–1725)', *Oxford Dictionary of National Biography*, Oxford University Press, 2004; M. G. Sullivan, 'Rapin, Hume and the Identity of the Historian in Eighteenth-century England', *History of European Ideas*, 28 (2002), 145–62; Okie, *Augustan Historical Writing*, pp. 47–74; Trevor-Roper, 'Whig Historian', pp. 249–65; Nelly Girard d'Albissin, *Un Précurseur de Montesquieu: Rapin-Thoyras, Premier historien français des institutions anglaises* (Paris: Éditions C. Klincksieck, 1969), pp. 18–25.

15 For the significance of learned journals, see Jonathan Israel, *Radical Enlightenment: Philosophy and the Making of Modernity, 1650–1750* (Oxford: Oxford University Press, 2002), pp. 142–55.

16 Thomas Rymer, *Foedera*, 20 vols (London, 1704–35). For Rapin's abridgement, see Thomas Rymer, *Foedera*, abr. Paul de Rapin de Thoyras, tr. Stephen Whatley, 4 vols (London, 1726–27). The word *foedera* is the Latin term for 'pacts' or 'treatises'.

17 For Whig politics, see H. T. Dickinson, *Liberty and Property: Political Ideology in Eighteenth-Century Britain* (London: Methuen, 1977); J. G. A. Pocock, 'The Varieties of Whiggism from Exclusion to Reform: A History of Ideology and Discourse', in *Virtue, Commerce*

and History: Essays on Political Thought and History, Chiefly in the Eighteenth Century (Cambridge: Cambridge University Press, 1985), pp. 215–52. On Whig ideas of political economy, see Steve Pincus, 'Rethinking Mercantilism: Political Economy, the British Empire, and the Atlantic World in the Seventeenth and Eighteenth Centuries', *The William and Mary Quarterly*, 69:1 (2012), 3–34; Steve Pincus, *1688: The First Modern Revolution* (New Haven, CT: Yale University Press, 2011), pp. 366–99.

18 See S.-J. Savonius, 'Locke in French: The *Du Government Civil* of 1691 and its Readers', *The Historical Journal*, 47:1 (2004), 47–79; Lisa Clark Diller, 'How Dangerous, the Protestant Stranger? Huguenots and the Formation of British Identity, c. 1685–1715', in D. J. B. Trim (ed.), *The Huguenots: History and Memory in Transnational Context* (Leiden: Brill, 2011), pp. 103–21 (p. 115). Among the important translations published and supported by Huguenots were John Locke, *Du Government Civil* (Amsterdam, 1691); Edmond Ludlow, *Les Mémoires d'Edmond Ludlow* (Amsterdam, 1699); Algernon Sidney, *Discours sur le gouvernement* (The Hague, 1702). For more on Huguenot links with radical Whiggism, see Margaret Jacob, *Radical Enlightenment: Pantheists, Freemasons, and Republicans* (London: Allen and Unwin, 1981).

19 Jean Leclerc, *Parrhasiana* (London, 1700). For Leclerc, see Samuel A. Golden, *Jean LeClerc* (New York: Twayne Publishers, 1972).

20 Hugo Grotius, *The Rights of War and Peace* (1625), ed. Richard Tuck (Indianapolis, IN: Liberty Fund, 2005), p. 111. For Grotius, see Richard Tuck, *Philosophy and Government 1572–1651* (Cambridge: Cambridge University Press, 1993), pp. 154–201; Richard Tuck, *The Rights of War and Peace: Political Thought and the International Order from Grotius to Kant* (Oxford: Oxford University Press, 1999), pp. 78–108.

21 Hugo Grotius, *Commentary on the Law of Prize and Booty*, ed. Martine Julia van Ittersum, tr. Gwladys L. Williams (Indianapolis, IN: Liberty Fund, 2006), p. 23.

22 Grotius, *Prize and Booty*, p. 27.

23 Leclerc, *Parrhasiana*, p. 138.

24 Leclerc, *Parrhasiana*, pp. 147–8. For Leclerc's comments on happiness, see pp. 157–8.

25 Leclerc, *Parrhasiana*, p. 158.

26 Leclerc, *Parrhasiana*, p. 205.

27 Leclerc, *Parrhasiana*, p. 216.

28 Leclerc, *Parrhasiana*, pp. 161, 160.

29 Leclerc, *Parrhasiana*, pp. 161–2.

30 Leclerc, *Parrhasiana*, p. 162.
31 Rapin, *History*, 1: ii, *Histoire*, 1: v.
32 The classic summary of the Brady controversy is to be found in J. G. A. Pocock, *The Ancient Constitution and the Feudal Law: A Study of English Historical Thought in the Seventeenth Century* (Cambridge: Cambridge University Press, 1987 [1957]), pp. 182–228. See also Hicks, *Neoclassical History*, pp. 83–98.
33 Rapin, *History*, 1: iii, *Histoire*, 1: vi.
34 Rapin, *History*, 1: iii, *Histoire*, 1: vi.
35 Rapin, *History*, 1: iv, *Histoire*, 1: vii.
36 Rapin, *History*, 1: iv, *Histoire*, 1: vii.
37 Richard Baker, *A Chronicle of the Kings of England* (London, 1643); Arthur Wilson, *The History of Great Britain* (London, 1653); Roger Coke, *A Detection of the Court and State of England* (1694), 3rd edn (London, 1697). Rapin ignores the major Royalist histories, including the works that William Sanderson discussed (see the previous chapter).
38 Rapin, *History*, 9: 334, *Histoire*, 7: 73; *History*, 9: 355–6, *Histoire*, 7: 87.
39 Rapin, *History*, 9: 386–7, *Histoire*, 7: 107–8.
40 Rapin, *History*, 9: 305, *Histoire*, 7: 53–4; Baker, *Chronicle*, part 4, p. 133.
41 Rapin, *History*, 9: 361–2, *Histoire*, 7: 90–1; Thomas Frankland, *The Annals of King James and Charles the First* (London, 1681).
42 Rapin, *History*, 9: 335, *Histoire*, 7: 74. The methods that James used are also discussed in detail in Rapin, *History*, 9: 356–8, *Histoire*, 7: 87–9, which paraphrases Coke, *Detection*, p. 54.
43 Rapin, *History*, 9: 311, *Histoire*, 7: 57–8; Coke, *Detection*, pp. 59–60.
44 Rapin, *History*, 9: 311–12, *Histoire*, 7: 58; Baker, *Chronicle*, part 4, p. 135.
45 Rapin, *History*, 9: 448–50, *Histoire*, 7: 149–51; Wilson, *History*, 155a–158b; Coke, *Detection*, p. 116. The page-numbering in Wilson's book is erratic; sometimes each page is numbered, on other occasions every second page is given a number. The 'a' above refers to the first page of a given number, the 'b' to the second page.
46 Rapin, *History*, 9: 360, *Histoire*, 7: 90.
47 Rapin, *History*, 9: 282, *Histoire*, 7: 38; Coke, *Detection*, p. 45.
48 Rapin *History*, 9: 312, *Histoire*, 7: 58; Baker, *Chronicle*, part 4, p. 135.
49 Rapin, *History*, 9: 388–91, *Histoire*, 7: 108–10; Coke, *Detection*, pp. 85–9.
50 Wilson, *History*, pp. 289–90.
51 E.g. Rapin, *History*, 9: 355, *Histoire*, 7: 87.

52 See Rapin, *History*, 9: 283, *Histoire*, 7: 39; *History*, 9: 408, *Histoire*, 7: 122; *History*, 9: 504, *Histoire*, 7: 187–8.
53 Rapin, *History*, 9: 506, *Histoire*, 7: 189. On the King's religion, see Rapin, *History*, 9: 611, *Histoire*, 7: 258.
54 Rapin, *History*, 9: 608, *Histoire*, 7: 256.
55 Rapin, *History*, 9: 433, *Histoire*, 7: 138. See also *History*, 9: 440–1, *Histoire*, 7: 143–4.
56 Rapin, *History*, 9: 612, *Histoire*, 7: 259.
57 For Alfred, see *History*, 1: 353, *Histoire*, 1: 322. For a discussion of his achievements with regard to commerce, see *History*, 1: 346, *Histoire*, 1: 317–18. For Edward III, see *History*, 4: 274, *Histoire*, 3: 200; *History*, 4: 341, *Histoire*, 3: 247–8. For an example of another high-taxing king, see Rapin's comments on Hardicanute: *History*, 2: 53–5, *Histoire*, 1: 420–1.
58 Rapin, *History*, 9: 23, *Histoire*, 6: 360.
59 Rapin, *History*, 9: 225, *Histoire*, 6: 496. For the felicitousness of Elizabeth's reign, see also *History*, 8: 294, *Histoire*, 6: 198.
60 Rapin, *History*, 9: 225, *Histoire*, 6: 496.
61 George Buchanan, *Rerum Scoticarum Historia* (Edinburgh, 1582); James Melville, *The memoires of Sir James Melvil of Hal-Hill* (London, 1683); François Eudes De Mézeray, *Histoire de France*, 3 vols (Paris, 1643–51); Hugo Grotius, *Annales et Historiæ de Rebus Belgicis*, ed. C. and P. de Groot (Amsterdam, 1658).
62 Rapin, *History*, 9: 175–6, *Histoire*, 6: 461; Camden, *Annales*, pp. 537–9.
63 Rapin, *History*, 9: 23, *Histoire*, 6: 361; Camden, *Annales*, pp. 273–4.
64 Rapin, *History*, 8: 398, *Histoire*, 6: 269; Camden, *Annales*, p. 119.
65 E.g. Rapin, *History*, 9: 137–9, *Histoire*, 6: 435–6; Camden, *Annales*, p. 440.
66 See Rapin, *History*, 9: 214–15, *Histoire*, 6: 488–9; Camden, *Annales*, pp. 635–6.
67 See Camden, *Annales*, pp. 235, 325, 397.
68 Camden, *Annales*, p. 32.
69 Rapin, *History*, 8: 259, *Histoire*, 6: 175.
70 Rapin, *History*, 8: 265, *Histoire*, 6: 178.
71 Rapin, *History*, 8: 509, *Histoire*, 6: 345; *History*, 9: 87, *Histoire*, 6: 403.
72 For France, see Rapin, *History*, 6: 351–2, *Histoire*, 4: 454–5; Rymer, *Foedera*, 12: 489. For Brittany: Rapin, *History*, 6: 279, 324–6, *Histoire*, 4: 403, 435–7; Rymer, *Foedera*, 12: 303, 362. For Spain: Rapin, *History*, 6: 439, *Histoire*, 4: 515; Rymer, *Foedera*, 13: 142. For Flanders: Rapin, *History*, 6: 388, *Histoire*, 4: 380; Rymer, *Foedera*, 12: 576–8. For the Holy Roman Empire: Rapin, *History*, 6: 422, *Histoire*, 4: 504; Rymer, *Foedera*, 13: 3, 6–22.

73 Rapin, *History*, 6: 323, *Histoire*, 4: 434.
74 Rapin, *History*, 6: 354, *Histoire*, 4: 457.
75 Bacon, *History*, p. 85.
76 Rapin, *History*, 6: 348, *Histoire*, 4: 452.
77 Rapin, *History*, 6: 348, *Histoire*, 4: 452; Bacon, *History*, p. 85.
78 Rapin, *History*, 6: 424–6, *Histoire*, 4: 505–6; Bacon, *History*, pp. 180–3.
79 E.g. Rapin, *History*, 6: 426–7, *Histoire*, 4: 506–7; Bacon, *History*, pp. 194–5.
80 Rapin, *History*, 6: 315, *Histoire*, 4: 428.
81 Rapin, *History*, 9: 452, *Histoire*, 7: 152.
82 Bacon, *History*, p. 133.
83 Rapin, *History*, 6: 433, *Histoire*, 4: 511.
84 Rapin, *History*, 6: 451, *Histoire*, 4: 524; *History*, 6: 424, *Histoire*, 4: 505.
85 Rapin, *History*, 6: 451, *Histoire*, 4: 524.
86 See Rapin, *Histoire*, 4: 523. Tindal mistranslated this section in the first edition as 'They are your Conquerors that make the greatest Kings', *History*, 6: 450. He corrected this in later editions to the more accurate: 'Conquerors do not always make the greatest kings', Rapin, *The History of England*, 4th edn, 12 vols., tr. and ed. Nicholas Tindal (London, 1757), 5: 363.
87 Rapin, *History*, 6: 450–1, *Histoire*, 4: 523.
88 Rapin, *History*, 6: 450, *Histoire*, 4: 523.
89 Rapin, *History*, 6: 451, *Histoire*, 4: 524.
90 Rapin, *Histoire*, 1: preface (my translation).
91 See Rapin, *History* (1757).
92 Rapin, *History* (1757), 5: 360, note b.
93 Rapin, *History* (1757), 7: 414, note y; 7: 455, note q; 7: 568, note j. For Russia, see 7: 325, note u.
94 For the influence of antiquarian writing on neoclassical history, see Hicks, *Neoclassical History*, pp. 30–6.
95 Illustrated discussions of coins were a standard feature of antiquarian histories. See, for example, Camden's *Britannia* (London, 1695), p. lxxxvii. They are less common within narrative histories, but some detailed material on 'médailles' can be found in the 'character' sections of Mézeray's lavishly illustrated works on the history of France. See, for example, Mézeray, *Histoire*, 3: 660–83.
96 Thomas Madox, *History and Antiquities of the Exchequer of the Kings of England* (London, 1711), p. 548. For Madox, see Harold Hazeltine, 'Thomas Madox as Constitutional and Legal Historian 1–2', *Legal Quarterly*, 32:3 (1916), 268–89; 32:4 (1916), 352–72.
97 On the importance of numbers and economic calculation in this

period, see William P. Deringer, 'Calculated Values: The Politics and Epistemology of Economic Numbers in Britain, 1688–1738' (PhD dissertation, Princeton University, 2012).

Chapter 6

1 Douglass C. North and Barry R. Weingast, 'Constitutions and Commitment: The Evolution of Institutional Governing Public Choice in Seventeenth-Century England', *Journal of Economic History*, 49:4 (1989), 803–32 (pp. 822–3). North and Weingast's post-1688 figures are derived from B. R. Mitchell, *British Historical Statistics* (Cambridge, Cambridge University Press, 1988).

2 On the guarantees that the bank was able to provide, see Joel Mokyr, *The Enlightened Economy: Britain and the Industrial Revolution, 1700–1850* (London: Penguin, 2011), p. 225. For paper money and the growth of the market in government bonds, see P. M. Deane, *The First Industrial Revolution*, 2nd edn (Cambridge: Cambridge University Press, 1989), pp. 184–5.

3 P. G. M. Dickson, *The Financial Revolution in England: A Study in the Development of Public Credit* (London: Macmillan, 1967), p. 457.

4 North and Weingast, 'Constitutions and Commitment', 822.

5 Karl Wennerlind, *Casualties of Credit, The English Financial Revolution, 1620–1720* (Cambridge, MA: Harvard University Press, 2011), pp. 5, 169. See also J. G. A. Pocock, *The Machiavellian Moment: Florentine Political Thought and the Atlantic Republican Tradition*, 2nd edn (Princeton, NJ: Princeton University Press, 2003 [1975]), pp. 425–6; Julian Hoppit, 'Attitudes to Credit in Britain, 1680–1790', *The Historical Journal*, 33:2 (1990), 305–22.

6 Wennerlind, *Casualties of Credit*, p. 169.

7 On Court Whig writing, see Isaac Kramnick, *Bolingbroke and his Circle: The Politics of Nostalgia in the Age of Walpole* (Ithaca, NY: Cornell University Press, 1992 [1968]), pp. 48–55; H. T. Dickinson, *Liberty and Property: Political Ideology in Eighteenth-Century Britain* (London: Methuen, 1977), pp. 121–62; Thomas Horne, 'Politics in a Corrupt Society: William Arnall's Defence of Robert Walpole', *Journal of the History of Ideas*, 41:4 (1980), 601–14; Reed Browning, *Political and Constitutional Ideas of the Court Whigs* (Baton Rouge, LA: Louisiana State University Press, 1982); Simon Targett, 'Government Ideology during the Age of the Whig Supremacy: The Political Argument of Sir Robert Walpole's Newspaper Propagandists', *Historical Journal*, 37:2 (1994), 289–317.

8 Anonymous, *Some Considerations on Publick Credit* (London, 1733),

p. 5. This passage has been widely discussed. See Kramnick, *Bolingbroke and his Circle*, p. 52; Dickinson, *Liberty and Property*, p. 151; Hoppit, 'Attitudes to Credit', 316–17.

9 *London Journal*, 666 (1 April 1732), quoted in Kramnick, *Bolingbroke and his Circle*, p. 53.

10 J. Hervey, *Ancient and Modern Liberty Stated and Compared* (London, 1734), p. 5.

11 Isaac Kramnick, 'Augustan Politics and English Historiography: The Debate on the English Past, 1700–1735', *History and Theory*, 6:1 (1967), 33–56 (p. 43). See James Harrington, *The Commonwealth of Oceana and a System of Politics*, ed. J. G. A. Pocock (Cambridge: Cambridge University Press, 1992).

12 *London Journal*, 768 (16 March 1734).

13 *London Journal*, 768 (16 March 1734).

14 Hervey, *Ancient and Modern Liberty*, p. 60.

15 For the Country/Patriot opposition, see Kramnick, *Bolingbroke and his Circle*; Quentin Skinner, 'The Principles and Practice of Opposition: The Case of Bolingbroke versus Walpole', in Neil McKendrick (ed.), *Historical Perspectives: Studies in English Thought and Society in Honour of J.H. Plumb* (London: Europa, 1974), pp. 93–128; Dickinson, *Liberty and Property*, pp. 163–92; Christine Gerrard, *The Patriot Opposition to Walpole: Politics, Poetry and National Myth, 1725–1742* (Oxford: Clarendon Press, 1994); David Armitage, 'Introduction', in *Bolingbroke: Political Writings*, ed. David Armitage (Cambridge: Cambridge University Press, 1997).

16 Dickinson, *Liberty and Property*, p. 168.

17 Lord Bolingbroke, *Remarks on the History of England* (London, 1743). It is worth adding, as Max Skjönsberg has noted, that 'almost all of Bolingbroke's political writings are historical to a greater or lesser degree'; Max Skjönsberg, 'Bolingbroke's Theory of Party and Opposition', *Historical Journal*, 59:4 (2016), 947–73 (p. 950).

18 Bolingbroke, *Remarks*, p. 28. For a detailed discussion of Bolingbroke's views on faction, see Pat Rogers, 'Swift and Bolingbroke on Faction', *Journal of British Studies*, 9:2 (1970), 71–101.

19 Bolingbroke, *Remarks*, p. 108.

20 Bolingbroke, *Remarks*, p. 138.

21 Bolingbroke, *Remarks*, p. 166.

22 Bolingbroke, *Remarks*, p. 211.

23 Bolingbroke, *Remarks*, p. 169.

24 Bolingbroke, *Remarks*, p. 211.

25 For Salmon's life, see Thompson Cooper, 'Salmon, Thomas (*bap.* 1679, *d.* 1767)', rev. Philip Carter, *Oxford Dictionary of National Biography*,

Oxford University Press, 2004. See also Laird Okie, *Augustan Historical Writing: Histories of England in the English Enlightenment* (Lanham, MD: University of America Press, 1991), pp. 99–113.

26 Thomas Salmon (ed.), *A Compleat Collection of State-tryals*, 4 vols (London, 1719). Salmon went on to edit *Tryals for High-treason, and other crimes*, 9 vols (London, 1720–31).

27 Thomas Salmon, *The Life of Her Late Majesty Queen Anne*, 2 vols (London, 1721).

28 Thomas Salmon, *An Impartial Examination of Bishop Burnet's History of His Own Times*, 2 vols (London, 1724).

29 This work had originally been published by Salmon's father. See Thomas Salmon (1648–1706), *Historical Collections* (London, 1706). His son added a new preface and altered the title, issuing the work as *The History of Great Britain* (London, 1725).

30 John Henley to Lord Carteret, 28 January 1724, SP 35/48 f. 68. For Henley, see Graham Midgley, *The Life of Orator Henley* (Oxford: Clarendon Press, 1973).

31 See *Evening Post*, 1 February, 1724.

32 John Henley to Lord Carteret, 4 February 1724, SP 35/48 f. 78.

33 John Henley to Lord Carteret, 4 February 1724, SP 35/48 f. 78.

34 *The Daily Post*, 19 May 1724. The *Post*'s account noted that 'Mr Rivington, Bookseller, and Mr Bethenham Printer, being concern'd in a Book entitled, *A Review of the History of England. By Mr Salmon*, appear'd in their Recognizances, and were discharg'd.'

35 Thomas Salmon, *Modern History, or the Present State of All Nations*, 31 vols (London, 1724–38).

36 Salmon, *Modern History*, 1: introduction.

37 This summary is from the dedication to the third edition of the text. Thomas Salmon, *Modern History*, 3rd edn, 3 vols (London, 1744), I: dedication.

38 *Universal Spectator and Weekly Journal*, 16 September 1732.

39 *Universal Spectator and Weekly Journal*, 16 September 1732.

40 Salmon, *The History of Great Britain*, preface.

41 Salmon, *The History of Great Britain*, preface.

42 Salmon, *The History of Great Britain*, preface.

43 Salmon, *The History of Great Britain*, preface.

44 Salmon, *Modern History*, 24: 41.

45 Salmon, *Modern History*, 26: 133. See Doohwan Ahn, 'The Anglo-French Treaty of Commerce of 1713: Tory Trade Politics and the Question of Dutch Decline', *History of European Ideas*, 36:2 (2010), 167–80. For the origins of anti-Dutch feeling, see Steven C.A. Pincus, *Protestantism and Patriotism: Ideologies and the Making of English*

Foreign Policy, 1650–1668 (Cambridge: Cambridge University Press, 1996), pp. 58–61. The most famous of the anti-Dutch texts is Jonathan Swift's *Conduct of the Allies and of the Late Ministry* (London, 1711).

46 Salmon, *Modern History*, 25: 102.
47 Salmon, *Modern History*, 26: 193.
48 Salmon, *Modern History*, 20: 21*; 20: 285.
49 John Strype, *Annals of the Reformation*, 4 vols (London, 1709–31). For examples of Salmon's references to Strype, see Salmon, *Modern History*, 20: 19, 25, 78. References are also made to Strype's *Life and Acts of John Whitgift* (London, 1718); see Salmon, *Modern History*, 20: 117.
50 See Salmon, *Modern History*, 15: 382–3.
51 Rapin, *History*, 8: 265, *Histoire*, 6: 178.
52 Salmon, *Modern History*, 20: 361.
53 Salmon, *Modern History*, 1: i.
54 Salmon, *Modern History*, 1: i.
55 Salmon, *Modern History*, 1: i.
56 For Russia, compare Salmon, *Modern History*, 20: 93–4; Camden, *Annales*, pp. 123–4. It is significant, however, that whereas Camden presented the interlopers who disrupted the company's trade as German, Salmon referred to them as Dutch. For the Huguenots, see Salmon, *Modern History*, 20: 91; Camden, *Annales*, p. 119. On sumptuary legislation, see Salmon, *Modern History*, 20: 136; Camden, *Annales*, pp. 243–4.
57 Salmon, *Modern History*, 20: 263.
58 Salmon, *Modern History*, 20: 93.
59 Salmon, *Modern History*, 20: 94.
60 Salmon, *Modern History*, 20: 37.
61 Salmon, *Modern History*, 20: 258.
62 Salmon, *Modern History*, 25: 102.
63 Salmon, *Modern History*, 18: 343.
64 For the excise bill, see Paul Langford, *The Excise Crisis: Society and Politics in the Age of Walpole* (Oxford: Clarendon Press, 1975); Michael Jubb, 'Economic Policy and Economic Development', in Jeremy Black (ed.), *Britain in the Age of Walpole* (Basingstoke: Macmillan, 1984), pp. 136–42.
65 Jubb, 'Economic Policy', p. 138.
66 The opposition campaign was led by the *Craftsman*, and the paper, aware of the government's plan for a 'general excise', devoted eight consecutive issues (330–7) to the matter between 28 October and 16 December 1732. The campaign was continued the following year, most notably through the republication of long excerpts from the

1706 pamphlet *Remarks on the horrible Oppressions, Insolencies, and unjustifiable Partialities of the Commissioners of the Excise* (*Craftsman*, 342). For examples of pamphlet literature, see Anonymous, *The Nature of the Present Excise*, 2nd edn (London, 1733); Anonymous, *Excise Anatomis'd* (London, 1733).

67 *The Craftsman*, 16 December 1732.

68 Anonymous, *Nature of the Present Excise*, p. 10. See also *An Excise Elegy, or the Dragon Demolish'd* (London, 1733), which argued that the right of officers to gage the 'stocks' of merchants not only threatened liberties, but also made it possible for officials to gage what lay under their wives' and daughters' smocks.

69 Salmon, *Modern History*, 18: 368. The passage quotes from Bacon, *History*, p. 182.

70 Salmon, *Modern History*, 18: 368.

71 Salmon, *Modern History*, 18: 368.

72 Salmon, *Modern History*, 18: 368.

73 Salmon went so far as to argue that it was Elizabeth who had 'granted more Monopolies, took up Money by Loans, Benevolences, and Privy-Seals out of Parliament, and imprison'd more Members for speaking disrespectfully of her Administration, and disobeying her Orders, than ever King *James* did'; Salmon, *Modern History*, 21: 31.

74 Salmon, *Modern History*, 21: 54.

75 Salmon, *Modern History*, 21: 33.

76 Salmon, *Modern History*, 20: 415.

77 Salmon, *Modern History*, 20: 415

78 Salmon, *Modern History*, 21: 55.

79 Salmon, *Modern History*, 21: 55.

80 Salmon, *Modern History*, 21: 55.

81 Salmon, *Modern History*, 21: 55.

82 Salmon, *Modern History*, 20: 451.

83 Salmon, *Modern History*, 20: 450.

84 Salmon, *Modern History*, 1: 368.

85 Salmon, *Modern History*, 1: 368.

86 Salmon, *Modern History*, 1: 237.

87 Salmon, *Modern History*, 1: 321.

88 Salmon, *Modern History*, 20: 420.

89 Salmon, *Modern History*, 20: 451.

Chapter 7

1 For Carte, see Paul Kléber Monod, 'Thomas Carte, the Druids and British National Identity', in Paul Kléber Monod, Murray Pittock and

Daniel Szechi (eds), *Loyalty and Identity: Jacobites at Home and Abroad* (Basingstoke: Palgrave, 2010), pp. 132–48; Laird Okie, *Augustan Historical Writing: Histories of England in the English Enlightenment* (Lanham, MD: University Press of America, 1991), pp. 135–54; Philip Hicks, *Neoclassical History and English Culture* (Basingstoke: Macmillan, 1996), pp. 159–69; Stuart Handley, 'Carte, Thomas (*bap*. 1686, *d*. 1754)', *Oxford Dictionary of National Biography*, Oxford University Press, 2004, online edn, May 2015. This paragraph and the next are based on these sources.

2 Thomas Carte, *History and Life of James Duke of Ormonde*, 3 vols (London, 1735–36); *General History of England*, 4 vols (1747–55).

3 See Eveline Cruickshanks and Howard Erskine Hill, *The Atterbury Plot* (Basingstoke: Palgrave, 2004), p. 157.

4 See Okie, *Augustan Historical Writing*, pp. 136–7.

5 Thomas Carte, *A Collection of Several Papers* (London, 1744), p. 6.

6 Monod, 'Thomas Carte', p. 135.

7 Whig supporters of the venture included the Speaker of the House of Commons, Arthur Onslow.

8 See *Jacobite's Journal*, 20 February 1748; 27 February 1748; *General Evening Post*, 14 January 1748. For Carte's response, see *General Evening Post*, 20 February 1748.

9 Okie, *Augustan Historical Writing*, p. 147.

10 Monod, 'Thomas Carte', p. 133. See also Colin Kidd, *British Identities before Nationalism: Ethnicity and Nationhood in the Atlantic World, 1600–1800* (Cambridge: Cambridge University Press, 2002); J. G. A. Pocock, *The Ancient Constitution and the Feudal Law: A Study of English Historical Thought in the Seventeenth Century*, 2nd edn (Cambridge: Cambridge University Press, 1987 [1957]), pp. 368–9.

11 Corbyn Morris, *A Letter from a Bystander to a Member of Parliament* (London, 1742). The date printed is 1741. Carte's reply was *A Full Answer to the Letter from a By-Stander* (London, 1742). Morris responded with *A letter to the Reverend Mr Thomas Carte* (London, 1743), and Carte concluded the spat with *A Full and Clear Vindication of the Full Answer to a Letter from A By-Stander* (London, 1743).

12 Morris, *A Letter*, p. 9.

13 Morris, *A Letter*, p. 28.

14 Morris, *A Letter*, pp. 15, 25.

15 Morris, *A Letter*, p. 31.

16 Morris, *A Letter*, pp. 33–4.

17 Morris, *A Letter*, p. 58.

18 Carte, *A Full Answer*, p. 177.

19 Carte, *A Full Answer*, pp. 11–12.

20 Carte, *A Full Answer*, p. 29.
21 Carte, *A Full Answer*, p. 29.
22 Carte, *A Full Answer*, p. 167.
23 Carte, *A Full Answer*, p. 168.
24 Carte, *A Full Answer*, p. 168.
25 Carte, *A Full Answer*, p. 200.
26 Morris, *A Letter*, p. 30
27 Robert Filmer, 'Anarchy', in *Patriarcha and Other Writings*, ed. Johann P. Sommerville (Cambridge: Cambridge University Press, 1991), p. 138.
28 Filmer, 'Anarchy', p. 138.
29 Filmer, 'Anarchy', p. 138.
30 Carte, *General History*, 1: 8.
31 Carte, *General History*, 1: 8.
32 Carte, *General History*, 1: 8.
33 Carte, *General History*, 1: 77.
34 Carte, *General History*, 1: 77.
35 Carte, *General History*, 1: 177.
36 Carte, *General History*, 1: 177.
37 Carte, *General History*, 1: 177.
38 Pocock, *The Ancient Constitution*, p. 369.
39 Carte, *General History*, 1: 376.
40 Carte, *General History*, 1: 363.
41 Carte, *General History*, 1: 363–4.
42 Carte, *General History*, 1: 14.
43 Carte, *General History*, 1: 14.
44 Carte, *General History*, 1: 21.
45 Carte, *General History*, 1: 21.
46 Carte, *General History*, 1: 75. See also 1: 25.
47 Carte, *General History*, 1: 321, 307.
48 Carte, *General History*, 4: 301.
49 Carte, *General History*, 4: 301.
50 Carte, *General History*, 4: 301.
51 Carte, *General History*, 4: 5.
52 Carte, *General History*, 4: 5; 4: 276.
53 Carte, *General History*, 4: 5.
54 Carte, *General History*, 4: 133; 4: 39. Similar comments are made at 3: 727.
55 Carte, *General History*, 3: 330.
56 Carte, *General History*, 3: 330.
57 Carte, *General History*, 3: 279.
58 Carte, *General History*, 3: 727.

59 Carte, *General History*, 3: 761.
60 Carte, *General History*, 4: 253.
61 Carte, *General History*, 4: 181.
62 Carte, *General History*, 4: 181.
63 Carte, *General History*, 4: 24.
64 Carte, *General History*, 4: 24.
65 Carte, *General History*, 4: 17.
66 Carte, *General History*, 3: 727.
67 Carte, *General History*, 4: 134.
68 Carte, *General History*, 4: 134.
69 Carte, *General History*, 4: 134.
70 Carte, *General History*, 4: 134.
71 Carte, *General History*, 4: 134. For Charles's abandonment of feudal duties, see *General History* 4: 187–8.
72 Carte, *General History*, 2: 866.
73 Carte, *General History*, 2: 865.
74 Carte, *General History*, 2: 866.
75 Carte, *General History*, 3: 1.
76 Carte, *General History*, 3: 1.
77 Carte, *General History*, 3: 699.
78 Carte, *General History*, 3: 700. On Russia, see Carte, *General History*, 3: 700, 577; Camden, *Annales*, pp. 102–4, 285–6. On Turkey, see Carte, *General History*, 3: 555; Camden, *Annales*, p. 235. On coin and copper (or 'brass' as both writers refer to it), see Carte, *General History*, 3: 398; Camden, *Annales*, pp. 48–9. On the benefits brought by Huguenot immigrants, see Carte, *General History*, 3: 481; Camden, *Annales*, p. 119.
79 Carte, *General History*, 3: 398; Camden, *Annales*, p. 49.
80 Carte, *General History*, 3: 398.
81 Carte, *General History*, 4: 129.
82 Carte, *General History*, 3: 784; Howes, *Annales*, p. 894.
83 Carte, *General History*, 3: 784; Howes, *Annales*, pp. 993–5.
84 Carte, *General History*, 3: 784–5; Howes, *Annales*, pp. 1018–21. The discussions of America were supplemented with material by the Flemish writer Emanuel van Meteren and the French diplomat Antoine Lefèvre de la Boderie.
85 Carte, *General History*, 4: 129.
86 Carte, *General History*, 4: 29.
87 Carte, *General History*, 4: 4.
88 Carte, *General History*, 4: 258.
89 Carte, *General History*, 4: 305.
90 Carte, *General History*, 3: 788.

91 Carte, *General History*, 3: 788.
92 Carte, *General History*, 3: 788.
93 Carte, *General History*, 3: 788.
94 Carte, *General History*, 3: 787.
95 Carte, *General History*, 3: 788.
96 For Carte's description of this process in relation to England's early history, see *General History*, 1: 78.
97 Carte, *General History*, 3: 789.
98 Carte, *General History*, 3: 789.
99 Carte, *General History*, 3: 788.
100 Carte, *General History*, 3: 788.
101 Carte, *General History*, 4: 129.

Chapter 8

1 See J. G. A. Pocock, *Barbarism and Religion, Volume 2: Narratives of Government* (Cambridge: Cambridge University Press, 1999), pp. 17–25; Karen O'Brien, *Narratives of Enlightenment: Cosmopolitan History from Voltaire to Gibbon* (Cambridge: Cambridge University Press, 1997), p. 11. O'Brien goes on to make the important point that attitudes to this assumption varied: 'the idea registers, in some instances as a glow of confidence in the historian's own age and country, but is more often received as a soberly responsible recognition of the benefits and limitations of living in a modern world, less spectacular, heroic or culturally innovative than that which had gone before'. For further discussion of eighteenth-century ideas of progress, see John Robertson, *The Case for Enlightenment: Scotland and Naples, 1680–1760* (Cambridge: Cambridge University Press, 2005), pp. 28–30; R. L. Meek, *Social Science and the Ignoble Savage* (Cambridge: Cambridge University Press, 1976).
2 The clearest account of the interconnectedness of different aspects of learning comes in Hume's essay 'Of Luxury', in *Political Discourses* (Edinburgh, 1752), pp. 23–40.
3 The literature on conjectural history is a voluminous one. See, for example, H. M. Hopfl, 'From Savage to Scotsman: Conjectural History in the Scottish Enlightenment', *Journal of British Studies*, 17:2 (1978), 19–40; Mark Salber Phillips, *Society and Sentiment: Genres of Historical Writing in Britain, 1740–1820* (Princeton, NJ: Princeton University Press, 2000), pp. 171–89. See also Frank Palmeri, *State of Nature, Stages of Society: Enlightenment Conjectural History and Modern Social Discourse* (New York: Columbia University Press, 2016).

4 Philip Hicks, *Neoclassical History and English Culture: From Clarendon to Hume* (Basingstoke: Macmillan, 1996), pp. 7–22.

5 Pierre le Moyne, *Of the Art of Writing & Judging of History*, cited by Hicks, *Neoclassical History*, p. 8.

6 James Boswell, *Life of Johnson*, ed. R. W. Chapman (Oxford: Oxford University Press, 1998), p. 85. For another account, see John Ramsay, *Scotland and Scotsmen in the Eighteenth Century from the MSS. of John Ramsay*, ed. Alexander Allardyce, 2 vols (Edinburgh: W. Blackwood and Sons, 1888), 2: 547–9. Modern discussions can be found in Duncan Forbes, *Hume's Philosophical Politics*, rev. edn (Cambridge: Cambridge University Press, 1978 [1975]), pp. 253–8; Laird Okie, *Augustan Historical Writing: Histories of England in the English Enlightenment* (Lanham, MD: University Press of America, 1991), pp. 171–95; Laird Okie, 'William Guthrie: Enlightenment Historian', *Historian*, 51:2 (1989), 221–38; Hicks, *Neoclassical History*, pp. 156–65. David Allan, 'Guthrie, William (1708?–1770)', *Oxford Dictionary of National Biography*, Oxford University Press, 2004; Gabriel Glickman, 'Cultures and Coteries in Mid-Century Toryism: Johnson in Oxford and London', in Jonathan Clark and Howard Erskine-Hill (eds), *The Politics of Samuel Johnson* (Basingstoke: Palgrave, 2012), pp. 57–89 (pp. 72–81).

7 For Guthrie and Johnson, see Peter Martin, *Samuel Johnson: A Biography* (London: Phoenix, 2008), pp. 155–7. See also Gillian Williamson, *British Masculinity and the Gentleman's Magazine* (Basingstoke: Palgrave, 2016), p. 22.

8 For Guthrie's involvement with the periodical press, see Laurence Hanson, *Government and the Press, 1695–1763* (Oxford: Clarendon Press, 1967 [1936]), pp. 119–20; Bob Harris, *A Patriot Press: National Politics and the London Press in the 1740s* (Oxford: Oxford University Press, 1997), pp. 38–42; Michael Harris, *London Newspapers in the Age of Walpole: A Study of the Origins of the Modern English Press* (London and Toronto: Associated University Presses, 1987), pp. 130–1. For *Common Sense*, see Thomas Lockwood, 'The Life and Death of *Common Sense*', *Prose Studies*, 16:1 (1993), 78–93.

9 See Bob Harris, *Politics and the Nation: Britain in the Mid-Eighteenth Century* (Oxford: Oxford University Press, 2002), pp. 42–3.

10 For the arrest warrant, see SP 36/60/1, f.86–87. The material taken from Guthrie can be found at TS 23/6. The *London Daily Post* of 23 March 1743 noted that 'Last Night William Guthrie, Esq.; the suppos'd Author of Old-England, or the Constitutional Journal, was discharged out of Custody.'

11 Public Records Office North Ireland, T 3158/251 and *Parliamentary*

History, xiii, 564–5, both quoted in Harris, *Politics and the Nation*, p. 43.

12 *Old England, or the Constitutional Journal*, 5 March 1743. A similar argument is made in relation to Henry III and Edward II in the number of *Old England* published on 31 March 1744.

13 *Old England*, 5 March 1743.

14 *Old England*, 5 March 1743.

15 *Old England*, 5 March 1743.

16 *Old England*, 5 March 1743.

17 *Old England*, 24 November 1744.

18 *Old England*, 24 November 1744.

19 *Old England*, 2 March 1745.

20 *Old England*, 2 March 1745.

21 *Old England*, 2 March 1745.

22 *Old England*, 2 March 1745.

23 *Old England*, 2 March 1745.

24 *Old England*, 2 March 1745.

25 *London Daily Post and General Advertiser*, 11 February 1744.

26 Hanson, *Government and the Press*, p. 119.

27 BL. Add. MS 35397, f. 53–5: Birch to Yorke, 11 July 1747, quoted in Harris, *A Patriot Press*, p. 42.

28 Guthrie, *General History*, 1: iv.

29 Guthrie, *General History*, 4: 1393.

30 Guthrie, *General History*, 2: 788.

31 Guthrie, *General History*, 2: 788.

32 Guthrie, *General History*, 4: 1394.

33 Guthrie, *General History*, 2: 795; Bacon, *History*, pp. 65–7; Guthrie, *General History*, 2: 803; Bacon, *History*, p. 86; Guthrie, *General History*, 2: 838; Bacon, *History*, pp. 174–8.

34 Guthrie, *General History*, 2: 832.

35 Guthrie, *General History*, 2: 796; Bacon, *History*, p. 67. See also the discussion of the regulation of silver coin (Guthrie, *General History*, 2: 841; Bacon, *History*, pp. 215–16) and the prohibition of the manufacture of silks (Guthrie, *General History*, 2: 841; Bacon, *History*, p. 841).

36 Guthrie, *General History*, 2: 849.

37 Guthrie, *General History*, 2: 771.

38 Guthrie, *General History*, 3: 834.

39 Bolingbroke, *Remarks*, p. 108.

40 Guthrie, *General History*, 3: 378. For further comparisons with Henry VII, see 3: 365.

41 Guthrie, *General History*, 3: 489.

42 Guthrie, *General History*, 3: 308; Camden, *Annales*, p. 119.
43 Guthrie, *General History*, 3: 401, 553; Camden, *Annales*, pp. 235, 596.
44 Guthrie, *General History*, 3: 301, 322, 420; Camden, *Annales*, pp. 103, 124, 285–6.
45 See Camden, *Annales*, pp. 102–4.
46 Guthrie, *General History*, 3: 301.
47 Camden, *Annales*, p. 169.
48 Guthrie, *General History*, 3: 357.
49 Guthrie, *General History*, 3: 471.
50 Guthrie, *General History*, 3: 471.
51 e.g. Guthrie, *General History*, 3: 625.
52 Guthrie, *General History*, 3: 380.
53 Guthrie, *General History*, 4: 819.
54 Guthrie, *General History*, 4: 642.
55 Guthrie, *General History*, 4: 691.
56 Guthrie, *General History*, 4: 669.
57 Guthrie, *General History*, 4: 683.
58 Guthrie, *General History*, 4: 683, 821.
59 Guthrie, *General History*, 4: 647.
60 Guthrie, *General History*, 4: 821.
61 Guthrie, *General History*, 4: 896.
62 Guthrie, *General History*, 4: 896.
63 Guthrie, *General History*, 4: 925–31.
64 Guthrie, *General History*, 4: 929.
65 Guthrie, *General History*, 4: 929–30.

Chapter 9

1 For biographical accounts of this period of Hume's life, see E. C. Mossner, *The Life of David Hume*, 2nd edn (Oxford: Clarendon Press, 1980 [1954]); John Robertson, 'Hume, David (1711–1776)', *Oxford Dictionary of National Biography*, Oxford University Press, 2004, online edn, January 2009; Ian Simpson Ross, 'The Emergence of Hume as a Political Economist', in Carl Wennerlind and Margaret Schabas (eds), *Hume's Political Economy* (London: Routledge, 2008), pp. 31–48. See also James A. Harris, *Hume: An Intellectual Biography* (Cambridge: Cambridge University Press, 2015).

2 For Hume's political economy, see Willie Henderson, *The Origins of David Hume's Economics* (London: Routledge, 2010); Istvan Hont, *The Jealousy of Trade: International Competition and the Nation-State in Historical Perspective* (Cambridge, MA: Harvard University Press, 2005); Carl Wennerlind and Margaret Schabas (eds), *David Hume's*

Political Economy (London: Routledge, 2008); Eugene Rotwein (ed.), *Writings on Economics: David Hume* (New Brunswick, NJ: Transaction Publishers, 2007); Andrew Skinner, 'Hume's Principles of Political Economy', in David Fate Norton and Jacqueline Taylor (eds), *The Cambridge Companion to David Hume* (Cambridge: Cambridge University Press, 2009), pp. 381–413. For a more general account of the development of political economy which contains useful discussion of Hume, see Donald Winch, *Riches and Poverty: An Intellectual History of Political Economy in Britain, 1750–1834* (Cambridge: Cambridge University Press, 1996).

3 David Hume, 'My Own Life', in Eugene F. Miller (ed.), *Essays Moral, Political and Literary* (Indianapolis, IN: Liberty Fund, 1985), pp. xxxi–xli (p. xxxvi).

4 These letters and others on economic themes are usefully collected in Rotwein, *Writings on Economics*, pp. 185–224. See also David Hume, *The Letters of David Hume*, ed. J. Y. T. Greig, 2 vols (Oxford: Clarendon Press, 1932).

5 David Hume, *The History of Great Britain, volume 1* (Edinburgh, 1754). Subsequent references to the *History* are given by a short form of the title and the year of publication (e.g. *History of Great Britain* (1754)). For Hume's early references to writing history, see Hume to Henry Home, 1747, *Letters*, 1: 98–100, Hume to James Oswald of Dunnikier, 29 January 1748, *Letters* 1: 108–10. Hume first mentions having commenced work on the project in Hume to Adam Smith, 24 September 1752, *Letters*, 1: 167–9.

6 David Hume, *The History of Great Britain, volume 2* (London, 1757); *England under the House of Tudor*, 2 vols (London, 1759). A revised version of the Stuart volumes also appeared in 1759.

7 David Hume, *The History of England from the Invasion of Julius Cæsar to the Accession of Henry VII*, 2 vols (London, 1761–62).

8 David Hume, *The History of England from the Invasion of Julius Cæsar to the Revolution in 1688*, 6 vols (London, 1762).

9 David Hume, *The History of England from the Invasion of Julius Cæsar to the Revolution in 1688*, 8 vols (London, 1770); *The History of England from the Invasion of Julius Cæsar to the Revolution in 1688*, 8 vols (London, 1773); *The History of England from the Invasion of Julius Cæsar to the Revolution in 1688*, 8 vols (London, 1778).

10 Alternative approaches to these issues can also be found in Constant Noble Stockton, 'Economics and the Mechanism of Historical Progress in Hume's *History*', in Donald W. Livingston and James T. King (eds), *Hume: A Re-Evaluation* (New York: Fordham University Press, 1976), pp. 296–322; John W. Danford,

'Hume's *History* and the Parameters of Economic Development', in Nicholas Capaldi and Donald W. Livingston (eds), *Liberty in Hume's History of England* (Dordecht: Kluwer, 1990), pp. 155–94.

11 Duncan Forbes, *Hume's Philosophical Politics*, rev. edn (Cambridge: Cambridge University Press, 1978 [1975]); Nicholas Phillipson, *David Hume: The Philosopher as Historian*, rev. edn (London: Penguin, 2011 [1989]); Harris, *Hume: An Intellectual Biography*, pp. 305–407. See also Mark G. Spencer (ed.), *David Hume: Historical Thinker, Historical Writer* (Philadelphia, PA: University of Pennsylvania Press, 2013). For the relevance of Hume's history to modern political theory, see Andrew Sabl, *Hume's Politics: Co-ordination and Crisis in the History of England* (Princeton, NJ: Princeton University Press, 2015).

12 Forbes, *Hume's Philosophical Politics*, p. x. It should be emphasised that while the idea that Hume was engaged in a political 'project' is a popular one in the critical literature, the nature of that project has been the subject of considerable debate. For a summary, see David Wootton, 'David Hume "The Historian"', in David Fate Norton and Jacqueline Taylor (eds), *The Cambridge Companion to David Hume* (Cambridge: Cambridge University Press, 2009), pp. 447–79 (pp. 465–6).

13 Forbes, *Hume's Philosophical Politics*, p. x.

14 Such a claim is, in part, in line with the work of Moritz Baumstark, who has argued that modern interpretations of Hume's work 'tend to hinge on the *Essays, Moral and Political* (1741–48), a work of political analysis in which Hume is deemed to have developed the basic elements of the historical views he was to expound in the *History of England*'. Such an approach, Baumstark notes, 'does not sufficiently take into account Hume's later views on subjects as varied as commerce, manners, and the history of religion, some of which are not foreshadowed in the *Treatise* or indeed the *Essays, Moral and Political*'. Moritz Baumstark, 'David Hume: The Making of a Philosophical History. A Reconsideration' (PhD dissertation, University of Edinburgh, 2007), p. 24.

15 David Hume, 'Of the Rise and Progress of the Arts and Sciences', in *Essays, Moral and Political, Volume II* (Edinburgh, 1742).

16 Hume, 'Arts and Sciences' (1742), p. 54.

17 Hume, 'Arts and Sciences' (1742), p. 54.

18 Hume, 'Arts and Sciences' (1742), pp. 55–6.

19 Hume, 'Arts and Sciences' (1742), p. 55.

20 Hume, 'Arts and Sciences' (1742), p. 56.

21 Hume, 'Arts and Sciences' (1742), p. 56.

22 Hume, 'Arts and Sciences' (1742), p. 56.

23 Hume, 'Arts and Sciences' (1742), pp. 57–8.

24 The Homer example is discussed in Hume, 'Arts and Sciences' (1742), pp. 58–9.
25 Hume, 'Arts and Sciences' (1742), p. 56,
26 Hume, 'Of Commerce', in *Political Discourses* (Edinburgh, 1752), p. 12.
27 Hume, 'Of Commerce' (1752), p. 16.
28 Hume, 'Of Commerce' (1752), p. 16.
29 Hume, 'Of Interest', in *Political Discourses* (1752), p. 75; 'Of the Balance of Trade', in *Political Discourses*, p. 80. Hume also used the term 'groundless' to describe the 'jealousy of trade': 'Of the Jealousy of Trade', in *Essays and Treatises on Several Subjects* (London, 1758), p. 187.
30 Hume, 'Of Commerce' (1752), pp. 2–3.
31 Hume, 'Of Commerce' (1752), p. 3.
32 Hume, 'Of Commerce' (1752), p. 3.
33 Hume, 'Of Money', in *Political Discourses* (1752), p. 59.
34 Hume, 'Of the Balance of Trade' (1752), pp. 97–8.
35 Hume, 'Of the Balance of Trade' (1752), p. 98.
36 Hume, 'Of Taxes', in *Political Discourses* (1752), p. 115.
37 J. G. A. Pocock, *Barbarism and Religion, Volume 2: Narratives of Government* (Cambridge: Cambridge University Press, 1999), p. 208.
38 For Hume's debts to classical ideas of history, see Philip Hicks, *Neoclassical History and English Culture: From Clarendon to Hume* (Basingstoke: Macmillan, 1996), pp. 177–82.
39 Hume to John Clephane, 5 January 1753, *Letters*, 1: 170.
40 Hume to John Clephane, 5 January 1753, *Letters*, 1: 169.
41 See Pocock, *Barbarism and Religion 2*, pp. 207–8; Mark Salber Phillips, *Society and Sentiment: Genres of Historical Writing in Britain, 1740–1820* (Princeton, NJ: Princeton University Press, 2000), pp. 48–55. While Pocock and Phillips both use the term 'philosophical history', their understandings of it are rather different. Phillips, building on the definition of Momigliano, presents 'philosophical history' as an account of general causes, and views its relationship with traditional narrative as one of 'critique'. Pocock, in contrast, sees 'philosophical history' as combining a 'narrative of state' with a 'narrative of manners' and, consequently, as a synthesis of traditional narrative history and more 'general' forms of cultural analysis. See Pocock, *Barbarism and Religion 2*, pp. 17–25; Arnaldo Momigliano, 'Eighteenth-Century Prelude to Mr Gibbon' (1976), in *Sesto Contributo Alla Storia Degli Studi Classici E Del Mondo Antico* (Rome: Edizioni di Storia e Letteratura, 1980).
42 Hume, *History of Great Britain* (1754), 1: 116.
43 Hume, *History of Great Britain* (1754), 1: 116.

44 Hume, *History of Great Britain* (1757), 2: 117.
45 See Hume to Adam Smith, 24 September 1752, *Letters*, 1: 167–8.
46 Hume, *History of Great Britain* (1754), 1: 15.
47 Hume, *History of Great Britain* (1754), 1: 15.
48 Hume, *History of Great Britain* (1754), 1: 15.
49 Hume, *History of Great Britain* (1754), 1: 15.
50 Hume, *History of Great Britain* (1754), 1: 33.
51 Hume, *History of Great Britain* (1754), 1: 34.
52 Hume, *History of Great Britain* (1754), 1: 34.
53 Hume, *History of Great Britain* (1754), 1: 34.
54 Hume, *History of Great Britain* (1754), 1: 34.
55 Hume, *History of Great Britain* (1754), 1: 34.
56 Hume, *History of Great Britain* (1754), 1: 16.
57 Hume, *History of Great Britain* (1754), 1: 35.
58 Hume, *History of Great Britain* (1754), 1: 35.
59 Hume, *History of Great Britain* (1754), 1: 35.
60 Hume, *History of Great Britain* (1754), 1: 35.
61 Hume, *History of Great Britain* (1754), 1: 34.
62 See Bolingbroke, *Remarks*, pp. 145, 247.
63 Hume, *History of Great Britain* (1754), 1: 130.
64 Hume, *History of Great Britain* (1754), 1: 131.
65 Hume, *History of Great Britain* (1754), 1: 131.
66 Hume, *History of Great Britain* (1754), 1: 131–2.
67 Thomas Rymer, *Foedera* (London, 1714–35). To estimate the number of seamen employed during this period, Hume turned to a work of economic literature, *The Trade's Increase* (London, 1615). He found this treatise in the *Harleian Miscellany*, a collection of material from the library of Robert Harley, Earl of Oxford. See *The Harleian Miscellany*, ed. William Oldys, 8 vols (London, 1744–46), 4: 202–20.
68 Hume, *History of Great Brita*in (1754), 1: 130. The passages that Hume quoted from are John Stow and Edmund Howes, *Annales, or General Chronicle of England* (London, 1631), pp. 895, 1021.
69 Hume, *History of Great Britain* (1754), 1: 131–3.
70 Hume, *History of Great Britain* (1754), 1: 132.
71 Hume, *History of Great Britain* (1754), 1: 133.
72 Hume, *History of Great Britain* (1754), 1: 134.
73 Hume, *History of Great Britain* (1754), 1: 134.
74 Hume, *History of Great Britain* (1754), 1: 135 (my italics). It is also worth noting that Hume's views on monopolistic trading companies, as expressed in the main body of his narrative, were diametrically opposed to those of Howes. Hume argued that James had done nothing to control these companies and that their monopolies constituted

an 'enormous grievance, the greatest which we read of in English [history]'. Howes, by contrast, as we saw in Chapter 3, was a semi-official employee of the trading companies, and a staunch defender of their interests. For Hume's comments, see *History of Great Britain* (1754), 1: 16–17.

75 Hume, *History of Great Britain* (1757), 2: 123.
76 Hume, *History of Great Britain* (1757), 2: 448.
77 Hume, *History of Great Britain* (1757), 2: 123.
78 Hume, *History of Great Britain* (1757), 2: 449.
79 Hume, *History of Great Britain* (1757), 2: 449.
80 See, for example, his discussion of the ill-effects of war with Spain on English merchants: Hume, *History of Great Britain* (1757), 2: 123.
81 Hume, *History of Great Britain* (1757), 2: 165.
82 Hume, *History of Great Britain* (1757), 2: 123.
83 Hume, *History of Great Britain* (1757), 2: 448.
84 Hume, *History of Great Britain* (1757), 2: 123.
85 Hume, *History of Great Britain* (1757), 2: 434.
86 David Hume to John Clephane, 2 September 1757, *Letters*, 1: 264.
87 David Hume, *The History of England under the House of Tudor*, 2 vols (London, 1759), 1: 54–6; Bacon, *History*, pp. 174–8.
88 Hume, *House of Tudor* (1759), 1: 139–40, 199–200, 264.
89 Simonds D'Ewes, *A Compleat Journal of the Notes, Speeches and Debates Both of the House of Lords and House of Commons, throughout the whole Reign of Queen Elizabeth, of glorious memory* (London, 1708).
90 Hume, *House of Tudor* (1759), 1: 56, 2: 706.
91 Hume, *House of Tudor* (1759), 2: 707.
92 Hume, *House of Tudor* (1759), 1: 56.
93 Hume, *House of Tudor* (1759), 1: 56.
94 Hume, *House of Tudor* (1759), 2: 706.
95 Hume, *House of Tudor* (1759), 1: 56.
96 Hume, *House of Tudor* (1759), 1: 264.
97 Hume, *House of Tudor* (1759), 2: 707.
98 Hume, *House of Tudor* (1759), 2: 707.
99 Hume, *House of Tudor* (1759), 2: 709–10. D'Ewes identifies the lachrymose Member of Parliament as Robert Wingfield (*A Compleat Journal*, p. 654) and the other as the Speaker of the House, John Croke (p. 657).
100 Hume, *House of Tudor* (1759), 2: 707.
101 Hume, *House of Tudor* (1759), 1: 65–6.
102 Hume, *House of Tudor* (1759), 1: 63.
103 Hume, *House of Tudor* (1759), 1: 63.
104 Hume, *House of Tudor* (1759), 1: 66.

105 Hume, *House of Tudor* (1759), 1: 61.
106 Hume, 'Of Commerce' (1752), p. 3.
107 Hume, *House of Tudor* (1759), 1: 61.
108 Hume, *House of Tudor* (1759), 1: 63.
109 Hume, *House of Tudor* (1759), 1: 63.
110 Hume, *House of Tudor* (1759), 1: 63.
111 Hume, *House of Tudor* (1759), 1: 64.
112 Hume, *House of Tudor* (1759), 1: 64.
113 Hume, *House of Tudor* (1759), 1: 65.
114 Hume, *House of Tudor* (1759), 1: 64.
115 Hume, 'Arts and Sciences' (1742), pp. 55–6
116 Bacon, *History*, pp. 67–8.
117 Hume, *House of Tudor* (1759), 1: 64.
118 Hume, *House of Tudor* (1759), 1: 63.
119 Hume, *House of Tudor* (1759), 2: 731.
120 Hume, *House of Tudor* (1759), 2: 732–3.
121 Hume, *House of Tudor* (1759), 2: 731.
122 Hume, *House of Tudor* (1759), 2: 731.
123 Hume, *House of Tudor* (1759), 2: 731.
124 Hume, *House of Tudor* (1759), 2: 731–2.
125 Hume, *House of Tudor* (1759), 2: 731–2; Camden, *Annales*, pp. 102–4, 123–5, 285–6.
126 Hume, *House of Tudor* (1759), 2: 732.
127 Guthrie, *General History*, 3: 420.
128 Carte, *General History*, 3: 576.
129 For the Saxons, see Hume, *History* (1761), 1: 146–9. For feudal government, see Hume, *History* (1761), 1: 420–1.
130 See Hume's comments on the Danes, for an example: Hume, *History* (1761), 1: 64.
131 Hume, *History* (1761), 1: 404.
132 Drawing on the accounts of Asser and Malmesbury, and treating them with a good deal less scepticism than, for example, Salmon had done, Hume argued that Alfred understood that commerce required not moralistic regulation, but encouragement. Through a combination of government investment and enthusiasm, the King had enabled individuals to benefit from their labours; this, in turn, had prompted improvements in manufacture, navigation and commerce. The introduction of 'the elegancies of life', meanwhile, which were brought to the King from the Mediterranean and the Indies, served to soften and refine the manners and morals of the people. As Hume observed: '[Alfred's] subjects, by seeing these productions of the peaceful arts, were taught to respect the virtues of justice and industry, from which

alone they could rise.' See Hume, *History* (1761), 1: 68–9. Others whose approach to commerce Hume saw as foreshadowing later developments included Athelstan and the participants in the Peasants' Revolt. See Hume, *History* (1761), 1: 75 and (1762), 2: 246.

133 For the low and languishing state of commerce, see Hume, *History* (1761), 1: 144; 1: 303; 1: 404; 1: 420; *History* (1762), 2: 56; 2: 153.

134 Hume, *History* (1761), 1: 22.

135 Hume, *History* (1761), 1: 22.

136 Hume, *History* (1761), 1: 115–16.

137 Hume, *History* (1762), 2: 89.

138 Hume, *History* (1762), 2: 89.

139 Hume, *History* (1761), 2: 90.

140 Hume, *History* (1762), 2: 93–4.

141 For a summary of the changes Hume made, see Graeme Slater, 'Hume's Revisions of the *History of England*', *Studies in Bibliography*, 45 (1992), 130–57.

142 For discussion of such issues, see Moritz Baumstark, 'The End of Empire and the Death of Religion', in Ruth Savage (ed.), *Philosophy and Religion in Enlightenment Britain: New Case Studies* (Oxford: Oxford University Press, 2012), pp. 231–57.

143 Hume, *History of Great Britain* (1754), 1: 35.

144 Hume, *History* (1762), 5: 33.

145 Hume, *History* (1762), 5: 33.

146 Hume, *History* (1762), 5: 33.

147 Hume, *History* (1773), 6: 50–1.

148 In the first edition of the *History*, Hume had argued that James's financial problems arose, in part, 'from want of oeconomy' (p. 125). This was revised to 'for want of a rigid oeconomy' in 1770. Similarly, the 1754 edition of the text had read 'The King, it must be owned, possessed not frugality, proportioned to the narrowness of his revenue' (p. 125). In all editions from 1763 onwards, Hume changed the latter part of this sentence to read: 'the extreme narrowness of his revenue' (p. 136). Finally, the original version of the *History* rejected the idea that James wished to become an arbitrary monarch, by arguing that his policies were contrary to those 'which [have] ever been practiced by all princes who studied the encrease of their authority'. These comments were supplemented with an extra clause in 1773: 'besides that he [James] had certainly laid no plan for extending his power' (p. 170).

149 Hume, *History of Great Britain* (1754), p. 121.

150 Hume, *History of Great Britain* (1754), p. 121.

151 Hume, *History* (1778), 6: 163.

Conclusion

1 *Monthly Review,* September 1790.
2 Robert Henry, *The History of Great Britain*, 6 vols (London, 1771–93), 1: vi.
3 Thomas Carte, *A Collection of Several Papers Published by Thomas Carte, in Relation to his History of England* (London, 1744), p. 7.
4 Carte, *A Collection*, p. 7.
5 Hugh Blair, *Lectures on Rhetoric and Belles Lettres*, 2 vols (London, 1783), 2: 288.
6 Hume, *History of England* (1770), 6: 205–6, 7: 363–4. Hume's source here is Adam Anderson's *An Historical and Chronological Deduction of the Origin of Commerce*, 2 vols (London, 1764). Indeed, while Hume refers to Misselden, the anonymous pamphlet *The Happy Future State of England* and Mun, as well as Anderson, all of the information used can be found in Anderson. See Anderson, *An Historical and Chronological Deduction*, 1: 490, 2: 3–4, 2: 7, 12.
7 Hume, *History of England* (1770), 6: 203. See also Anderson, *An Historical and Chronological Deduction*, 1: 461.
8 Hume, *History of England* (1770), 7: 364.
9 Catharine Macaulay, *The History of England from the accession of James I to that of the Brunswick line*, 8 vols (London, 1763–83), 1: 277. For a brief discussion of Macaulay's views on commerce, see Karen O'Brien, *Women and Enlightenment in Eighteenth-Century Britain* (Cambridge: Cambridge University Press, 2009), pp. 159–60.
10 See Henry, *History of Great Britain*, 1: General Preface.
11 John Sinclair, *The History of the Public Revenue of the British Empire*, 3 parts (London, 1785–90).
12 Anderson, *An Historical and Chronological Deduction*, 1: v.
13 Anderson, *An Historical and Chronological Deduction*, 1: v.
14 See, for example, Anderson, *An Historical and Chronological Deduction*, 1: 313.
15 See Adam Smith, *An Inquiry into the Nature and Causes of the Wealth of Nations* (1776), ed. R. H. Campbell, A. S. Skinner and W. B. Todd, 2 vols (Indianapolis, IN: Liberty Fund, 1981), Book III (I: 376–427), Book IV (1: 429–2: 662).

Bibliography

Primary texts

Anderson, A., *An Historical and Chronological Deduction of the Origin of Commerce*, 2 vols (London, 1764)

Anonymous, *An Excise Elegy, or the Dragon Demolish'd* (London, 1733)

Anonymous, *Excise Anatomis'd* (London, 1733)

Anonymous, *The Life of the Great Statesman, William Cecil, Lord Burghley*, ed. A. Collins (London, 1732)

Anonymous, *The Nature of the Present Excise*, 2nd edn (London, 1733)

Anonymous, *Some Considerations on Publick Credit* (London, 1733)

Anonymous, *The Trade's Increase* (London, 1615)

Aristotle, *Nicomachean Ethics*, tr. D. Ross (Oxford: Oxford University Press, 1980)

Aristotle, *Politics*, tr. E. Baker, rev. tr. R. F. Stalley (Oxford: Oxford University Press, 1995)

Bacon, F., *The Advancement of Learning*, ed. M. Kiernan (Oxford: Oxford University Press, 2000)

Bacon, F., *De Augmentis Scientiarum*, in *The Philosophical Works of Francis Bacon*, ed. J. M. Robertson (Freeport, NY: Books for Libraries Press, 1970), pp. 413–638

Bacon, F., *The Essays*, ed. J. Pitcher (London: Penguin, 1985)

Bacon, F., *The History of the Reign of King Henry VII* (1622), ed. B. Vickers (Cambridge: Cambridge University Press, 1998)

Bacon, F., 'Of the True Greatness of the Kingdom of Britain', in *The Works of Francis Bacon*, vol. 7, ed. J. Spedding (London: Longmans, 1872)

Baker, R., *A Chronicle of the Kings of England* (London, 1643)

Barclay, A. (ed.), *Here begynneth the famous cronycle of the warre by Sallust*, tr. A. Barclay (London, 1525)

Blair, H., *Lectures on Rhetoric and Belles Lettres*, 2 vols (London, 1783)

Blundeville, T., *The True Order and Methode of Wryting and Reading Hystories* (London, 1574)

Bolingbroke, *Remarks on the History of England* (London, 1743)

Boswell, J., *Life of Johnson* (1791), ed. R. W. Chapman (Oxford: Oxford University Press, 1998)

Botero, G., *A Treatise, Concerning the Causes of the Magnificencie and greatnes of cities*, tr. R. Peterson (London, 1606)

Brady, R., *A Complete History of England*, 2 vols (London, 1685–1700)

Buchanan, G., *Rerum Scoticarum Historia* (Edinburgh, 1582)

Camden, W., *Britannia*, ed. D. F. Sutton (2004), www.philological.bham.ac.uk/cambrit

Camden, W., *The History of the Most Renowned and Victorious Princess Elizabeth Late Queen of England* (1615, 1625), 4th edn (London, 1688)

Carte, T., *A Collection of Several Papers Published by Thomas Carte, in Relation to his History of England* (London, 1744)

Carte, T., *A Full Answer to the Letter from a By-Stander* (London, 1742)

Carte, T., *A Full and Clear Vindication of the Full Answer to a Letter from A By-Stander* (London, 1743)

Carte, T., *A General History of England*, 4 vols (London, 1747–55)

Carte, T., *History and Life of James Duke of Ormonde*, 3 vols (London, 1735–36)

Coke, R., *Detection of the Court and State of England*, 2 vols, 3rd edn (London, 1697 [1694])

Coke, R., *A Discourse of Trade* (London, 1670)

Coke, R., *England's Improvements* (London, 1675)

Coke, R., *Reflections upon the East-Indy and Royal African Countries* (London, 1695)

Coke, R., *A Treatise Concerning the Regulation of English Coin* (London, 1696)

D'Ewes, S., *A Compleat Journal of the Notes, Speeches and Debates Both of the House of Lords and House of Commons, throughout the whole Reign of Queen Elizabeth, of glorious memory* (London, 1708)

Filmer, R., 'The Anarchy of a Limited or Mixed Monarchy' (1648), in *Patriarcha and Other Writings*, ed. J. P. Sommerville (Cambridge: Cambridge University Press, 1991), pp. 131–71

Frankland, T., *Annals of King James* (London, 1680)

Fuller, T., *The Appeal of Iniured Innocence* (London, 1659)

Grotius, H., *Annales et Historiæ de Rebus Belgicis*, ed. C. and P. de Groot (Amsterdam, 1657)

Grotius, H., *Commentary on the Law of Prize and Booty* (1868), ed. M. J. van Ittersum, tr. G. L. Williams (Indianapolis, IN: Liberty Fund, 2006)

Grotius, H., *The Rights of War and Peace* (1625), ed. R. Tuck (Indianapolis, IN: Liberty Fund, 2005)
Guthrie, W., *A General History of England*, 4 vols (London, 1744–51)
Hakluyt, R., *The Principal Navigations, Voiages and Discoveries of the English Nation, made by Sea or Over Land* (London, 1589)
Hall, E., *The Union of the Famous and Illustre Families of Lancastre and York* (London, 1548)
Hayward, J., *The Life and Reign of King Edward the Sixt* (London, 1630)
Henry, R., *The History of Great Britain*, 6 vols (London, 1771–93)
Hervey, J., *Ancient and Modern Liberty Stated and Compared* (London, 1734)
Heylyn, P., *Observations on the Historie of the Reign of King Charles* (London, 1656)
Holinshed, R., *The First Volume of the Chronicles of England* (London, 1577)
Hughes, J. (ed.), *A Complete History of England, Volumes 1 and 2* (London, 1706)
Hume, D., *England under the House of Tudor*, 2 vols (London, 1759)
Hume, D., *Essays, Moral and Political, Volume II* (Edinburgh, 1742)
Hume, D., *The History of England from the Invasion of Julius Cæsar to the Accession of Henry VII*, 2 vols (London, 1761–62)
Hume, D., *The History of England from the Invasion of Julius Cæsar to the Revolution in 1688*, 6 vols (London, 1762)
Hume, D., *The History of England from the Invasion of Julius Cæsar to the Revolution in 1688*, 8 vols (London, 1770)
Hume, D., *The History of England from the Invasion of Julius Cæsar to the Revolution in 1688*, 8 vols (London, 1773)
Hume, D., *The History of England from the Invasion of Julius Cæsar to the Revolution in 1688*, 8 vols (London, 1778)
Hume, D., *The History of Great Britain, volume 1* (Edinburgh, 1754)
Hume, D., *The History of Great Britain, volume 2* (London, 1757)
Hume, D., *The Letters of David Hume*, ed. J. Y. T. Greig, 2 vols (Oxford: Clarendon Press, 1932)
Hume, D., 'My Own Life', in *Essays Moral, Political and Literary*, ed. E. F. Miller (Indianapolis, IN: Liberty Fund, 1985), pp. xxxi–xli
Hume, D., *Political Discourses* (Edinburgh, 1752)
Johnson, R., 'Of Histories', in *Essaies, or Rather Imperfect Offers* (London, 1601)
Jourdain, S., *A Plaine Description of the Barmudas* (London, 1613)
Kennet, W., *A Complete History of England, Volume 3* (London, 1706)
Leclerc, J., *Parrhasiana* (London, 1700)
L'Estrange, H., *The Reign of King Charles: An History* (London, 1655)
Lipsius, J., *Sixe Bookes of Politickes or Civil Doctrine*, tr. W. Jones (London, 1594)

Livy, *The Rise of Rome, Books 1–5*, tr. R. J. Luce (Oxford: Oxford University Press, 1998)
Lockman, J., *A New History of England, in English and French by question and answer. Extracted from the most celebrated English historians particularly M. de Rapin Thoyras* (London, 1729)
Macaulay, C., *The History of England from the accession of James I to that of the Brunswick line*, 8 vols (London, 1763–83)
Machiavelli, N., *Discourses on Livy* (1531), tr. J. C. Bondanella and P. Bondanella (Oxford: Oxford University Press, 2008)
Machiavelli, N., *The Prince*, tr. and ed. P. Bondanella (Oxford: Oxford University Press, 2005), distributed from c. 1513
Madox, T., *History and Antiquities of the Exchequer of the Kings of England* (London, 1711)
Malynes, G., *The Maintenance of Free Trade* (London, 1622)
Malynes, G., *Saint George for England* (London, 1601)
Malynes, G., *A Treatise of the Canker of Englands Commonwealth* (London, 1601)
May, T., *The History of the Parliament of England* (London, 1647)
Melville, J., *The memoires of Sir James Melvil of Hal-Hill* (London, 1683)
Mézeray, F. E. de, *Histoire de France*, 3 vols (Paris, 1643)
Milton, J., *The History of Britain* (London, 1670)
Misselden, E., *The Circle of Commerce. Or the Ballance of Trade* (London, 1623)
Misselden, E., *Free Trade. Or, The Means to Make Trade Flourish* (London, 1622)
More, T., *The History of King Richard III and Selections from the English and Latin Poems* (1513–18), ed. R. S. Sylvester (New Haven, CT: Yale University Press, 1976)
Morris, C., *A Letter from a Bystander to a Member of Parliament* (London, 1742)
Morris, C., *A letter to the Reverend Mr Thomas Carte* (London, 1743)
Mun, T., *England's Treasure by Forraign Trade* (London, 1664)
Oldys, W. (ed.), *The Harleian Miscellany*, 8 vols (London, 1744–46)
Polybius, *The Histories*, tr. R. Waterfield (Oxford: Oxford University Press, 2010)
Raleigh, C., *Observations upon some particular persons and passages* (London, 1656)
Ramsay, J., *Scotland and Scotsmen in the Eighteenth Century from the MSS. of John Ramsay*, ed. A. Allardyce, 2 vols (Edinburgh: W. Blackwood and Sons, 1888)
Rapin de Thoyras, P. de, *Histoire d'Angleterre depuis l'invasion de Jules César*, 13 vols (La Haye, 1724–27)

Rapin de Thoyras, P. de, *The History of England*, tr. and ed. N. Tindal, 15 vols (London, 1725–31)
Rapin de Thoyras, P. de, *The History of England*, tr. and ed. J. Kelly and J. Morgan, 3 vols (London, 1732–37)
Rapin de Thoyras, P. de, *The History of England*, tr. and ed. J. Templeman, 2 vols (London, 1734)
Rapin de Thoyras, P. de, *The History of England*, 4th edn, 12 vols, tr. and ed. N. Tindal (London, 1757)
Rapin de Thoyras, P. de, and Robertson, H., *The History of England from the earliest periods*, tr. and ed. H. Robertson, 2 vols (London, 1820)
Rapin de Thoyras, P. de, and Tindal, N., *The History of England*, tr. N. Tindal, 2 vols (London, 1744–47)
Rymer, T., *Foedera*, 20 vols (London, 1704–35)
Rymer, T., *Foedera*, abr. P. de Rapin de Thoyras, tr. S. Whatley, 4 vols (London, 1726–27)
Salmon, T. (1648–1706), *Historical Collections* (London, 1706)
Salmon, T. (1648–1706), and Salmon, T., *The History of Great Britain* (London, 1725)
Salmon, T., *An Impartial Examination of Bishop Burnet's History of His Own Times*, 2 vols (London, 1724)
Salmon, T., *The Life of Her Late Majesty Queen Anne*, 2 vols (London, 1721)
Salmon, T., *Modern History, or the Present State of all Nations*, 31 vols (London, 1724–38)
Salmon, T., *Modern History, or the Present State of All Nations*, 3rd edn, 3 vols (London, 1744)
Salmon, T. (ed.), *A Compleat Collection of State-tryals*, 4 vols (London, 1719)
Salmon, T. (ed.), *Tryals for High-treason, and other crimes*, 9 vols (London, 1720–31)
Sanderson, W., *An Answer to a Scurrilous Pamphlet* (1656)
Sanderson, W., *Aulicus Coquinariæ, or a Vindication in Answer to a Pamphlet, entitled the Court and Character of King James* (London, 1650)
Sanderson, W., *A Compleat History of the Life and Raigne of King Charles* (London, 1658)
Sanderson, W., *A Compleat History of the Lives and Reigns of Mary Queen of Scotland, And of Her Son and Successor James the Sixth, King of Scotland; And (After Queen Elizabeth) King of Great Britain, France, and Ireland* (London, 1656)
Sanderson, W., *Graphice: Or, the Use of the Pen and Pencil* (London, 1658)
Sinclair, J., *The History of the Public Revenue of the British Empire*, 3 parts (London, 1785–90)
Smith, A., *An Inquiry into the Origins and Causes of the Wealth of Nations*

(1776), ed. R. H. Campbell, A. S. Skinner and W. B. Todd, 2 vols (Indianapolis, IN: Liberty Press, 1981)

Smith, J., *The Generall Historie of Virginia, new-England, and the Summer Islands* (London, 1624)

Smith, J., *A Map of Virginia* (London, 1612)

Sparke, M., *The Narrative History of King James for the first fourteen years* (London, 1651)

Speed, J., *History of Great Britaine* (London, 1611)

Stow, J., *The Annales of England* (London, 1592)

Stow, J., *A Summarie of the Chronicles of Englande* (London, 1570)

Stow, J., *A Summarie of the Chronicles of England* (London, 1575)

Stow J., and Howes, E., *The Abridgement of the English Chronicle* (London, 1611)

Stow J., and Howes, E., *The Abridgement of the English Chronicle* (London, 1618)

Stow J., and Howes, E., *The Abridgement or Summarie of the English Chronicle* (London, 1607)

Stow J., and Howes, E., *Annales, or, a generall chronicle of England* (London, 1615)

Stow J., and Howes, E., *Annales or a General Chronicle of England* (London, 1631)

Stow J., and Howes, E., *Annales, or, a generall chronicle of England* (London, 1632)

Strype, J., *Annals of the Reformation*, 4 vols (London, 1709–31)

Strype, J., *Life and Acts of John Whitgift* (London, 1718)

Suetonius Tranquillus, G., *The Twelve Caesars*, tr. R. Graves, rev. J. B. Rives (London: Penguin, 2007)

Swift, J., *Conduct of the Allies and of the Late Ministry* (London, 1711)

Tacitus, *The Annals of Imperial Rome*, tr. M. Grant (London: Penguin, 1996)

Temple, W., *An Introduction to the History of England* (London, 1695)

Tyrrell, J., *General History of England, both ecclesiastical and civil*, 3 vols (London, 1696–1704)

Vergil, P., *Anglica Historia*, tr. D. F. Sutton, philological.bham.ac.uk/polverg/1e.html, based on the 1555 version of the text

Vergil, P., *The Anglica Historia of Polydore Vergil*, ed. and tr. D. Hay (London: Office of the Royal Historical Society, 1950), based on the 1513 version of the text

Vergilii, P., *Anglicæ Historiæ* (Basel, 1532)

Weldon, A., *The Court and Character of King James, written and taken by sir A.W.* (London, 1650)

Wilson, A., *The History of Great Britain* (London, 1653)

Wilson, A., 'Observations of God's Providence', in F. Peck (ed.), *Desiderata curiosa*, new edn, 2 vols in 1 (1779), pp. 460–83.

Selected secondary bibliography

I have divided this selected bibliography of secondary sources into five sections. The first lists a series of works that are of general relevance either to seventeenth- and eighteenth-century historiography, or to the wider study of history. Sections 2–4 list more period-specific accounts of historical writing. The final section is concerned with discussions of commerce, finance and political economy.

1. General studies

Burrow, J., *A History of Histories: Epics, Chronicles, Romances and Inquiries from Herodotus to the Twentieth Century* (London: Penguin, 2007)

Dew, B., and Price, F. (eds), *Historical Writing in Britain, 1688–1830: Visions of History* (Basingstoke: Palgrave, 2014)

Grafton, A., *The Art of History in Early Modern Europe* (Cambridge: Cambridge University Press, 2007)

Gras, N. S. B., 'The Rise and Development of Economic History', *Economic History Review*, 1:1 (1927), 12–34

Hicks, P., *Neoclassical History and English Culture: From Clarendon to Hume* (Basingstoke: Macmillan, 1996)

Looser, D., *British Women Writers and the Writing of History, 1670–1820* (Baltimore, MD: Johns Hopkins University Press, 2000)

Momigliano, A., 'Eighteenth-century Prelude to Mr Gibbon', in *Sesto Contributo Alla Storia Degli Studi Classici E Del Mondo Antico* (Rome: Edizioni di Storia e Letteratura, 1980)

O'Brien, K., 'The History Market in Eighteenth-Century England', in I. Rivers (ed.), *Books and their Readers in Eighteenth-Century England: New Essays* (London: Continuum, 2003), pp. 105–34

Okie, L., *Augustan Historical Writing: Histories of England in the English Enlightenment* (Lanham, MD: University Press of America, 1991)

Phillips, M. S., *On Historical Distance* (New Haven, CT: Yale University Press, 2013)

Phillips, M. S., *Society and Sentiment: Genres of Historical Writing in Britain, 1740–1820* (Princeton, NJ: Princeton University Press, 2000)

Pocock, J. G. A., *The Ancient Constitution and the Feudal Law: A Study of English Historical Thought in the Seventeenth Century*, 2nd edn (Cambridge: Cambridge University Press, 1987 [1957])

Pocock, J. G. A., *Barbarism and Religion*, 6 vols (Cambridge: Cambridge University Press, 1999–2015)
Pocock, J. G. A., *The Machiavellian Moment: Florentine Political Thought and the Atlantic Republican Tradition*, 2nd edn (Princeton, NJ: Princeton University Press, 2003 [1975])

2. Historical writing, c. 1500–c. 1650

Beer, B. L., *Tudor England Observed: The World of John Stow* (Stroud: Sutton Publishing, 1998)
Bradford, A. T., 'Absolutism and the "Utility" of Tacitus', *Huntingdon Library Quarterly*, 46:2 (1983), 127–55
Brownley, M. W., 'Sir Richard Baker's "Chronicle" and Later Seventeenth-Century English Historiography', *Huntingdon Library Quarterly*, 52:4 (1989), 481–500
Burke, P., 'A Survey of the Popularity of the Ancient Historians', *History and Theory*, 5:2 (1966), 135–52
Gajda, A., 'Tacitus and Political Thought in Early Modern Europe, c. 1530–c. 1640', in A. J. Woodman (ed.), *The Cambridge Companion to Tacitus* (Cambridge: Cambridge University Press, 2008), pp. 253–68
Gransden, A., *Historical Writing in England ii, c. 1307 to the Early Sixteenth Century* (London: Routledge Kegan Paul, 1982)
Hadfield, A., *Literature, Travel and Colonial Writing in the English Renaissance* (Oxford: Oxford University Press, 2007)
Herendeen, W. H., *William Camden: A Life in Context* (Woodbridge: Boydell Press, 2007)
Jardine, L., *Francis Bacon: Discovery and the Art of Discourse* (Cambridge: Cambridge University Press, 1974)
Levy, F. J., 'Hayward, Daniel, and the Beginnings of Politic History in England', *Huntington Library Quarterly*, 50:1 (1987), 1–34
Levy, F. J., 'The Making of Camden's *Britannia*', *Bibliothèque d'Humanisme et Renaissance*, 26 (1964), 70–97
Levy, F. J., *Tudor Historical Thought* (San Marino, CA: Huntingdon Library, 1967)
Peltonen, M., 'Bacon's Political Philosophy', in M. Peltonen (ed.), *The Cambridge Companion to Bacon* (Cambridge: Cambridge University Press, 1996), pp. 283–310
Peltonen, M., *Classical Humanism and Republicanism in English Political Thought, 1570–1640* (Cambridge: Cambridge University Press, 1995)
Sharpe, K., *Politics and Ideas in Early Stuart England* (London: Pinter, 1989)
Trevor-Roper, H., *Elizabeth's First Historian: William Camden and the Beginnings of English 'Civil History'* (London: Jonathan Cape, 1971)

Woolf, D., *The Idea of History in Early-Stuart England: Erudition, Ideology and the Light of Truth* (Toronto: University of Toronto Press, 1990)

3. Historical writing, c. 1650–c. 1750

Earl, D. W. L., 'Procrustean Feudalism: An Interpretive Dilemma in English Historical Narration, 1700–1725', *The Historical Journal*, 19:1 (1976), 33–51

Gallagher, N., *Historical Literatures: Writing about the Past in England, 1660–1740* (Manchester: Manchester University Press, 2012)

Girard d'Albissin, N., *Un Précurseur de Montesquieu: Rapin-Thoyras, Premier historien français des institutions anglaises* (Paris: Éditions C. Klincksieck, 1969)

Kramnick, I., 'Augustan Politics and English Historiography: The Debate on the English Past, 1700–1735', *History and Theory*, 6:1 (1967), 33–56

Macgillivray, R., *Restoration Historians and the English Civil War* (The Hague: Martinus Nijhoff, 1974)

Monod, P. K., 'Thomas Carte, the Druids and British National Identity', in P. K. Monod, M. Pittock and D. Szechi (eds), *Loyalty and Identity: Jacobites at Home and Abroad* (Basingstoke: Palgrave, 2010), pp. 132–48

Norbrook, D., 'The English Revolution and English Historiography', in N. H. Keble (ed.), *The Cambridge Companion to the Writing of the English Revolution* (Cambridge: Cambridge University Press), pp. 233–50

Schwarz, M. L., 'James I and the Historians: Toward a Reconsideration', *Journal of British Studies*, 13:2 (1974), 114–34

Stephan, D., 'Laurence Echard – Whig Historian', *Historical Journal*, 32:4 (1989), 843–66

Stryer, S., 'The Style of Discontinuity: Prose Patterning and Historical Change in Paul de Rapin de Thoyras and Thomas Salmon', *Clio: A Journal of Literature Philosophy and the Philosophy of History*, 42:2 (2013), 137–60

Sullivan, M. G., 'Rapin, Hume and the Identity of the Historian in Eighteenth-century England', *History of European Ideas*, 28 (2002), 145–62

Trevor-Roper, H., 'Our First Whig Historian', in *From Counter-Reformation to Glorious Revolution* (London: Secker and Warburg, 1992), pp. 249–65

4. Enlightenment historical writing

Baumstark, M., 'The End of Empire and the Death of Religion', in R. Savage (ed.), *Philosophy and Religion in Enlightenment Britain: New Case Studies* (Oxford: Oxford University Press, 2012), pp. 231–57

Danford, J. W., 'Hume's *History* and the Parameters of Economic

Development', in N. Capaldi and D. W. Livingston (eds), *Liberty in Hume's History of England* (Dordecht: Kluwer, 1990), pp. 155–94.
Forbes, D., *Hume's Philosophical Politics*, rev. edn (Cambridge: Cambridge University Press, 1978 [1975])
Harris, J. A., *Hume: An Intellectual Biography* (Cambridge: Cambridge University Press, 2015)
Hopfl, H. M., 'From Savage to Scotsman: Conjectural History in the Scottish Enlightenment', *Journal of British Studies*, 17:2 (1978), 19–40
Meek, R. L., *Social Science and the Ignoble Savage* (Cambridge: Cambridge University Press, 1976)
O'Brien, K., *Narratives of Enlightenment: Cosmopolitan History from Voltaire to Gibbon* (Cambridge: Cambridge University Press, 1997)
Okie, L., 'William Guthrie: Enlightenment Historian', *Historian*, 51:2 (1989), 221–38
Phillipson, N., *David Hume: The Philosopher as Historian*, rev. edn (London: Penguin, 2011 [1989])
Robertson, J., *The Case for Enlightenment: Scotland and Naples, 1680–1760* (Cambridge: Cambridge University Press, 2005)
Slater, G., 'Hume's Revisions of the *History of England*', *Studies in Bibliography*, 45 (1992), 130–57
Stockton, C. N., 'Economics and the Mechanism of Historical Progress in Hume's *History*', in D. W. Livingston and J. T. King (eds), *Hume: A Re-Evaluation* (New York: Fordham University Press, 1976), pp. 296–322
Wootton, D., 'David Hume "The Historian"', in D. F. Norton and J. Taylor (eds), *The Cambridge Companion to David Hume* (Cambridge: Cambridge University Press, 2009), pp. 447–79

5. Commerce, finance and political economy

Armitage, D., *The Ideological Origins of the British Empire* (Cambridge: Cambridge University Press, 2000)
Cramsie, J., 'Commercial Projects and the Fiscal Policy of James VI and I', *The Historical Journal*, 43:2 (2000), 345–64
Deane, P. M., *The First Industrial Revolution*, 2nd edn (Cambridge: Cambridge University Press, 1989)
Dickson, P. G. M., *The Financial Revolution in England: A Study in the Development of Public Credit* (London: Macmillan, 1967)
Dietz, F. C., *English Public Finance, 1558–1641* (London: Frank Cass, 1964 [1932])
Hont, I., *The Jealousy of Trade: International Competition and the Nation-State*

in Historical Perspective (Cambridge, MA: Harvard University Press, 2005)

Hont, I., and Ignatieff, M. (eds), *Wealth and Virtue: The Shaping of Political Economy in the Scottish Enlightenment* (Cambridge: Cambridge University Press, 1983)

Hoppit, J., 'Attitudes to Credit in Britain, 1680–1790', *The Historical Journal*, 33:2 (1990), 305–22

Hoppitt, J., 'The Context and Contours of British Economic Literature', *Historical Journal*, 49:1 (2006), 79–110

Jubb, M., 'Economic Policy and Economic Development', in J. Black (ed.), *Britain in the Age of Walpole* (Basingstoke: Macmillan, 1984), pp. 136–42

Jurdjevic, M., 'Virtue, Commerce, and the Enduring Florentine Republican Moment: Reintegrating Italy into the Atlantic Republican Debate', *Journal of the History of Ideas*, 62:4 (2001), 721–43

Langford, P., *The Excise Crisis: Society and Politics in the Age of Walpole* (Oxford: Clarendon Press, 1975)

Magnusson, L., *Mercantilism: The Shaping of an Economic Language* (London: Routledge, 1994)

Mokyr, J., *The Enlightened Economy: Britain and the Industrial Revolution, 1700–1850* (London: Penguin, 2011)

North, D. C., and Weingast, B.R, 'Constitutions and Commitment: The Evolution of Institutional Governing Public Choice in Seventeenth-Century England', *The Journal of Economic History*, 49:4 (1989), 803–32

Pincus, S., *1688: The First Modern Revolution* (New Haven, CT: Yale University Press, 2009)

Pincus, S., 'Neither Machiavellian Moment nor Possessive Individualism: Commercial Society and Defenders of the English Commonwealth', *American Historical Review*, 103 (1998), 705–36

Pincus, S., 'Rethinking Mercantilism: Political Economy, the British Empire, and the Atlantic World in the Seventeenth and Eighteenth Centuries', *William and Mary Quarterly*, 69:1 (2012), 3–34

Pocock, J. G. A., *Virtue, Commerce and History* (Cambridge: Cambridge University Press, 1985)

Reinert, S. A., *Translating Empire: Emulation and the Origins of Political Economy* (Cambridge, MA: Harvard University Press, 2011)

Sacks, D. H., 'The Countervailing of Benefits: Monopoly, Liberty, and Benevolence in Elizabethan England', in D. Hoak (ed.), *Tudor Political Culture* (Cambridge: Cambridge University Press, 1995), pp. 272–91

Wennerlind, K., *Casualties of Credit, The English Financial Revolution, 1620–1720* (Cambridge, MA: Harvard University Press, 2011)

Winch, D., *Riches and Poverty: An Intellectual History of Political Economy in Britain, 1750–1834* (Cambridge: Cambridge University Press, 1996)

Index

EU authorised representative for GPSR:
Easy Access System Europe, Mustamäe tee 50,
10621 Tallinn, Estonia
gpsr.requests@easproject.com

www.ingramcontent.com/pod-product-compliance
Ingram Content Group UK Ltd.
Pitfield, Milton Keynes, MK11 3LW, UK
UKHW011005120926
8556IPUK00027B/94
* 9 7 8 1 7 8 4 9 9 2 9 6 5 *